P9-DEW-083

The Contemporary American Family

The Contemporary American Family

Edited with an Introduction by

William J. Goode

A NEW YORK TIMES BOOK

Quadrangle Books
CHICAGO

THE CONTEMPORARY AMERICAN FAMILY. Copyright © 1971 by
The New York Times Company. All rights reserved, including
the right to reproduce this book or portions thereof in any
form. For information, address: Quadrangle Books, Inc.,
12 East Delaware Place, Chicago 60611. Manufactured in the
United States of America. Published simultaneously in Canada
by Burns and MacEachern Ltd., Toronto.

Library of Congress Catalog Card Number: 79-124510
SBN   cloth   8129-0149-5
SBN   paper   8129-6125-0

The publishers are grateful to the contributors herein for
permission to reprint their articles.

Contents

3. Husbands and Wives

4. Parents and Children

5. Family Problems

6. New Family Forms

The Contemporary American Family

Introduction

IN THIS most industrialized society where our prime motivations are alleged to be the purely individualistic goals of money and occupational success, where the divorce rate is one of the highest in the world, and where commentators and social analysts constantly predict the decline if not the disappearance of the American family, that institution continues to exert its power over almost everyone. Men with attractive job offers turn them down because they do not fit the needs and wishes of their families. People who divorce remarry as soon as possible. Not only in rural but also in urban areas, not merely the nuclear family but the extended kin network is strong and active. Although adolescent peer groups are thought to dominate the opinions and attitudes of a rebellious American youth, in fact young people gradually come to believe in the values of their parents, who generally shape their plans for marriage and jobs more than their teen-age friends do. Both love and hate split families asunder, and family life is pervaded by both, yet few people wish to cut their family ties. Thus, while the media each day inform us about supposedly "important" public events in politics, war, and business, the private and seemingly humdrum processes of the family continue to dominate much of our lives.

But though all of us spend much of our time and emotional attention on our family relations, our daily experiences do not ordinarily transform us into objective analysts. Most of us have had only a narrow, if intense, slice of family life before our eyes, and we have not observed the family life of other ethnic groups or classes. We have not seen even the family life of people who live a few blocks from us. If we are reared in conservative social networks, we have probably not observed the wide range of family behavior that is characteristic of contemporary American life. Nor are we likely to be acquainted with the family patterns of even the recent past. In addition, we are all emotionally so involved in our own observations that we are not good observers. Our comments are all too likely to be self-justifications and rationalizations rather than cool attempts to find out how even our own family has operated. Husbands and wives, for instance, describe a very different reality in talking about family life, and the reality their children experience seems different from both of these.

Complicating the analysis of the American family still further is a set of what may be called "social myths" which describe the family as it is or once was, but for which there are little supporting data. We have already noted one such myth: the widespread belief that somehow the American family is unstable and is declining rapidly; but there are others. It is true of course that American families were once mainly rural, but along with this truth go many myths about what that rural family was. It is untrue, for example, that the average age at marriage was very low in the United States. Here, as in most Western countries, the norm has been that young couples should be able to live independently, and since most young people could not establish themselves independently at an early age, the average marital age was generally higher than at the present time. It is untrue that American parents once fully controlled the courtship of their children, and chose their future spouses for them. Indeed, the earliest European observers remarked how free courtship was in America. Doubtless the authority of the father has fallen over the last century, but the literary picture that has been handed down to us—of the autocratic, all powerful, remote Victorian father—is essentially a portrait of the English upper-middle-class and upper-class father. We have no reason to suppose that the authoritarian father was typical in ordinary American farm families in the past, and certainly it has not been an accurate picture of the urban lower-class father in recent times or even over the past half-century.

We cannot assume that we understand the family adequately merely because we have strong opinions about it, or have ourselves lived in families. We must, then, be prepared to discover that many of our most cherished beliefs about American family patterns are only partially correct and that future research may well disclose that still other of our beliefs about American family life may also turn out to be incorrect.

Although this book focuses primarily on the contemporary American family, it is useful occasionally to glance at other societies, whether contemporary or historical, because in doing so we thereby ascertain more clearly the extent to which the American family may be the vanguard of future family developments in other countries, or may instead be peculiar to our own society. For example, falling in love is given far greater importance in our own society than in almost any other. American parents punish their children physically far more than Japanese parents do, and are probably stricter in general than most primitive societies have been. Our divorce rate is one of the highest among industrialized nations, but in the past other nations have had higher rates, and most primitive societies probably had even higher rates still. A broader perspective sometimes helps us better to understand our own family system.

In this broader perspective, the family still looms large as a major kind of social arrangement in all societies, not just in our own. Many societies do not have formal organizations for making war. Many do not have a formal leader or chief, or any clearly organized lawmaking body. A goodly number of societies do not have markets as we know them; many have economic systems that are not at all separated from the family patterns. But all societies, however primitive or industrialized, have family and kinship structures with the following major functions: (1) reproduction of the young, (2) the physical maintenance of family members, (3) the placement of the child in the social structure, (4) socialization, and (5) social control.

In any society, one could imagine separating each of these

functions from the other. Those who bear children do not have to take care of them physically, nor is there any *logical* necessity that requires children to be placed in the social structure on the basis of their parents' positions. One group could feed the children, but not socialize them. One group could control the children, but still not be engaged in their physical maintenance.

Yet however easy it is to imagine that all of these functions could be separated from one another, in fact they never are separated, unless it is by a formal legal act, such as the creation of the Israeli kibbutz, the Russian experiments in communal living, the Chinese communes, and some utopian experiments in the United States. In other words, no such system for separating these functions has ever evolved historically and naturally out of the aspirations and needs of a whole society. Where they have existed, they have instead been imposed by a set of leaders, or created by a small sect intent on establishing a new utopia.

Characteristic of other family systems, too, is the fact that although people are not typically required to participate in family life after their childhood, almost everyone does. We can easily escape religious responsibilities, and a very large portion of the American population does. On the other hand, we cannot escape military obligations, legal restrictions, or the threat of starvation if we do not work. These latter responsibilities are imposed upon us under severe physical threats. By contrast, such punishments do not occur in the realm of the family. Nevertheless, almost everyone feels the inner necessity to found a family on his own, and to maintain his own family ties. This is no less true in the United States than in other societies round the world.

If we examine the five major functions of the family noted above, we see first that all of these seem to be necessary. After all, the child must be *produced* as an organism, but thereafter he must be *maintained;* and so on. It is not particularly useful to argue that one of these functions is more important than another. Nor is it even possible to argue that it must be the family that carries them out, since in fact all of them also to some extent take place outside the family: many children are born out of wedlock; various people are physically maintained in institutions of various kinds, such as orphanages, homes for the aged, penitentiaries, and so on; many social institutions help to place children in the social structure. In addition, we are all *socialized* and under the pressures of *social control* in most of our interaction with other people outside the family. None of this will happen unless the child is given a position in the social structure.

Nevertheless, in some ways the most spectacular activity of the family consists in transforming a squalling blob of red protoplasm into an adult human being, capable of acting with some autonomy and effectiveness in a very complex world. Indeed, so necessary is this process of socialization that we are now fairly sure that the human animal does not even become human unless he is socialized in some type of family-like situation. This being the case, it is useful to discuss the biological foundations of the family.

Biological Foundations of the Family

As we learn more about how animals live in their natural surroundings, it becomes clear that most of our human characteristics are shared by one or more animal groups. Yet man is biologically an extreme species of animal in several respects. First, as far as we know man has no *instincts* at all. He has many *reflexes,* such as the eye blink or the sucking reflex; and he has some *drives,* such as hunger and thirst. He has, however, no preset, linked mechanisms which can be triggered to solve any major problem for him when he is born; nor do any of these appear later in his life (as, for example, nest-building does in birds). Instead, he must learn almost everything. Coupled with this is his long infancy. No other animal remains helpless as long as man does. Grazing animals, of course, are able to survive alone fairly early in their lives, though they may easily fall prey to predators. By contrast, predators have a somewhat longer infancy, since they need to learn how to kill. Nevertheless, over a two-year span any predator has learned enough to survive. Man at two years of age remains helpless in almost every way. His learning process has barely begun.

Whether one argues that man has a large brain because he has no instincts to guide him, or that his instincts began to drop out of his repertoire as his brain developed, the important fact is that some type of social unit was needed to take charge of this helpless animal and teach him both appropriate techniques for coping with a hostile natural environment and the appropriate social attitudes for getting along within the social unit itself.

These peculiarities of man's biological heritage pose great difficulties when we try to understand the relationship between nature and nurture, or biological and social factors. We simply do not know what man is "naturally"—that is, without the changes wrought in him by socialization. Nor can we find out, because it is only after some socialization has taken place that we can adequately evaluate the human being, and by that time these social factors have already altered his responses.

It is not even easy to pin down precisely the male and female differences which might require very different patterns of family behavior. For example, though it is clear that only women can menstruate, bear children, and nurse, it does not follow *biologically* that women must rear the children, cook the food, take care of the domestic needs of the husband, and so forth. As is especially clear in the United States today, we continue to define as "children" people who are rather mature biologically. We object to very early marriages, and impose many social norms and pressures to persuade young people that they should not try to establish a home before they have an occupation. But these patterns are not determined by biological elements. Man's biological heritage may permit a very wide range of family patterns, since there is no family system that is definitely determined by biological elements.

On the other hand, many human traits that are important for the family might be labeled "bio-social" and are to be found among all the higher animals (though these animals do not have either a language or a culture). Some are learned; and others are acquired as the animal matures biologically. They are not, in a strict technical sense, *normative;* that is, animals do not feel they *should* carry out these patterns, and do not feel ashamed if they fail to do so. Instead, these traits are likely to be backed by force or by biological links which we do not yet fully understand.

In any event, they are all social, and they affect human family patterns.

First, the higher animals typically move in some kind of family grouping, often composed of an adult male, one or more adult females, some adolescents, and a few still younger members. Second, among most animals there is a fairly strong pattern of territoriality—that is, each family remains in a particular territory, and will defend that territory fiercely if it is invaded. Third, the adult male is typically jealous of male intruders, and among some animals the female is also jealous. Fourth, in such groupings there is a pattern of dominance or hierarchy. This is sometimes called a "pecking order": the dominant animal (usually a male) can force the other animals to get out of the way, while the animal at the second rank of dominance can force all the others to get out of the way except the first-ranked animal; and so on. Such a pattern yields a kind of social order in that each animal comes to know what to expect of the others. The dominant animal is likely to decide when to move on to a new feeding ground, when to stand and face an intruder, or when to bed down for the night. Yet there are no rules, as there are in a human family, that state that the dominant person *should* have this authority.

In this broader biological and social perspective, the crucial point is that the human infant cannot become a fully normal adult unless he is reared in some kind of close and continuing social unit. If he is not given warmth, attention, and affection, he does not grow up to be a "natural biological human being," but much more likely an emotionally disturbed or otherwise aberrant person. Some social unit, therefore, must have the responsibility of accepting the human infant and providing it with a long period of physical and emotional care, and a substantial input of knowledge. Since people do things mainly because they have been socialized to *want* to do them, this means that each generation of adults must not only care for the next generation, their own children, but also train them in turn *to want* to procreate and to socialize a succeeding generation. If the society is to continue, the infant must also be gradually taught to want to behave like the adults he has known, which means to found a family of his own and to rear children when he himself is grown.

It is in this broader biosocial context, then, that we must consider the types of relations between males and females in American society, the current and continuing debates and arguments about what is the "natural" or "right" form of the family, the rights and obligations of parents and children, the problem of population expansion, and the best techniques for rearing children in so rapidly changing a society.

Biological Bases of Sex Roles in the Family

In any society even the casual observer can see that men and women act differently, work at different tasks, play different roles in the family, and almost everyone firmly believes that biological differences determine these social patterns. But simple observation is not in this instance a reliable guide to accurate analysis: after thousands of years of attentive man-watching by women, and woman-watching by men, we still are not sure to what extent the biological differences between men and women shape their behavior.

In every society the division of labor is partly based upon sex, and at first glance physical differences do seem to determine how these tasks are divided. The hunting of large mammals, rock-quarrying, and heavy work with timber, for example, are all men's tasks. Nursing infants, maintaining a fire, and cooking are typically women's tasks. A second, more skeptical look at such a division of labor, however, always casts doubt upon such a simple formulation. In the first place, what is defined as a man's task in one society—pottery-making, say, or buying and selling in the market—may in another society be defined as a woman's task. Once we move away from tasks where great physical strength and endurance are required, we find that biological differences cannot account for all the ways in which men and women have allocated the work in their society. Clearly, then, such allocations must be in part based upon social definitions.

Perhaps the most immediately striking difference is that whatever jobs are defined as dramatic, interesting, and challenging are assigned to men. Tasks that may be physically hard but monotonous and offer much less freedom are more likely to be female tasks. Although many books and essays still refer to "matriarchies," no society has yet been discovered in which women were unequivocally in charge of the important work and decisions. Indeed, one might even argue that since women are "by nature" not as strong as men, and since all psychological tests show that women are as intelligent as men, men should carry out all of the jobs in society that require strength and endurance—that is, the unskilled work—while women should be in charge of the higher-level positions, where physical ability is of no consequence. Moreover, since women are "by nature" said to be much more sensitive to personal and social relations, the tasks of administration and management should fall to them, in which case women would be in controlling positions at the highest levels of corporations, governments, and military organizations. In addition, since women are known to be more "emotional" than men, they should be trained to become poets, artists, and composers—aesthetic tasks especially requiring the expression of emotion. These changes might be logical consequences of the traditional clichés about the social traits assigned to women and men.

But if we consider only the biological differences that appear to be important for family patterns, the most obvious ones are female menstruation, child-bearing, and lactation. Men cannot do any of these. On the other hand, it is clear that none of these female functions requires that the women take care of the children during their infancy and childhood, cook and keep house, sew and shop, or defer to their husbands. Menstruation does slightly reduce the work effectiveness of many women, but in fact the overall absenteeism record of women is no worse than that of men. Pregnancy also reduces work effectiveness, but only for part of the period of gestation; and, in any event, most women are not pregnant that many times during their lives. In sum, women do not appear to have any special biological endowment that makes them better able to care for children than men, or for that matter any less able to hold down jobs.

It is not possible to measure just what effect men's greater muscular strength and endurance has upon the relations between the sexes. Nevertheless, we can at least guess that one unmeasured element in the dominance of men over women in all societies and in all family systems lies in part in the superior fighting equipment of males. We must, however, be skeptical of another supposedly biologically based difference between the sexes—the so-called "later physical maturation of males." This has sometimes been used to explain why males marry later than females in most societies. It also explains why in America girls of thirteen or fourteen are encouraged to date and engage in an active social life, while many parents of boys at the same age are rather pleased if their sons devote their energies instead to sports and studies. Just which sex "matures later" depends upon what standard one uses for maturation. Very likely, girls produce a viable egg at about the same time that boys produce viable sperm. If we look at specific traits, such as height at different ages, it is true that some girls will grow faster than boys (e.g., puberty), while boys will grow faster at another age. In their early teens, boys can breed the next generation without harm to their bodies, while girls are likely to be harmed somewhat by early pregnancy.

On the other hand, it is clear that social values are fundamental to the definition of what is "mature." For the purposes of dating and courtship, little is asked of the girl other than that she be attractive and exhibit the appropriate secondary sex characteristics (curves, full breasts, and so on). The girl is likely to be able to handle the tasks of housekeeper and mother and to be in command of the appropriate social graces in her teens. By contrast, a boy of the same age is barely defined as an appropriate date for her. His "maturity" is measured by a different adult standard: Is he earning an adequate salary?

Exploring further the biological differences between men and women, in an effort to ascertain which of them might be important for family patterns, we must note that both men and women (unlike most animals) have a continuing sex drive rather than a single periodic rutting season. Moreover, there seem to be no differences in the biological capacity for sexual enjoyment; if differences exist, the superiority clearly lies on the side of the female. Both of these traits press toward the constant association of the sexes.

By contrast, however, an important sex difference is reflected in the social definitions of male and female role behavior; the male must feel some sexual desire in order to engage in sexual intercourse, and ejaculation must precede conception. By contrast, the female can become pregnant without any desire or orgasm.

This difference is reflected in the fact that in almost all societies, including our own until very recently, the woman's sexual pleasure was given relatively little attention. If her earlier socialization makes her sufficiently docile, so that she will accept the marriage arrangements her elders have made for her, she can become pregnant and continue the family line. In general men have been given a slightly wider choice of mates, in that they have been permitted to take wives from lower classes or sub-castes; and they have been given greater freedom of choice even when the marriages were mostly arranged by their elders. Note that this difference is not caused by the biological factor noted above, but it does suggest that societies have paid more attention to the man's motivation.

Such differences do not, of course, exhaust the many biological differences between men and women. As we have seen, biological differences do not actually determine the immense variation in sex roles from one society to another, or from one historical age to another. True, they limit somewhat the forms that the family can take, but fundamentally they are insufficient to guide the human animal in his almost totally learned family behavior. Thus we must be very cautious about accepting any given American family pattern as somehow "natural" or "rooted in biology."

American Kinship Structure

More than 200 million people in the United States live under such a wide variety of family arrangements that it is impossible to characterize them all by a simple formula. Most do follow similar patterns, however, and we can describe them in a general way by noting how at many points they differ from other family systems of the world.

First, of course, the American system is technically monogamous. It has sometimes been called "serial monogamy," since every year several hundred thousand people divorce and soon remarry, and of course a small percentage of these people may have a succession of spouses over their lifetimes. Nevertheless, the structure of daily marital living is very different from a system in which one man is married to several wives (polygyny) or the much rarer system in which one woman is married to two or more husbands (polyandry), since life with a single spouse is much more intense. In point of fact, in most polygamous systems the ordinary person is usually married to only one spouse; even when marriage to two or more wives is approved, only the powerful and well-to-do have the resources to achieve that blissful state. It should also be kept in mind that in such great civilizations as India, China, Japan, and those Western European countries where monogamy has been the legal norm, the aristocratic and the rich have been able to indulge their wish to enjoy mistresses and concubines without fear of punishment. On the other hand, in all these societies the rules against a woman's enjoying the same privilege have always been very strict.

The American family system is also based on the independent family unit, in which a married couple and their children are expected to live physically separated from their kin and from their parents. In most instances, even older parents prefer to live alone if they have the financial means to do so. Here again our system differs from that of many other societies, such as China, Japan, India, and Arabic Islam, in which a couple might continue to reside for years in either a joint household or under some other kind of shared economic arrangement. To be sure, this kind of living arrangement was always more common among the upper classes, who could more easily afford to take care of a young dependent couple. In most societies a young man has not been able to afford a marriage until he achieved economic independence. Formerly this independence came with owning land; now it comes with holding a job. Nevertheless, in most societies the ideal, if not the universal, practice was one large family unit in which several family units were linked closely together.

Because of the American emphasis upon the independence of the family unit, the age at which people marry in the United States has been somewhat higher than in Eastern countries, though lower than in most European countries. The average age of American males at marriage is approximately twenty-two years of age; that of females is approximately twenty. Thus the majority of American women marry when they are still in their late teens. As noted earlier, the average marital age in the United States was higher fifty years ago. At present, most young women work for a while before they marry. Men who marry young typically have jobs that pay low wages, but they are not as economically dependent upon their parents as rural people were a hundred years ago, when owning land was necessary for making a living.

In the last two decades a slightly new pattern has emerged, which might be considered the spread of an *older* upper-class pattern: middle-class youngsters have married increasingly earlier but remained economically dependent on their parents. In practice this has meant that young men and women who are in college are permitted to marry, but still continue to receive all or most of their income from their parents. Socially, this pattern overlaps with a deviant arrangement, in which a young middle-class couple lives together with the tacit approval and financial support of their parents, who may or may not hope that the two will ultimately legitimate their union by formal marriage.

Although the American system is still patronymic, since the name of the family line comes from the male side, it is neither a patrilineal nor matrilineal society but a *bilateral* one in which kinship is equally traced through both male and female parents. All of the major civilizations that we know of have been patrilineal, in that the lineage is traced primarily through the male line. Modern research, however, clearly reveals that in all major civilizations at least the informal links with the female side have often counted very heavily.

Patrilineal societies are also likely to give far more authority to the male and, in some societies, to the eldest living male ancestor. In the American system the husband does indeed have more authority than the wife, especially in major decisions, but not only do many women manage to achieve considerable influence in all family relations, but the modern movement in favor of liberating women continues to press for still greater decision-making power for wives.

This marks a difference from most other major societies in the past, and of course represents a substantial departure from America's own historical pattern. For years in the United States wives were not permitted to make contracts on their own. If they possessed real estate when they entered the marriage, the husband could legally use that real estate in order to earn money on his own. It was extremely difficult for a woman to leave her own home without being charged with "abandoning her domicile." She could not gain custody of her children, since children belonged to the husband's line. She could not sue. Along with these and many other legal disabilities, the near impossibility of earning an adequate salary by herself meant that the wife ultimately had to obey the authority of her husband, if he chose to exercise it.

The American kinship system has also been one of equal inheritance, as contrasted with those traditional social systems in which all of the family estate went to a single male heir (as in upper-class England and Japan) or in which the males shared equally (as in China), or in which the male received a larger share than the female children (as in Arabic Islam). In the United States the allocation of an inheritance is largely a problem of the more affluent social strata, and indeed our social patterns place less and less importance on the notion of "building an estate for the children."

Although equal inheritance is the legal norm, in fact there are many informal rules which alter this arrangement. If the family owns a business it is likely that a son, not a daughter, will enter it. If there are two sons, it is likely that the son who enters the business will inherit it, with some financial provision being made for the other son. Sons are likely to receive loans or gifts of money, while daughters are more likely to be left trust funds which give them much less autonomy in financial matters.

The American kinship system is also characterized by "free courtship," which in the adolescent phase of dating to some degree resembles the Polynesian societies in its emphasis upon romance. Perhaps the only European societies that come close to it are the Scandinavian ones, though parental influence in the ultimate choice of the spouse may be greater in those countries than in America. In practice, as is well known, our system permits rather early dating, great freedom of physical movement, privacy, and almost no chaperonage whatsoever. In America, too, there is no sharp line between dating and courtship; the social assumption is that people who go together are merely dating unless they announce that they are serious about their future plans.

The informal assumption of our courtship system is that people date one another on the basis of personal attraction. Yet many researchers have shown the extent to which people are actually participating in a kind of limited "marriage market," in which one excludes most of the population and accepts only people with characteristics very similar to one's own. The element of choice in dating is wider than in marriage, but most people never date across broad caste, religious, class, or age lines. Both parents and peer groups support these restrictions, by cajoling, threats of social ostracism, refusals of invitations, and financial inducements. Thus, technically, anyone may marry almost anyone else who is not barred by incest rules, but in fact informal family patterns confine most people within a fairly narrow pool of eligible dating or marriage partners who share a similar background. Moreover, when people do cross these lines successfully, for the most part they do so only when they have already lost some of the traits that are associated with their particular caste, ethnic group, or class. Thus, for example, a girl from the lower class who has gone to college may well have lost most of the social traits of her own class, and have acquired those of the middle class. Similarly, those who cross religious lines are likely to be less intense in their devotion to the religion in which they were reared, and to move in social circles where religion is not considered very important.

Most family systems of the great civilizations have (or have had) either a dowry system or a bride-price system, but the American kinship pattern has dropped this sort of marriage gift. In Western countries the dowry has been fairly standard, and in Europe it is not uncommon even today in some upper-middle-class circles. When it was in full operation, a family with many daughters might be unable to marry all of them off to husbands of the appropriate class, because such husbands would expect an adequate amount of money, and there might not be enough to divide among all the daughters. A family with sons was of course in a more fortunate position. Under some dowry systems, the money actually went to the elders or to the family estate rather than to the husband himself.

Note, however, that both the dowry and the bride-price system ultimately depend upon a high degree of stability in the marriage itself. When elders have no assurance that the marriage they are helping to arrange and pay for will continue for any length of time, they are less likely to be willing to make substantial cash investments in it. In any event, over the past century such arrangements have come to be viewed as degrading, for they suggest that the woman is worthless in herself and is valuable only for the money she brings in.

It could be argued that in fact the American family system does operate under a dowry arrangement, though it is not a legal requirement and is never spoken of as a dowry. It is, however, clear that not only are there strong pressures on the part of both parents to contribute as much money and goods to the young couple as possible, but the bride's family is clearly expected to contribute far more than the groom's. Supposedly, the side with the most money contributes most, but this rule is tempered by the social pressure on the bride's parents to contribute more. Not only are they expected to pay for the wedding and reception, which may be elaborate and expensive, but they are expected in addition to come up with other sums and gifts beyond those expected of the groom's parents.

As with the traditional Japanese and Arabic Islamic family, the American system exhibits a high rate of instability. For technical reasons it is difficult to calculate the rate of this instability with any exactitude. Nevertheless, various estimates suggest that approximately one-fourth of all American marriages end in divorce. The divorce figure is certainly lower in rural areas than in urban areas, lower among Catholics than among Protestants, lower among whites than among blacks.

America's high marital instability has in turn meant a high "turnover"—that is, most of those who become divorced or who lose their spouses through death are likely to remarry. As a consequence, the dating and courtship system is not confined to the young, as it traditionally was in European and earlier American society. Other industrial nations are experiencing rapid increases in their divorce rate, but theirs are not as high as that of the United States. Over the past fifty years the social disapproval of divorce in America has dropped substantially, men can obtain most of the services their wives provide by simply buying them (laundry, housekeeping, and so forth), and wives in turn can support themselves by getting jobs on their own. In very few circles these days would a man or woman be ostracized for seeking a divorce.

Crucial to any account of marriage in contemporary America is the great emphasis that Americans place upon individual happiness. Since the supposed purpose of marriage is "happiness through love," and since any relationship of this kind is not likely to continue to yield the same intense feeling year after year, far more is expected of marriage than it can possibly produce. In fact, most American marriages carry too heavy an emotional burden. In this context, divorce serves as an escape valve for all the tensions of a highly intimate, emotionally overloaded relationship from which far too much has been expected.

Another difference between the American kinship system and that of most great civilizations of the past has to do with the position our system accords the elderly. In traditional societies the eldest male has been viewed as head of the family, a figure endowed with great authority and paid enormous deference. In some societies he was thought to be in touch with the spirits of the dead, to control magic, and to be the possessor of considerable wisdom. In the older societies, where most technical procedures and problems might be relatively simple and similar from one decade to another, very likely the older men did in fact have much useful knowledge.

While American society does not withdraw respect from older people, as is obvious to anyone who looks at the age distributions of powerful or esteemed politicians, judges, or corporate executives, nevertheless age itself commands little deference. In the American kinship system the position of the elderly is ambiguous. Few obligations or responsibilities are prescribed by age. The grandfather of sixty may, if he wishes, move to another state, take up water skiing, go to nightclubs, adopt the newest fashions, or even decide to start a new career without much social disapproval. He may also, if he wishes, play a much more traditionally grand-fatherly role, again without much criticism. This arrangement has advantages as well as disadvantages. The older kinsman has in effect earned very little credit. Certainly he cannot rest upon his laurels. If he wishes to keep his kin network alive and active, he will have to take the initiative and continue to contribute to the ongoing flow of affection, services, and funds that characterize family life. He cannot expect his kinsmen to flock around him, as they might once have done to a revered elder. On the other hand, the older kinsman now can shake off some of his traditional responsibilities if he does not wish to maintain them, and can start an almost entirely new life without expecting more than mild joshing or a comment or two about "acting his age."

Mating, Dating, and Courtship

Moving from this broad perspective to a closer view of the American courtship system, its dynamics become clearer. All courtship systems are "marriage markets," but the American version differs from others in the extent to which each individual tries to sell his own wares and carry out his or her own negotiations. In many traditional societies, by contrast, elder kinsmen made these arrangements for younger people.

In America everyone is permitted to marry as early or as late as he chooses. If he chooses early, his marriage may well fall short of his ideal expectations. This would be especially likely if he is upwardly mobile, for a marriage with someone of his own class origin might prove embarrassing once he had moved up into a higher class. If a man marries late, the marriage market will have been severely narrowed, and his ideal spouse may have already married. If a man desires to marry a pretty, rich, talented woman, he is certainly permitted to make the attempt; but if he has no equivalent gifts to offer, he is likely to be rejected. In order to avoid that risk, he may instead court a young woman whose qualities are worth much less in the market than his own. Although kinsmen and friends will usually offer some advice about his choice, there are no official "go-betweens," or matchmakers, whose responsibility it is to investigate the prospective bride or groom so as to prevent foolish errors of judgment.

Several processes in the American "free-courtship" system can be distinguished. One is the ordinary market process of supply and demand. Some people ask for more than they can get on the market, and others ask less, but in general brides and grooms are likely to be roughly similar in their traits and assets. A girl who is physically attractive can marry a young man who is less handsome but upwardly mobile. A young man in a higher social class is most likely to marry a woman from his own class, but he may go outside his class to choose someone who has money or beauty. An older man is most likely to marry a woman younger than himself (but still in an older age bracket); but if he is rich or influential, he has a good chance of marrying a much younger woman who is very attractive. In general, marital choices are homogamous: like marry like, and discrepancies are likely to be balanced off.

However, underlying all marital choices is a set of preferences, or values, which tend toward homogamy. Everyone is socialized to value certain traits, and thus a man (and his kinsmen and friends who influence his choices) sees others as more or less attractive to the extent to which they possess these traits. The talented young assistant professor of economics may seem very attractive to his female students, but he may appear pretentious, unmanly, and boring to a lower-class woman. People who have been reared mainly within one ethnic or religious group are not only less likely to meet and date outsiders; they are also less likely to enjoy being in an intimate situation with them. Thus the apparently "free" American system of individual courtship presses toward homogamy.

None of this is meant to deny the importance of love. Indeed, until recently, when their own courtship systems became closer to our own, European social commentators often ridiculed Americans for allowing love so large a role in marital choice. The theme of love has for decades pervaded American movies, popular music, literature, and advertising, and is one of the commonest topics of gossip. Perhaps no other major nation ever gave so prominent a position to love; specifically, only Americans have assumed it to be necessary (if not altogether sufficient) for marriage.

By contrast, in some societies love is viewed as a threat to the orderly processes of mate choice, since the choice of a mate is carried out by elder kinsmen, and so strong an attraction between a young man and woman might well thwart those negotiations. In these societies love is rather to be isolated or curbed, either by marrying young people off very early or by controlling access to jobs or land so as to prevent free choice. In still other societies love is not viewed as an aberration or a threat; instead, it is thought acceptable as long as it does not interfere unduly with the marriage arrangements made by kinsmen. This can usually be accomplished by seeing to it that only young men and women who belong to the appropriate class or kinship line have any opportunity of meeting, and hence of falling in love with one another. Our own society, of course, permits love a very large role in marital choice, though the extent to which the likelihood of falling in love is constricted by social and economic factors is great.

Some social analysts have argued that love motivates young people, who after all do not know each other very well, to adjust to one another's foibles and idiosyncracies in the early stages of marriage. It also motivates them to leave their parents and establish their own home. This is especially important in that in our system few people have much stake in maintaining the marriage— at least as compared with people living in those systems in which a large kin network may actually have an economic investment in the marriage. Many couples are disappointed when the high excitement of courtship diminishes, leaving them with a drab and rather humdrum existence. Marital counselors and others point out that if the relationship between men and women is pervaded by love before marriage, it is difficult to tell married people afterwards that it is of secondary importance. In any event love will continue to be of central significance to the American marriage far into the future.

Husbands and Wives

A famous actress once protested that what's wrong with getting married is that after the honeymoon husbands always want to go home with their wives. This objection to the day-to-day boredom of marital adjustment is found in many barbed comments from social philosophers, whether professors or cab drivers. On the other hand, every study of marital adjustment reveals that a large majority of husbands and wives claim that they are either "happy" or "very happy" in their marriages. Since the American marriage system encourages maximum closeness between husbands and wives, the opportunities for disagreement are also maximized. How then do they adjust to one another's different behavior in the various areas of married life, such as the division of labor, power and authority, sex, attitudes toward work, and children?

In the traditional Hindu marriage—to look once again at other cultures—a young girl is married in her early teens to an older man and goes to live with her husband's family before the union is finally consummated. Thus she has few resources with which to resist their authority, and is either forced or persuaded to learn the ways to please her husband and his kin. Relieving these pressures somewhat was the custom of fairly long visits to her own relatives, who assured her that her duty was to adjust. In the old Chinese kinship system, the young woman also lost the potential support of her own kin since she moved to the village or area where her husband's family lived, and, like the Hindu girl, she was given no options: divorce was nearly impossible, and she found herself surrounded by older and more powerful people who in any dispute were likely to side with her husband. In addition, both systems prescribed certain tasks that were appropriate to males and females. The young husband had his own duties, and these were clearly separate from those of his wife. If each carried out his or her own traditional duties, then there could be little conflict. The amount of daily contact between the young husband and wife was reduced to a minimum. The young wife cooperated with her female relatives and the young husband carried out male tasks with his male relatives. In these ways the importance of the husband-wife bond was reduced.

In most such traditional kinship systems, again in contrast to our own, the notion of "love and happiness" was simply not the aim of married life at all. The officially supported aims of marriage were continuing the family line, honoring ancestors, contributing to the economic well-being of the larger kin unit, or living a harmonious life according to established religious precepts. By setting a much lower standard of emotional attachment between husband and wife, and by emphasizing specific duties and tasks, such systems made it possible for most people to reconcile themselves to the humdrum qualities of daily married life.

The advantage of such a system is that it prescribes actions, rather than a loving emotion. We *can* will conformity to the former, but not the latter. It is also easier to fulfill marital obligations if both husband and wife agree on what those obligations are, but the American system is probably less clear than almost any other in its specification of what each partner in a marriage is supposed to do. There is thus a wider area of action in which conflict is at least potential: each couple must work out for themselves just who is responsible for what. There are husbands who refuse to help at any household task and others who are willing to share in all of these tasks, from cooking to redecorating the home.

It may be objected that the two great areas of "earning a living" and "taking care of the children" are clear role obligations that are divided by sex. Indeed, it is true that it would be difficult to find many homes in which the wife goes out to earn a living, while the husband stays at home to care for the house and children. Yet if a group of men and women were asked individually to write down a fairly complete list of all the tasks in a marriage, designating which ought to be carried out by the husband and which by the wife, it would soon become apparent that even in a fairly homogeneous group, disagreement is likely to be very large and full of tension. Even in a household where both husband and wife know what in general the other expects, both may also harbor considerable resentments about the way these jobs are allocated.

Husbands and wives, of course, begin the adjustment of such differences as early as their first date together and may continue the process throughout their marriage. From their very first meetings, young men and women inform each other by subtle or not so subtle cues or even full-blown philosophical discussions of how they feel about what husbands and wives ought to do, in areas ranging from sexual relations to how many children a couple should have. Although each may be trying to impress the other, or to present his or her best self, the other is generally able to penetrate these disguises to a considerable extent—certainly to the point where it can be ascertained whether the other's views are traditional or radical, egalitarian or patriarchal, flexible or rigid. By the time they have actually begun their married life together, most of the larger issues have at least been confronted in one way or another, if not actually settled.

No matter how intimate their exploration of each other was before marriage, most couples experience the first year of marriage as a set of discoveries. Some of these are delightful, while others create chagrin and dismay. Like all great alterations in status, the change from single to married life holds surprises that few can anticipate. Some men can be effective and masterful in the dating situation, but once married expect to be fully taken care of by their wives. Some young women seem soft and yielding before their marriages, but these traits often turn out to conceal ruthless ambition and a deep need to dominate. On the other hand, some husbands and wives, once the anxieties and tensions of courtship and early marriage are over, enjoy the relaxation of building a home together and the security of an emotional solidarity in which each takes real pleasure in pleasing the other.

Most couples at least strive to make a go of marriage, and most do stay married until the union is broken by death. If few attain the ecstatic bliss portrayed in TV commercials and popular romances, most do manage to work out a tolerable situation. Husbands and wives learn what will anger or soothe the other, what the other can or will not do, and adjusts his or her actions to these realities of the relationship in so far as possible.

The general form of that adjustment is determined by the values brought to bear by the larger society. We are socialized to believe in monogamy and to avoid divorce if possible; we live as couples in independent households; we have two or three children; we give more authority in large decisions to the husband and expect him to earn most or all of the family income; we expect the wife to manage the household and the children; and so on.

Within each class, ethnic group, neighborhood, or social circle still other values and expectations create pressures toward more specific adjustmental patterns: wives with younger children should not hold full-time jobs unless the economic need is great; young parents should keep in close contact with their parents if possible; to maintain their social standing, husbands and wives should encourage and press their children to go to church or synagogue; it may be permissible for the husband to neglect his wife because he works late hours; and so on. Needless to say, in many circles one or more of these items would be rejected.

Husbands and wives also work out still more detailed adjustments of their own, from the choice of friendship and kinship visits, to sexual and other expectations. Moreover, they may (in private or public) simply ignore some of the directives of the larger society. Couples may agree on these personal adjustments from the beginning, or grow into them gradually, but most are the slow result of many trials, tentative probings, disagreements, errors, and successes.

If two people are to adjust, both must yield somewhat, but it is obvious that who yields in which areas is determined by who has the most resources and who has the greatest will to win. The husband or wife who has a lesser stake in the union will care less whether his or her spouse is displeased, and thus have a greater chance of imposing his or her will. The wife whose husband loves her more than she loves him is more likely to have her whims obeyed. Husbands who enjoy fighting will win more often, at least as long as the marriage lasts. Wives with an independent income are in a better position to act autonomously and to gain their ends. It is not surprising, then, to learn that wives make more adjustments in marriage than do husbands, since their resources are less. Lower-class wives enjoy more influence than do wives closer to the upper social strata, since the discrepancy between their earnings and those of their husbands is less. Women who work full time enjoy a stronger voice in family decisions than those who do not. Husbands who are better educated than their wives have more influence than those with less education.

Such factors continue to affect husband-wife relations throughout the life cycle of the family, and vary according to the area of family life. Other things being equal, wives are listened to more in the realms of children's religious education than in choosing family friends; decisions about small purchases than large ones; about where to spend vacations than whether to move elsewhere for a better job opportunity.

Social change has also transformed the areas in which personal adjustments between spouses can or must be made. The American economic and legal systems have given new options to wives, for example: independent ownership and management of property, custody of the children, graduate education, higher-level occupations, and so forth, thus creating new areas for adjustments as well as potential conflicts. A century ago, husbands and wives had almost no chance of getting a divorce, and thus felt a greater need to make a go of the only marriage they were ever likely to have. New choices expand opportunities for both spouses, but also create new problems of getting along together.

An example is the area of sexual relations. Until well after World War I, it is likely that, although sex relations were not satisfying to a high percentage of husbands and wives, the problem of adjustment was minimal. More husbands than wives felt that sexual intercourse was too rare. For a high percentage of wives—the figure varies from one sample to another—possibly as much as one half, the pleasure of orgasm was not a typical experience. As a holdover from the Victorian period, husbands were not greatly concerned with their wives' enjoyment, and many would still have argued at that time that a real lady should tolerate sex but not exult in it. Husbands were not, however, so likely as wives to be satisfied with a marriage in which the degree of sexual pleasure was low, since women expected less of sex, and other areas of family life counted for more in their eyes. In any case, neither husbands nor wives typically felt sex a problem they had to solve. More accurately it might rather be called a burden which many had to live with. Some wives or husbands went to physicians, and others hoped that time and patience might remedy matters, but in general husbands and wives felt that little could be done about sexual difficulties.

Now this situation has changed radically. The pill and other effective contraceptives have largely removed the fear of pregnancy that so often tainted sexual relations in the past. Hundreds of books explain to anyone who can read how to improve their sexual technique. Much of this information trickles from the upper middle class down, and it is explained and disseminated by the mass media, including films. Of their sex lives, wives and husbands are told frequently that they can and should "do something about it." Young people experiment with sex in order to gain pleasure and sexual competence before settling down to married life. It is safe to say that at the present time a far higher percentage of husbands and wives actually derive pleasure from sex than ever before; yet a far higher percentage of married people also feel frustrated by the need to solve sexual problems that in marriages of fifty years ago would have demanded no special effort because they were not thought capable of solution. Beyond question, far more husbands and wives now expect more pleasure from sex, and may well be disappointed when, as so frequently happens, sex turns out to be no substitute for the need for adjustment in other areas of family living.

Parents and Children

No nation has ever produced or consumed so much advice as America on how to rear children. Whether the result has justified all the outpouring of guess and fact, or even whether parents put into practice much of this advice, is not known. For obvious reasons, true experiments in socialization are almost never attempted. Judging, however, from the complexity of the problem and the difficulty of learning just *which* experiences have had *which* effects on children, perhaps a cautious conclusion would be that we now at least know what are some of the worst ways of rearing a child, but we are much less sure of how to do it well.

Some couples want fewer children than they have, and others

want more than they have had or are able to have, but only a tiny percentage want no children at all. Although this fact may seem obvious, it deserves some attention for the light that it throws not only on socialization but also on the world population problem—one of the central social problems created by the family structure. It may be argued that when Americans were farmers, children served as cheap labor and thus were economically profitable. In many societies, in addition, children are still believed to be a form of old-age insurance. But today, given the cost of rearing a child in America, children probably represent an economic loss to most families. From a national perspective, as some of the articles in the pages to follow show in more detail, the quality of living would be improved if our population were to become stationary or even if it decreased. But in fact it continues to grow.

As noted earlier, one of the pervasive themes of socialization is that children shall grow up some day to become parents themselves. Thus girls are taught to mother dolls and babies; boys are prepared to become breadwinners and fathers. In the past, socialization in all societies pressed toward high fertility. Since most traditional societies lost from 20 to 50 per cent of their infants in the first year after birth, and were threatened by occasional pestilence or famine or war, the encouragement of high fertility insured the rapid replacement of population after any calamity.

By contrast, in modern times, even in technologically less developed nations, public health measures reduce not only the infant mortality rate but the general death rate as well. The threat of pestilence or famine has become negligible. War rarely destroys more than a small percentage of the total population. Despite all this, fertility continues to be encouraged.

Consequently, most efforts to reduce the birthrate in any serious way have not met with much success. As the death rate drops substantially, the birthrate remains high. To reduce the birthrate requires changes in individual attitudes that were in fact created by a socialization process of two decades earlier, when the current generation of young adults were infants or children. Parents want to have children because they were taught to want them, and thus reducing the birthrate requires individual actions and decisions—in contrast to the public or mass kinds of actions that brought about the reduction of the death rate. The consequence of the rising population, of course, is that many nations are fighting a losing battle to improve their standard of living: their gross national product does not increase as fast as their population. Even in as rich a country as the United States, the amount of living space is constantly being diminished, and such resources as minerals, water, recreation areas, national parks, and just plain space are rapidly being used up. Indeed, the limits on rich nations are in a sense even more severe, since the per capita consumption of water, the production of wastes and pollution, and the psychological need for space may be even greater. Here, then, we see a neat illustration of the extent to which the dramatic variables of the family and socialization generate a significant social problem which threatens the quality of American living in the next generation.

Couples have children and rear them because they have been socialized to want to do so. In the process of socialization, they face the same problem that parents must solve in every society: the transformation of a resistant, changing human animal into an adult whose values, attitudes, and behavior will fit the demands of its parents. Needless to say, most couples fail, but the result is still a new generation of adults who maintain the social structure very much as it was when they were infants. How does this happen?

All mammals learn from experience, but socialization differs from even the social learning observable among the higher mammals in at least two respects. First, although monkeys can learn from others to wash potatoes in seawater, and crows learn to tease or attack cats or owls, only human beings must learn to behave in situations they have not yet encountered. Only men can deliberately communicate to each other about a wide range of problems that are outside their immediate observation.

Second, human beings transmit not just information to one another and to their children, but *norms* and values. Children must learn not only to avoid wrongdoing and to behave according to the rules of their family and group but to *want* to do so. More deeply, socialization makes us embarrassed or conscience-stricken if we do wrong, and pleased with ourselves if we do right. To illustrate the difference, the young gorilla is not taught that he *ought* to show respect to the older silver-backed gorilla leader. His learning does not contain any element of legitimacy, or of the normative. Instead, if he gets in the way of, or otherwise annoys, the dominant leader, the latter will simply cuff him aside.

The basis of both these aspects of socialization is the infant's early experience that whatever good or ill happens comes through *social interaction:* first with his mother, later through other members of the family, and still later through neighbors and the school. He comes to need the approval of others, and to be willing to behave in certain ways—smiling, talking, eating properly, showing affection, obeying—because thereby his own physical and psychological needs are better satisfied. Of course, much of his learning is simply information: matches burn, cars kill, people get angry if they are hurt, people will punish him if he steals. But at a deeper level, much of this is absorbed and becomes part of the child's autonomous feelings and responses. He himself comes to believe that behaving in certain ways is desirable.

Love is a necessary part of the socialization process, for without love an automated "child-teaching machine" that would punish or reward the infant strictly according to his performances would only create a psychopath: someone who would obey the rules because he knows he would get caught, but who has no inner sense of right or wrong. The threat of police action cannot be the only foundation of the social structure. Even in the most primitive of social circles, the maintenance of social patterns depends on inner belief that some forms of behavior are right, graceful, mannerly, or admirable, while others are wrong, awkward, rude, or despicable. Unless the child receives love, and thus comes to identify to some extent with his parents, the chances of his accepting their values are greatly reduced. Perhaps, needless to say, this also holds for his later experiences with other children and adults, in school and in the larger society.

Although parents differ in their philosophy of child-rearing, most parents have absorbed enough knowledge or folk wisdom to understand what makes for an effective way of rearing their child. For example, American parents would probably agree that they should give love and emotional security, but encourage independence; pay respect to the child's wishes, but require that it respect others as well; reward the child for living up to difficult standards, ethics, or morals, but also serve as models by living up to those standards themselves; teach children to help others, but also to have enough self-esteem to make their own legitimate demands on others; encourage them to work competently, but also to enjoy play and relaxation; and so on. Unfortunately, few parents can achieve so ideal a goal, because their own needs make its attainment so difficult and because children are not plastic or putty to be molded easily: each child has his own resistances, his own responses to a particular way of behaving. A mother may be aware that she should love her children and cuddle them, but simply be too tired or irritated by her situation in life to do so more than on rare occasions. A father may know that he creates a poor model to follow if he drinks heavily, loses his job, and is generally unreliable; yet he may nonetheless be unable to break his old habits.

Infants are lovable, but with each passing month they develop more definite wills of their own. Children in a crib may create crises frequently during the day, but they are small crises. As they grow older, they generate fewer problems, but the problems are bigger ones, and parents find it increasingly harder to retrace their steps and correct the mistakes they made years earlier in their attempts to socialize their children.

People in different social classes may have different resources with which to handle the problems of child-rearing. A divorced mother with several children, trying to eke out a living with a part-time or full-time job, hardly has the capacity to cope with all the problems her children create. By contrast, an upper-class family with many servants, the financial ability to segregate their children from outside influences through tutors or private schools, and greater rewards with which to induce conformity in their children can more easily shape their social environment and thus the influences that are important in their children's lives. They may fail, of course, because they do not know how to achieve their objective, but at least their resources are greater.

In most ghettos, a child's street companions give advice and encouragement in directions that parents and teachers deplore, but the latter do not have the resources with which to combat those influences. Children instead learn that their chances of getting out of their situation are small, except through a stroke of great luck, shady or criminal dealings, or personal strength. Children are likely to believe that much of what parents and teachers actually tell them is irrelevant or foolish, because they see before their eyes that these ideal images do not correspond with reality.

Therefore it is not surprising that studies of child-rearing show that different classes socialize their children somewhat differently —partly in response to the opportunities and resources available to them, and partly in response to different values and goals. Middle classes, for example, are more likely to give reasons to the child when they demand obedience, and are less likely to make demands on the basis of simple power alone. They are less likely to use physical punishment, and more likely to use such control devices as guilt and the withdrawal of love. Lower-class parents are much more tolerant about letting their children stay out late at night or permitting them to go to movies alone, but middle-class parents are more likely to allow their children to go downtown alone. Lower-class parents are more likely to be preoccupied with problems of survival, and thus to demand that children take care of themselves. They are also less likely to be consistent in their socialization—in part because the ideals they proclaim are likely to be pierced or shattered from time to time by the harsh realities that the family faces. As might be expected, lower-class parents are more likely than middle-class parents to approve when their child learns to fight back in a conflict with other children. Middle-class parents are more likely to emphasize high performance in school, a strong motivation to achieve, and verbal skills. Obviously, these differences partly reflect a somewhat different set of goals, but much more fundamentally a response to different life situations.

As has been emphasized *ad nauseam,* the contemporary era is one of great parent-youth conflict. In a broader sense, of course, there is a perennial conflict between parents and children, since children at an early age wish to follow their own goals and needs, while parents wish to impose their own upon their children. However, we are now in a period of great social change, in which large numbers of young people express their political and social objections to the values, goals, attitudes, and general behavior of their parents and of other parents.

Conflict of this kind is less common in most primitive societies. Although in some of these societies children have in fact been reared more permissively than in our own, when there is no great difference in the life situations of parents and that of their children when they become adults, the wisdom and accumulated knowledge of the parents is useful. To be sure, there is always a life-cycle conflict between parents and children: the child of five or the youth of fifteen cannot view his problems in quite the same perspective as his parents do. In a time of great social change, to this normal life-cycle conflict is added the conflict that arises because the youngster feels that his parents' grasp of the world is either irrelevant or wrong. Thus the speed of social change intensifies normal parent-youth conflict. To take an obvious example, many modern parents have tried some of the outlawed drugs that are part of the youth scene, but none has grown up in the so-called "drug culture." Nor did the current generation of parents grow up in a culture in which the contraceptive pill was taken for granted. On the political side, only since World War II has the United States maintained a large standing army and a large military complex that makes up much of the industrial system. In all these and other ways, the life situation of the contemporary adolescent is very different from that of his parents, and it is not surprising that as a consequence he rejects much of their advice.

In the modern era, too, in part because of the mass media, it is much easier for young people to organize themselves. This has been true in the past only when great social movements were under way, such as the Bolshevik revolution, the Nazi period, or the long period during which the Chinese Communists were gradually gaining power.

Being more affluent, and able to obtain jobs more easily without the help of their parents, the young can survive economically more easily than in previous generations. Parents will not usually cut their ties and abandon their child even when he is rebellious. Adolescents can move out and join communes or simply live with friends' families.

In a period of fast social change, the young find many models to follow, whose philosophies differ from that of the society. Adolescents seize on new ideas and styles of life that are presented on television, and the mass media contain many exhortations to new and radical ways of organizing the social structure. The dissident youngster can find many supports and many companions in his rebellion.

It is too early to know how far this parent-child conflict will go, and whether the generation now growing up will in fact alter in a major way the social institutions of the United States. In the past, we know that many young people rebelled but later became sober and docile members of the society. Moreover, active rebels form only a small percentage of the total population of even the college youth. On the other hand, since among those who do revolt are to be found many of the future leaders of the nation, and since even though their present philosophies may not be fully put into action in the future, these young people may not entirely change their ideas when they assume positions of power, it is at least arguable that the social institutions and organizations of this country may well be changed as an outcome of contemporary parent-youth conflict. As a consequence, the nation may gradually shift its aims from a continually increasing gross national product to a more definite focus on the human quality of social life.

Problems of the Family

Since the family is linked at so many points with other social institutions, it not only generates many problems internally, but also creates problems in the larger society. In turn, it develops many problems in response to pressures from the social structure. We have just seen, for example, that the socialization practices of many families create numerous psychological problems, often producing adults who do not function adequately in the larger society. Illegitimacy must be considered as one type of family problem, even though in this instance the family unit cannot be said to have actually dissolved since it never formally existed to begin with. In cases of illegitimate birth, the "father-husband" does not fulfill his obligations, and a major factor in high illegitimacy rates is the failure of members of the families of both the mother and father of the illegitimate child to socialize their children properly.

We have noted in passing—and a later article in this book will deal with the problem at greater length—that the continued fertility of American families creates a major population problem which the present social structure is not equipped to solve. We have noted the extent to which the larger social structure and socialization practices in individual families create a large-scale parent-youth conflict in our time. In the various forms of family dissolution, such as annulment, desertion, separation, and divorce, both the internal strains created by members of the family and the external pressures from the larger society interact to push these rates higher every decade. On a smaller scale, of course, are the various internal catastrophes which result when one member of the family cannot fulfill his normal obligations because of severe mental retardation, or mental or physical breakdown.

There exists, then, a wide range of family problems which encompass a large segment of the American population, and these are intertwined in complex ways both with the individual personalities of family members and the broader contemporary social currents. Rather than treat all of these problems in a glancing way, let us look at the phenomenon of divorce in some detail.

Several countries in the past have had higher divorce rates than the United States, but presently the United States has the highest divorce rate among all Western nations. Although the American rate has varied over the past century, it has been consistently on the rise. Its general tendency has been to drop during depressions and to increase during periods of prosperity. It increases after major wars, largely because the number of marriages is greater at such times. It is difficult to calculate precisely how many American marriages end in divorce, but various estimates suggest that between one-fifth and one-fourth of all marriages do, and over the past decade there has been more than one divorce for every four marriage ceremonies. (Keep in mind, however, that for the most part these divorces did not arise from the same set of marriage ceremonies, but merely occurred in the same year.)

Most countries with relatively low divorce rates are those in which controls have been fairly high; that is, if marriages were not always arranged by parents, the parents at least took a strong hand in their children's decision to marry and continued to exert their influence afterward. In American society, many changes have taken place over the past hundred years to create a higher divorce rate. Most fundamental, of course, have been alterations in *values* about the stability of marriage. Divorce has come to be viewed as a kind of escape valve for family tensions that cannot be solved by the individuals, and those who divorce are no longer ostracized from their social circles. Perhaps the extent of this change can best be noted by recalling that a hundred years ago a husband and wife who felt that they were caught in a bad marriage simply did not view divorce as a possibility. Since that time the laws themselves have not changed radically, but the interpretation of an acceptable level of pain in a marriage before divorce ought to be sought has dropped sharply.

Some might view this change as a move toward selfishness, or individualism, or even self-fulfillment. The essential factor, however, is that individuals no longer see divorce as so immoral as to be beyond contemplation, and this applies as well to almost all religious segments of the population. Accompanying this change is another: social pressures from friends and kin have altered fundamentally. Since they themselves no longer believe that a bad marriage must be endured, and since they do not have a large stake in the continuation of any particular marriage, people are much less inclined to press the husband or wife into remaining together. Moreover, although divorce always creates some awkwardness among in-laws, kin, and friends, no longer is there any concerted or organized decision to view either husband or wife as the major culprit, and so a divorce can be achieved without grave social consequences for either party.

Of equal importance is the fact that now there are many alternatives. Obviously, if many people divorce, then the number of potential spouses available for anyone who does leave his marriage increases. The loss of a wife is not so disastrous as it once was, especially when America was more rural than it now is and so many tasks had to be carried out by the wife in and around the household so that the husband could till the fields. Perhaps the change for the woman is even greater, since it was once nearly impossible for a woman to survive alone at any respectable standard of living. Few jobs were available for women, and most of those were unskilled or semi-skilled factory jobs paying a pittance wage. Although women do earn less at any given level of competence in our society than do men, it is nevertheless now possible for a divorced wife to earn a salary that will permit her to face life alone.

Along with this change, of course, is the lesser willingness of women to adjust to inequality. Although women have not achieved liberation, and may well never achieve it, the past century has seen (especially in the United States) a steady spread of an egalitarian philosophy that demands greater rights for women both in the larger society and within the family. These attitudes are part of broader social changes in our society, which create individuals who enter marriage with different philosophies and attitudes than those held by previous generations. The ambiguous role of woman in American life seems likely to increase the possibilities of stress between husbands and wives, and hence to increase the possibilities of divorce.

In a sense, then, the "cause" of many divorces can be found in the larger social structure. It is rarely possible to pin down the precise cause of even a single divorce, much less the causes of the roughly 534,000 divorces that occur in the United States year after year. One might say that not only does every member of a family contribute to a given divorce, but so do kin and friends as well as the pressures and influences of TV and films, magazines and newspapers, economic depression and war, and indeed almost every other major factor in the larger society.

The Future of the American Family

In response to the apparent rapid social change in our era, hundreds of essays and books have sketched the future of the American family. Many predict that it will change in major ways over the next two generations, although the safest prophecy about any social institution is that it will alter somewhat but not much. If we chart our daily lives, or assess our personalities truthfully, we can see that we are not transformed from one week to the next or even from one year to the next. Our habits, both good and bad, maintain their vigor. So it is with great institutions. Technology has indeed been transformed over the past hundred years, but it is difficult to point to many really substantial alterations in most of our social institutions. If we look back at the American family of a century ago, its basic outlines look very similar to our own, though of course they have been somewhat modified over the years.

Americans marry at younger ages now than a hundred years ago, and they divorce at a higher rate. The population has a longer life expectancy, and so more people live to become sixty-five years of age or older, and there are more couples living together who are elderly. These couples expect to live with each other when they are old rather than with their children. The use of contraceptives is widespread among all religious faiths. The illegitimacy rate is somewhat higher among the white population than it once was. Abortion is becoming legally permissible. Couples expect to enjoy sex in marriage, and most do.

But merely to list such changes is to raise the problem of defining what a radical change in the family really is. Has the American family system fundamentally altered since the Civil War? If it changes as much during the next hundred years as it has over the past hundred, will we be able to consider its fundamental transformation? A hundred years ago divorce was uncommon because it was financially and legally very difficult, but people could and did separate permanently. Modern contraceptives had not been invented, but American couples began to limit the number of their children as early as the beginning of the nineteenth century. Courtship is freer now, and young people are less chaperoned, but European travelers well over a century ago remarked on how little control American parents had over their children. Today, American parents still have a large voice in their children's marriage choices. Young people are less respectful to their elders than they used to be, but the values and attitudes they come to accept are usually quite close to those of their parents just the same. Husbands still have a controlling voice in family decisions, while wives and children typically do not.

The American family has moved in certain directions during the past hundred years, which it may well follow in the next few generations, and these quantitative differences are not negligible. The question is, however, whether these changes in family life comprise a serious transformation of the institution of the family itself.

At first glance it would seem safe to predict that in the future the American family will continue to change as it has in the past. Yet certain major cautions should be kept in mind. The downward trend of the age of marriage, for example, will not maintain itself forever. Young people have more voice in family decisions than they used to, but it is unlikely that this will persist to the point where they rule the family. The basic weakness in any prediction that social trends will persist in their present direction is that we often simply do not know what the fundamental factors are that are *causing* the trends in the first place. For example, the United States experienced a long-term decline in the birthrate that extended well over a century. The birthrate rose during prosperity, and declined during depression, but overall continued downward. During the last depression, demographers predicted that the downward trend would persist through the 1940's and 1950's. All their predictions fell far short of reality, for the birthrate in fact spurted upward. The problem was, and remains, that we do not fully understand precisely which variables reduce or increase the birthrate, just as we do not understand which factors have created changes in the American family system up to this point.

Because the family is so closely linked to all other social institutions it is difficult to predict what will become of it without knowing how the larger social structure will itself be altered in the future. During past decades we have witnessed a "revolution" of blacks, of youth, and of women. With this in mind, some analysts have maintained that we have arrived at a watershed, a major bifurcation in the history of our country, and that the years to come will see radical changes in the social structure of America.

If, for example, the United States begins to care less about an ever-increasing gross national product and instead concentrates upon the quality of its human relations and daily living, then obviously the family will change along with the rest of society. At the moment, people have come to be concerned about pollution. If a serious campaign is mounted to clean our environment, it will require radical changes in the present social and economic patterns of the United States. Since World War II, for the first time in the history of the United States, much of the national economy has been devoted to military production in one way or another. If that were to change, much else in the society would change. In short, if a prophet's predictions about the American family are to be correct, he must also risk some guesses about the direction of changes in the American social structure, and of course no one can know with any certainty where American society will be two or three decades from now.

With such cautions in mind, several areas in which the American family seems likely to change in the future can be suggested.

As the farm population of the United States has dwindled, the place of the elderly in the family system has changed. What their position will be in the future is not clear. In a traditional agricultural society, the elderly are given more respect, for the good reason that they have more social and technical knowledge relevant to the affairs of the family and farm than anyone else. They do not simply retire at age sixty-five but continue to be of use on the farm, working at less strenuous tasks. Typically, they retain ownership of the property they have been farming all along. Consequently, in the family structure the elderly have resources that are of the utmost importance, and hence command far more respect than in an urban society where they are defined as useless after age sixty-five. In some primitive societies the elderly were also thought to be in touch with the gods or sacred ancestors, whom they would soon join, and were believed to be in command of whatever magic the society possessed. Consequently they were not likely to be cast aside in favor of the young.

Because the birthrate has declined over several generations while a few years have been added to the average life span, the overall percentage of elderly in the population has increased. They represent a significant political force, and various attempts have been made to create a social insurance system that would guarantee them some security. In part, the need for such insurance may reflect a lessening of commitment on the part of the younger generation to take care of their elders, though it also reflects an understanding that many elderly people simply do not have any kin on whom to rely. Since family attitudes in the United States have emphasized the independence of the household, both young married couples and elderly couples prefer to live in their own households, with modern transportation and communication facilities making it possible for them to be in frequent contact.

Perhaps the central change in the family role of the elderly has been a blurring of role obligations of the elderly and members of their families. Quite a range of options is open to the elderly. They may sell their house and move to Florida or California, where they may start a different mode of life. It is now taken for granted that they may wish to spend their accumulated earnings, and not merely "build an estate" for the younger generation. They may take up new sports. Or, instead, they may play the traditional role of grandparents, and make no attempt to get in tune with modern times. Many men retire and decay. Others start new businesses, continue their occupation or profession in a different locality, or go back to school for training in a new job. While less protected by their own adult children than they once were, the elderly are also permitted to choose among a wider range of options.

Of course, in all societies the roles of the elderly have ranged widely. Some heads of families are vigorous patriarchs until they die, while other men retire into contemplation or senility. Such a range is in large part a simple function of an older person's health and financial resources. America is the first society, however, in which "retirement" has become typical, and it is perhaps ironic that this has occurred in a society in which work has been the major justification for a man's existence. To some extent, work as a justification for living applies to the wife as well. Thus many elderly couples are, in effect, left dangling by a system that often enforces their retirement at a point in their lives when they are still vigorous and still feel the need to be useful.

This change, which may be expected to continue in the future, may also have some effect upon the divorce rate among older people. Couples who have been married many years are not necessarily happier. Indeed, there is often a slow decline in marital adjustment, at least in the sense that both partners to the marriage are less concerned emotionally about the relationship. With retirement, however, some women find that "having a man around the house" all day long is intolerable, and especially so since the man himself may begin to take an interest in matters in which his wife had previously reigned. Decisions may have to be made about selling the house or moving their residence, or even taking new jobs. Retirement breaks a lifetime of habit, and this new phase of adjustment convinces many people that the marriage itself need not be prolonged.

A similarly jarring change may occur in the future with respect to sexual relations. Most women still believe that with the onset of menopause sexual relations should either stop or decline sharply. This attitude has traditionally been coupled with a widespread feeling that sexual relations between the elderly or even the late middle-aged were obscene if not ridiculous: grandparents, after all, should not engage in sexual relations.

While women in the past have been more willing to give up sexual relations than men have, an increasing percentage of the female population will doubtless be convinced by modern studies that their sexual drive should continue throughout their lifetime and that sexual pleasure is possible even after age sixty-five. We can expect, therefore, that in the near future there will be an increasing amount of sexual conflict between people who are technically thought of as elderly.

Quite possibly, this change will be linked to still another possibility—that a larger percentage of widows will remarry in the future. At the present time, elderly men have a substantial advantage over elderly women in their marriage options. It is not considered ridiculous for a man of sixty-five to marry a woman of forty-five, though it is so considered for a woman of the same age to marry a much younger man. This curious duality comes about mainly because of the belief that older women who show an interest in sex are somehow perverse or funny. Yet to the extent that it is taken for granted that older women are sexually responsive, and to the extent that a greater equality between men and women is created, it may well be that the remarriage rate among older women will eventually approach that of older men.

Although women may well be the last group to be liberated, it is possible that the modern drive toward women's equality will have an important effect upon family relations in the United States of the future. A half-century has passed since women won the right to vote in the United States, but it is not at all clear that their basic position in the family or in the larger society has changed much. In the traditional professions, the percentage of women has changed little over the years. The percentage of women college graduates who become professionals has in fact probably declined. There is evidence that the wage discrepancy between men and women has increased rather than decreased over the past two decades. Although women have nearly closed the gap in education, and have entered many new occupations, even at middle levels of achievement women complain rightly that they are not given the kind of personal respect that men would command in similar positions. Correspondingly, as in all situations of subordination and superordination, men are not only reluctant to grant equality to their wives; they are even reluctant to concede that a discrepancy exists.

As a consequence, across the nation women are beginning to organize in formal and informal groups to protest their treatment —both at the hands of employers and of their own husbands. No specific program is likely to capture the allegiance of even a majority of American women, but many proposals, ranging from the modest to the radical, are being supported by one or another different groups. These proposals range from that which calls for women simply to cut off social relations with men and rely upon each other and upon masturbation for sexual pleasure, to suggestions for facilities for child care which would enable women to work full time. Some proposals have called for new modes of household living, equivalent to communes, in which there would be no discrimination based on sex. Girl children would not be pushed to become owners of dolls and carriages, and boys who prefer to engage in such activities would not be discouraged from doing so.

Generally, an increasing number of women are demanding that they be treated as human beings, and not merely as sexual objects, that they be given a full voice in family decisions; that they have the right to the use of their own bodies, whether in sexual relations or abortion; that they not be required to carry the whole burden of nurturance, home care, child-rearing, shopping, and so on, but that these activities properly be the obligation of men and women equally. Some groups show great hostility toward all men, and it is fair to say that as women become more aware, through such group activities, of the extent to which they have been discriminated against, far more hostility against men will be released in the future, as has occurred in the relations between blacks and whites in the United States. Since most men are emotionally dependent upon a flow of tender "feminine" gestures and acts, this change is likely to generate much conflict between husbands and wives in the near future.

To the extent that women acquire a firmer economic base, they can become much more independent of their husbands. As their skills are further developed by increasing job responsibilities, they will be better able to command a larger share of decision-making in the family. As more of them reject the older notion that chastity is more incumbent upon wives than husbands, far more will reject or ignore this norm, and men will either adjust or be plunged into more conflict than at present. When women are in fuller control of the decision to bear a child, almost certainly the birthrate will fall somewhat. And, in the near future, an increasing number of young men and women would be wise to feel each other out on how each feels about these recently emergent issues.

It is too soon to say what a marriage under the new dispensation might be like. Some women now reject marriage entirely, but are nevertheless willing to live with a man they love. Perhaps, as one social analyst suggests, men and women must give up either the notion of exclusivity or that of stability. Under such an arrangement they can opt for stability and permit each other various temporary or long-term relationships outside the marriage; or they can engage in a succession of exclusive and intense relationships. The harmony between men and women in such a future family would not, presumably, be based upon a sexual division of labor; for example, the man might well stay home and take care of the children while the woman went out to work, if that were required. Presumably a higher percentage of women would enter the labor force. Perhaps some men would welcome the option of rejecting the masculine ego-image, which calls for being bold, courageous, dominating, and so on. Certainly many women would welcome the opportunity to drop the feminine ego-image. Perhaps there will have to be many varieties of "adult homes," where men and women can easily make the acquaintance of new potential mates in the periods between more intense relationships. In such institutions they could gain solace from one another and assuage loneliness in the periods before or after entering into some kind of "marriage."

Such a new version of the family may not necessarily emerge. But choices and patterns of this kind are currently being presented as new options, and indeed are already being followed by many men and women in contemporary society. Moreover, it seems unlikely that the women's liberation movement will decline greatly over the next decade. The pressure from women is more likely to increase, and millions of men will be dominated, cajoled, or reasoned into acquiescence. Doubtless, the changes will be greatest in economic and occupational spheres, where they can be implemented most easily, but such changes will inevitably alter the resources, commitments, and ability of men and women to the point where their positions in the family will also change.

Although the drive toward women's liberation is a much more radical change than the increase in parent-youth conflict discussed earlier, both contain one element that does affect the future of the family—the changing sexual patterns in the United States. Nearly two decades ago, Kinsey noted a marked shift in sexual behavior among people who had matured before World War I and those who became adults afterward. Clearly this change has become much more profound within the last decade, though many published studies have shown that most Americans have not yet radically altered their sexual mores.

In sexual relations several general patterns are relevant in any analysis of what is now taking place. In general, in the past lower-class youth have taken part in sexual relations much earlier than middle- or upper-class youngsters. They have also engaged much less in masturbation. When they have engaged in extramarital relations, these are more likely to occur in the early years of marriage. By contrast, middle- and upper-class men have been much more likely to engage in extra-marital relations later in their marriages. Women have been much less inclined to engage in either pre-marital or extra-marital affairs, although a substantial percentage (perhaps as high as one-fourth) of women in all classes have been pregnant at the time of their marriage ceremony. Finally, the middle classes engage in sexual relations less frequently but with a wider range of sexual techniques than do lower-class men and women.

Most of the American population does not participate to any great extent in the new sexual patterns being promulgated by a minority of style-setters. But more and more people are beginning to accept the terms of debate about social patterns of the future. Some of the new patterns may be found in contemporary communes, in which it is assumed that everyone may engage in sexual relations with anyone else, male or female. In many social circles a similar philosophy is beginning to be heard. Although sexual relations with a beloved is viewed as ideal, love is not viewed as essential, and of course marriage is also considered inessential. Sexual relations are for pleasure, and under the best of circumstances may be a "mode of communication" in which people experience one another at a deep level. The new philosophy clearly proclaims that sex is by no means to be confined to marriage.

Clearly, there has been a substantial shift toward permissiveness in sexual attitudes. Tens of thousands of parents know that their daughters or sons are going off on a lengthy trip with someone of the opposite sex, but they no longer feel that they have the right or the ability to forbid them to do so. Most parents do not arrange for their adolescent daughters to have access to the contraceptive pill, but an increasing number of parents in fact do just that. Although quantitative data are not available, and would be most difficult to obtain, it is clear that in every large city there are thousands of men and women who are living together in quasi-marriage, and finding full acceptance in their social circles while doing so. Increasingly, young men and women in college are living together, often with the knowledge of university authorities, sometimes without the knowledge of parents, and usually without anyone making any major objection. Graduate students, of course, had preceded them in adopting this kind of arrangement.

Here again, it is too soon to predict what effect such changes would have upon the family if they were to be accepted by a substantial percentage of the population. It seems unlikely that men and women in love can avoid the feelings of jealousy when someone else threatens the possession of what is, in a sense, their sexual property. To the extent that sexual relations are often caused by, and in turn sometimes cause, an intense love relationship, it hardly seems possible to argue that under the new arrangements people would simply "not mind" if their beloved partner spent the night with someone else. Alternatively, it is possible that sex relations could become imbued with much less affect, so that within a very wide range of behavior most couples would not view these activities any more of a threat than they would if their spouses were to share a cup of coffee with someone else. It does not seem likely, on the other hand, that our society will somehow follow a "pendulum course" and simply become more and then less conservative in sexual matters over the next two generations. Without any question, however, there will be intensified conflict within the family over these matters. People who have been reared to believe in a relatively conservative philosophy will be unable to accept the changes; and those who espouse a more radical version will continue to fight for what they view as their freedom.

Although we have made mention of such new family arrangements as communes, at the present time it seems highly unlikely that such communities will be accepted by any large proportion of the American population in the foreseeable future. On the other hand, they have continued to attract a small percentage of idealists for well over a century. Americans tend to forget that this country has at different times tolerated various utopias, some of them quite radical.* In the quite successful Oneida community, older people introduced younger people to sexual relations; highly intense relationships between two individuals were not permitted; and everyone, presumably, was sexually available. A decision by the elders was made as to who might be mother and father of a child, but there was considerable permissiveness in sexual relations, whose aim was clearly pleasure. The Mormon community permitted polygyny. The Shaker community forbade sexual relations altogether. Some past American utopian societies were truly communalistic with respect to property, meals, and household arrangements, as when several couples share an apartment, sleep together, or pool their resources. Others tried to establish rural retreats, believing that only by some isolation could they remain intact, in the meanwhile adjusting themselves to a lower standard of living than they might have if they lived in the city. Unlike most nineteenth-century utopias, the modern attempts at new family arrangements typically espouse a philosophy that rejects the materialism of our culture. These communities extol the principles of love and giving. The older utopias attempted to create a full-scale village or community with an elaborate division of labor. The modern aim is rather to simplify.

The communal rearing of children is of course partly practiced in any traditional society. In most Polynesian societies, for example, it was taken for granted that any adult could scold any

---

* One of the more delightful accounts of such utopias can be found in Charles Nordhoff, *The Communistic Societies of the United States,* New York, Schocken Books, 1965.

youngster who was guilty of some transgression, and almost anyone might pick up a wandering child and cuddle him for a while. Communal patterns of child-rearing have been tried in China, the Soviet Union, and Israel, and of course some type of cooperative child-rearing has been proposed by many women's liberation groups as part of the effort to free the woman from the burden of child care. On a large scale, as in the Soviet Union or in Israel, such arrangements never grow organically, or develop naturally out of prior institutions. They are always imposed by fiat, created by an administrative act, or established out of necessity. It would be incorrect to say that such facilities have failed in Russia and Israel. But neither have they achieved what they originally set out to achieve. Far from freeing women for tasks that might be better suited to their needs, women have increasingly been moved to the traditional female tasks in the Israeli kibbutzim. It is not possible to say how much change there has been in recent decades in the Soviet Union, but the extent to which men are found in the most responsible positions, leaving women to fill lesser positions, is evident in that nation's occupational statistics.

More important, the development of communal child-care facilities has not fundamentally altered the family structure. If anything, there has been a gradual drift back toward more traditional family arrangements. Parents have wanted to spend more time with their own children, just as many husbands and wives prefer to spend more time together rather than enjoying life in the collectivity. In the midst of a social setting which gives high priority and approval to communal arrangements of all kinds, the resurgence of the intimate family unit may suggest that communal child-rearing is not a sufficient first step in transforming the contemporary family. Of course, none of the experiments can tell us what the limits of family arrangements are, since they are typically carried out within a larger society and executed by people who were themselves reared in a traditional family pattern. It may well be that people reared under different social arrangements will not only accept but feel happier under far more radical family arrangements than any now being organized.

In the United States almost all alternative family structures exist within, and indeed depend upon, a surrounding social structure in which older family patterns are maintained. This means that while members may drift away at any time that they feel under pressure to do so, they are subjected to all of the persuasion of the mass media as well as their "square" friends to view any new family arrangements they might enter into as essentially an episode, a temporary situation.

Yet to the extent that the strains and problems we have been discussing are widespread among American families, and in so far as the contemporary era demonstrates a deep conflict of social points of view, we can expect a continuing escape of some Americans for longer or shorter periods into such alternative family arrangements as communes. Present family arrangements obviously seem inadequate to a large minority of the population. To a smaller minority, they seem even damaging to human personalities. It may well be that, given what we know of human nature, no alternative family arrangement would work so well as the one we now live under. One thing is certain: we cannot return to such traditional modes of family living as once existed in China, Japan, India, or even England. Our society is clearly not likely to retreat back into an agricultural system. Consequently, the next generation will live under such family strains, and will continue to attempt to work out new arrangements or to live under what we now have.

Finally, we should not lose sight of the fact that a goodly number of American family members *do* live in alternative family structures. Many husbands and wives know—and far more suspect—that their spouses have some type of nearly regularized relation with someone else. Many husbands rear children they did not father. Since divorce is widespread, hundreds of flexible patterns of alternative child-rearing arrangements have evolved—not all of them, to be sure, happy ones. Quasi-communes of extended kin sometimes live within the same apartment house or the same block. Whether any of these phenomena will evolve as an attractive goal for a large number of the American population cannot be prophesied at the present time, though in the main the evidence would seem to be against it. Our social structure continues to make the husband-wife-child household the most convenient; and besides, most people are socialized to accept it, even if grudgingly.

A small minority of the American population believes that the problems of the family are so extreme, and its influence is so destructive, that it not only should be destroyed but indeed that new family forms are already emerging which will effectively replace it. A much larger percentage of the population doubtless believes that the American family is indeed going rapidly downhill, that the old order is dissolving completely, and that all the values they have so long respected will no longer be adhered to by the new generation. The reality of the situation seems much more complex than either description allows. In fact, all family systems both generate and partially solve many human problems. No family system has ever been evolved that made a vast majority of the population happy. Perhaps people were somewhat more contented in a traditional system in which everyone at least knew what he was supposed to do, even if he did not like it. We have, however, no reliable data about any such a system in the past, and all our cherished beliefs about contentment of the old days may well be erroneous. Certainly it is relatively easy to imagine that in systems where concubines were permitted, wives were jealous and miserable when such women were introduced into the household. Young people fought the domination of their elders in the past as they do today. While people divorced far less in the past, that is no index to the amount of misery people suffered in marriages from which they saw no escape.

We also see that within our own system an immense number of variations are worked out by individuals without any public recognition of the fact. Husbands and wives separate informally. Children go to live with other relatives, or with friends of the family. Many adjustments are made—to be sure, not all of them leading to happiness—within the broad structure of the present system. Moreover, such variations have always been found in traditional societies as well. Not everyone obeyed the rules.

We also note that although individuals, or even small groups, can create different family arrangements, large-scale changes in family systems are rather difficult, because each person has been socialized to accept the contemporary family structure as being the most desirable. People are jealous if their spouses are unfaithful. Few people are accustomed to group living, or wish to see other adults chastise their children for transgressions. Few people can break a long-standing marriage without some hurt. Changes in fertility patterns are difficult to achieve. Knowing how sacred the present family structure appears to be held, few laws have been proposed that would effect major changes in American family patterns.

In emphasizing the problems of the family, we have not so much attempted to bring out its weaknesses as to use its strains and pressures to show the social processes affecting the American family. By noting the point of conflict, by indicating the junctures at which people's values and goals come into conflict with one another, we can better see how the social structure operates to mold the American family as we know it.

Part 1

BIOSOCIAL BASES OF THE FAMILY

IN READING the following selections, the main points of the Introduction should be kept in mind. One of the authors ranges in his subject matter from animal behavior to that of primitive societies. The other considers differences between boys and girls as they appear in our society at different ages. Although both sets of descriptions do throw some light on the biological foundations of the family, they must be analyzed cautiously.

First, even when we can find many parallels between our own family behavior and that of the higher animals—mothers nurse and groom their children, and try to protect them from external dangers, males are typically dominant and jealous; family groups maintain a territory, etc.—these are not based upon cultural *norms*. Animals learn how to behave because they are rewarded if they behave correctly, and punished if they do not. But animals are not taught a general attitude or norm which they must follow in situations they have not encountered. As far as we know, they do not suffer from pangs of conscience if they do something wrong and are not caught at it. Moreover, no animal (unless porpoises and whales are exceptions) has a genuine language. This limits considerably the range of culture that they can transmit from one generation to the next.

More important, animal species differ considerably in the family patterns they exhibit, so that we cannot extrapolate from their systems to our own. Thus the gibbon seems to be a monogamous animal, but the baboon is not. Most of the higher animals are strong in the defense of their territory, but gorillas do not seem to be much offended if family groups encounter one another in their native habitat. In short, as we move from one species to another, we are likely to find a wide variety of family arrangements, so that we cannot easily fix on one as the "natural form of the family."

Similarly, when we consider the wide range of family patterns among the hundreds of primitive societies, some large differences emerge that are widespread. (We have taken note of some of these earlier, in the Introduction.) Of course men more typically are permitted to enjoy the tasks that are challenging, physically dangerous, require heavy lifting, and demand long trips. Women are more likely to be given tasks that keep them close to the hearth. On the other hand, in many societies women do a multitude of heavy tasks, such as carrying wood or water, hoeing and gardening, or even traveling great distances to buy and sell. In short, there is a wide area of overlap in which societies differ about what is the appropriate definition of sex roles. Consequently, we cannot easily infer from such patterns what the biological foundations of sex role are. More cautiously, since family patterns vary so much, we must conclude that biological foundations do not effectively determine which family system a society will follow. It is for this reason that arguments in American society about what men and women ought to do, or how children ought to behave, are likely to become fierce: In fact, the data are obscure and conflicting.

With reference to the actual differences that are observable between boys and girls, the topic investigated by Stanley F. Yolles in the section that follows, it is important to keep in mind that by the time the child is available for psychological testing or other social observation, he or she has gone through years of socialization. During that period, boys have learned to be boys, and girls to be girls. Boys have been urged to explore, to attempt dangerous and challenging physical tasks, and to some extent even to be boisterous and aggressive. Girls have been taught to be docile, neat, clean, and to cajole or to be coy when attempting to get their way. Girls have been encouraged in verbal facility, but have not been encouraged to develop their talents at spatial or mathematical thinking. Consequently, such differences do emerge in a wide variety of tests, but we are unsure of their origins.

It is equally clear that no matter which trait is under observation, some boys will rank higher on one or more "feminine traits" than most girls do, and vice versa. Sometimes this occurs because the boy has been reared among girls, or the girl has been reared among many brothers. Sometimes, parents have wanted a boy very much, and have treated their daughter as though she were a boy. Most analysts would now claim, however, that to the extent that such differences are rooted in the biological inheritance, inevitably some girls will rank high on so-called masculine traits and vice versa. In American society, as in most societies, boys are discouraged from developing their "feminine traits," as girls are discouraged from developing "masculine traits."

These cautions are not to be construed as arguing that there are no differences between boys and girls, or that the differences that exist are not important. Instead, what must be kept in mind is that a social structure can build upon a wide variety of biological and psychological patterns—as indeed it must if it is to accommodate all the range of human potential that is born in any cohort of children. Philosophically, this suggests that perhaps many of our prejudices and stereotypes about masculinity and femininity are incorrect if we suppose that they are based upon biological differences. Perhaps much or most of the difference may come from the different ways that societies socialize male and female children.

The Evolution of Human Sexual Behavior

by Robin Fox

HUMAN SEXUAL BEHAVIOR is as much the end product of evolution as human sexual anatomy. But while we have grown used to the idea that the body has evolved, we are only beginning to understand the implications of extending to behavior the same kind of analysis that has proved successful with flesh and bone. Indeed, it must seem at first glance that this is an impossible task. The evolution of human anatomy can be studied from the various fossil forms that have been discovered, and the gradual transition from ape-man to man-ape to true man can be discerned with some accuracy. But we have only the sketchiest idea of what these creatures were *doing,* so how can we ask about the evolution of their behavior?

Nevertheless, we know that there must have been such an evolution. In the same way as there was a gradual transition from apelike to manlike form there must have been a similar gradual transition from apelike to manlike function. Our bodies testify to the first change—as any simple comparison of man with other primates will show. To what extent does our behavior testify to the second?

From the *New York Times Magazine,* March 24, 1968, copyright © 1968 by The New York Times Company

At least one school of zoologists would claim that the study of the evolution of behavior can be more instructive than that of the evolution of anatomy. The science of ethology—defined by one of its practitioners as "the biological study of behavior" —which has flourished under the leadership of such men as Konrad Lorenz in Germany and Nikolaas Tinbergen in Britain, is one of the youngest branches of zoology. Its stance is "neo-Darwinian" and in essence it points up the fact that natural selection operates on the *performance* of the animal. Structure therefore evolves in order that the creature may function in ways that give it selective advantage in the struggle for survival.

In the case of certain gross motor activities this may seem obvious: Speed enables animals to chase and to flee, etc. But the ethologists have concentrated mainly on the *signaling* abilities of animals, showing how these social signals serve to enhance threat behavior, inhibit aggression, attract mates and so on. The point about these signals, whether they be structural—such as bright coloring—or purely behavioral—such as specific postures —is that they are evolved by the process of natural selection and hence have become part of the genetic "repertoire" of the animal.

When a black-headed gull is defending its nesting site during the breeding season the presence of any other animal is clearly threatening to it. Male and female black-headed gulls look pretty much alike, so even when a prospective mate lands on the site, the male's aggressive instinct of territorial defense is aroused. However, if the female does not stare at the male but turns her head aside, then the male's aggression is inhibited and the preliminaries of mating become possible.

This "looking away" gesture of the gull is only one of many in its total "ethogram" of postures and gestures which are as much a part of its genetic endowment as feathers and wings— and just as necessary to its survival and success. The ethologists have found that by careful comparison of closely related species, they can arrive at answers to the question: "Why does this particular species behave in this particular way?"

Ethologists have, until very recently, confined their attention to lowlier forms of life, such as birds, fish and small mammals. In these the genetically based behaviors are easy to ascertain.

But what of the more complex, higher mammals—and what of man?

Some very careful studies of our primate cousins over the past decade have given us much-needed comparative material from closely related species. But these species prove to be much more complex than the little creatures familiar to ethology. It is not that they are without genetically programmed predispositions, but that their range of behavior is extended by programming to take more advantage of their learning ability than is the case with lower forms.

At the pinnacle of this development stands man, with the greatest learning capacity of all animals. His behavior has evolved, it is true, but this evolution has been toward greater flexibility. To put it paradoxically, man's greatest instinct is the instinct to learn. It is therefore "natural" to man to be "unnatural"—to go beyond nature and supplement the genetically endowed predispositions of behavior with cultural forms not built into the chromosomes.

This has been regarded by some observers as the ultimate stumbling block to our understanding of human behavior on ethological lines. And it is true that if we stick rigidly to the methods of the ethologists we will learn only a limited amount about ourselves. Nevertheless, things are not so black. What the flexible learning ability of man allows him to do is to extend the range of his behavior, but only within well-defined limits. His genetic behavioral inheritance lays down for him a limited number of things to do, but he can vary enormously the ways in which he does them.

For example, as with many other animals, man prefaces the formation of a stable mating arrangement with some form of "courting" activity. The form of this activity, however, can be extremely varied and consists of a great many postures, gestures and sounds that are traditional rather than genetic. The black-headed gull can "look away" and a few other things, but it cannot write sonnets, dance the frug or wear an engagement ring. The difference can perhaps be expressed in a metaphor: Animal behavior is like filling in a form; in some animals there are a lot of instructions on the form but only a limited space for answers, while in other animals there are an equal number of instructions but the space for answers is large and the range of possible answers is wide. It is not that animals have "instincts" while man does not, but that man can do more things about his instincts than other animals.

If, then, we want to look at the basic sexual behavior of man as the end product of a long process of natural selection, what information have we? We have the fossil record; we have the behavior of related species; we have the behavior of the creature itself. From a judicious survey of the evidence from these three sources we should perhaps be able to reconstruct the evolution of human sexual behavior. (I am confining this analysis to heterosexual behavior.)

It may seem absurd, but perhaps the greatest gap in our knowledge is our lack of information on the "natural" sexual behavior of man. A great deal of our knowledge here is inferential; we know very little about sex despite our seeming obsession with it. But at a fairly gross level we know enough to start with, even if the knowledge is not of the detailed kind that the ethologist would need. What then are some of the main characteristics of human sexual behavior?

There is the striking fact of a lack of an oestrous cycle in the female; she does not go into heat. It is usually phrased as "permanent sexual receptivity" in the human female—which may seem a little extreme and overoptimistic. Such evidence as there is on female receptivity indicates that it is at its height just before and just after menstruation. This is curious in that the peak in other primates comes halfway between menstrual periods—that is, during ovulation. In other words, most primate females are most receptive at the time when they are most likely to conceive, while the human primate female is most receptive when she is least likely to conceive. There may be the evolution of some kind of birth-control device lurking here, but it is difficult to see this as being very efficacious unless the female determines the timing of intercourse according to her own physiological state of readiness—an interesting but unlikely theory.

The lack of heat goes along with the lack of a breeding season. This is not peculiar to man, but it does put him into the category of primates which have continual sexual activity. True, there are "birth peaks" in most societies which show that breeding is to some extent seasonal (in Christian countries the peak comes nine months after Christmas, as a rule), but there is no rutting season as such in man. This year-round activity is probably also connected with another feature—namely, the high level of sexual activity and the drive for novelty and variety in sexual experience. Compared, say, with the gorilla, man exhibits a level of sexual activity which is quite phenomenal.

Insofar as the end product of sexual activity is offspring—and in man this is not always the case—then the "breeding-pair" is the most typical unit for this purpose. Like many fish, birds and mammals which establish "pair bonds," man does not just mate promiscuously and then leave the female to rear the young. Rather, he tends to associate regular sexual activity and at least some degree of emotional attachment with the rearing of offspring.

One way of looking at this—favored, for example, by Desmond Morris—is to see the "pair-bond" phenomenon among animals duplicated in man by the process of "falling in love"—a behavioral mechanism for keeping the pair together. Other observers (including this one) see more of a "contractual" element in the male-female relationship when it comes to the business of forming a family and rearing children. Love and marriage may go together like a horse and carriage, but let us not forget that the horse has to be broken and harnessed.

Strong bonds between mated pairs are certainly common enough in Homo sapiens, but this is by no means the whole of the story. These bonds are not necessarily the result of a primitive "pair-bonding" instinct, and indeed seem very variable in intensity. They are primarily an adolescent phenomenon and obviously have to do with giving impetus to the breeding process. But once this is under way the relationship becomes very complex indeed, and the bond between the pair is as much an outcome of their role as "parents" as of their roles as "lovers." The "tenacity of the pair bond" which Morris seems so anxious to establish is as much a tenacity of the parental bond as anything else. There are obviously good evolutionary reasons for this. But the bond is not exclusive; there is no reason why it should be and many reasons why it could not have been.

The starting point for the analysis of the biological evolution of any human social behavior is obvious: the brain. Apart perhaps from the precision grip of the hand and the bones and muscles devoted to the striding walk, this is man's only major biological specialization.

The question we must then ask is a typical one of chicken or egg. Did the growth of the brain lead to the capacity for greater social complexity or vice versa? I think the answer is undoubtedly that as certain kinds of animals developed complex social systems as weapons in the struggle for survival, there was pressure in the direction of selecting out those animals with the best brains. These were the animals better able to cope with the complexities of life in a social group. But in our particular family of animals—the primates—what kind of social system was involved?

Here we must introduce another of our three kinds of evidence: the social behavior of primates. This is, as we might expect, enormously varied. But certain constant features stand out in those primates which, like ourselves, have an organized social system, and particularly in those which, again like ourselves, have spent a considerable portion of their evolution outside the forest environment in which the earliest primates were nurtured. Typical examples are the baboons and macaques.

A baboon group usually comprises about 40 animals which wander about in search of food, always keeping together. This cohesion is of enormous advantage to animals like these living in open savanna and subject to attacks from predators. A single baboon is not much of a match for the big cats, but a group of baboons stands a pretty good chance of beating off attacks with concerted action.

The social system, however, is anything but democratic. Power in the group lies with the biggest and most successful of the males. These (never more than about six in number however large the total group) stay at the center with the females and young. Around this central core will wander a number of "cadets"—young males who are candidates for membership in the hierarchy. At the edge of the horde are the "peripheral males" —unsuccessful and immature animals who have not yet made it. Many never will. Some even wander off and become solitaries —the dropouts of the monkey rat race. These peripheral males act as first line of defense and a kind of living radar for the group. The big males of the hierarchy are the ultimate deterrent, and also they keep order within the group, and are especially solicitous of the welfare of the young.

This is a very sketchy account of a "typical" society of ground-dwelling primates. We must now look at its dynamics. How do young males get into the hierarchy and what is the significance of this? The significance is overwhelming in terms of the evolution of the group because *it is only the males of the hierarchy that do the breeding*. While the cadets and peripheral males may get a chance to copulate with a female during her infertile periods, only the hierarchical males mate with the females at the peak of oestrus—that is, during ovulation. Therefore, only these males are going to pass on genes to the next generation. It is of tremendous significance then to know what characterizes the "successful" males.

Before answering this question we must note that there is another form of terrestrial primate society that has to be reckoned with. This is typical of baboons living on dry desert savanna, as opposed to those living in woodland savanna. The horde is not divided into the components we have just described, but rather into a series of polygamous families in which one male collects a number of females (usually four) and monopolizes these the whole time. Still, however, there are the unsuccessful males at the edge waiting to get in, and we still have to ask how they do it and who succeeds.

Not to put too fine a point on it, we can say that it is the smart ones who make it. But what constitutes smartness? Basically, it is the ability to control and time responses—to understand the consequences of one's actions. The British ethologist Michael Chance has described the process as "equilibration"; thus, an animal caught between the desire to copulate with an oestrous female on the one hand, and the desire to escape attack from a dominant male on the other, must be able to inhibit his sexual response and bide his time. If he fails to do so often enough, he is at worst either going to be killed or driven out, or at best will fail to ingratiate himself with his superiors and be tolerated by them. The stupid animal, then, one that blunders about, following without foresight the dictates of his lustful and aggressive appetites, will never make it to the top. The cunning animal, on the other hand, that can forgo present indulgence in anticipation of future reward, will be more likely to get there.

Of course, he has to have other qualities. He must be sociable and able to cooperate, or the big males will not accept him. He must also be acceptable to the females, it seems, hence his capacities as a baby minder (and the rank of his mother) are important. Besides possessing these charming attributes, he must also be tough and aggressive in order to assert his rights as a hierarchy member. It is easy to see the evolutionary advantages of such a process. It is a breeding system which puts at a premium those qualities in the male most advantageous to the survival of the group.

If this kind of social system was in fact typical of our ancestors, then it gives us some powerful clues concerning the evolution of the brain. Clearly, it was those animals with the best brains which were going to do the breeding, and each generation would see a ruthless selection of the best-brained males, with the dumbest and weakest going to the wall. And it was the *controlling* aspects of the brain which were being so strongly selected. The more the emotions of aggression and lust came under cortical control, the better chance the animal had of surviving and passing on his genes to the next generation.

But the expanding brain had to cope with other things than sex and aggression. Predominant among these were the use of tools and the development of language. Large areas of the cerebellum are concerned with the control of the hand, and growth of this center must have been a response to the demands of tool-making. Control over the emotions was one thing; control of the environment through tools and weapons was, however, equally important. Selection favored the controlled and *skillful* animal. It also favored the animal which could *communicate* best. Up to a point a series of nonlinguistic signals will do, but after a certain point of social complexity is reached, cooperation is impossible without a more flexible code. Large areas of the brain, then, are devoted to speech.

Many commentators have stressed these two aspects of brain evolution, but few have taken the breeding problem seriously. Yet without this component the major puzzle in brain evolution remains unanswered: How did the hominid brain manage to evolve so quickly? About a million years ago, the brain of one of the earliest recognizable hominids (the family which includes man and his extinct relatives and ancestors) was little larger than that of the chimpanzee. Within that million years it trebled in size—an almost unprecedented rate of evolution.

Now, whatever the pressures in favor of a larger "thinking" brain exerted by the demands for better technicians and speakers, the question still remains: By what kind of breeding system were these newly acquired traits so quickly developed? Given that the prespeech and pretools system had, built into it, the breeding mechanisms we have described, then we only have to add that the successful breeders needed to be not only controlled, but also eloquent and skillful. The system would then insure that these were the males who passed on the essential genes, and the rapid (in evolutionary terms) development of the large forebrain would be insured.

This suggests that throughout the evolution of the hominid lines which eventually led to Homo sapiens, the social system was one in which the majority of the breeding was done by a minority of the males, with the least successful males being largely shut out of the breeding system. In other words, a system based on the polygyny of the powerful. And note that this polygyny has not to do primarily with sexual appetite. It has to do with dominance and the relation of males to males. The survival value of the system is obvious.

Here we must turn to the most controversial and difficult part of our evidence: the fossil record. We can know that the model of the society of the ground-dwelling primates is applicable to our own evolution only if we can show that it plausibly fits our earliest ancestors. We know that the hominid line evolved from monkeylike forms which moved from forest to savanna, and hence must have been in some ways like contemporary savanna-dwelling primates. We also know that those earliest hominids of a million years ago on the East African savanna were elementary hunters, and that this trait increased in complexity and importance as time went by. Hence to the qualities that went into being a dominant male we must add skill in hunting. Indeed, it may have been the pressures of the chase that accelerated the demand for more advanced tools and speech.

Some writers have seized upon the fact that our earliest manlike ancestors were hunters to "prove" many things about the changes from the apelike to the human in sexual behavior. But we must remember that the changes did not occur overnight, and that there was much in the old vegetarian ape that was useful to his omnivorous successor. Some things certainly changed. The female presumably became less and less under the control of the oestrous cycle, and the "permanent sexual receptivity" phenomenon emerged.

It has been suggested that this happened as a result of the pressures exerted by the need for cooperative hunting. Hunters need a fixed home base. The females stay in this base with the young; the males return and provision them—a practice unheard of among vegetarian primates, but common, for example, among hunting carnivores, such as wolves. It has been argued that with such a system the old primate dominance hierarchy could not operate, since this depended on females coming in and out of heat and being monopolized by the top males during ovulation. If the males had to be away a good deal of the time then this would not work, it is argued.

What is more, if the male needed a female to work for him—cooking, skinning, gathering vegetable food, etc.—he would want her "attached" for more of the time than just when she was feeling sexy. Similarly, she would want the constant attention of the male for provisioning herself and her young. If she were constantly available for sexual intercourse this would be more likely to happen. The high level of sexuality would make the relationship more rewarding to the partners and hence keep them "bonded." Thus many features of "human" sexuality would emerge as responses to the demands of the hunting situation.

This is fine until it is pushed one step further, as it usually is, and the evolving hominid is credited with instinctive tendencies to form "monogamous nuclear families." I never cease to be amazed by the ingenuity that speculative writers resort to in an effort to prove that deep in man's nature is a Saturday Evening Post family: Dad, Mom and the kids. Their assertiveness on this point has often a rather frantic air to it, and what they never do is ask what the consequences would have been if our earliest protohuman ancestors had allowed fair shares for all in the mating game. It seems unimaginative, to say the least, to pin these enterprising creatures down to dreary monogamy.

The point here is that none of the features of human sexuality that have developed are incompatible with a breeding system based on the relative dominance of a few males. If a male can attach one female to him for the reasons advanced, he can attach several just as easily, provided he can maintain his harem against all comers. Insofar as only a minor part of the food intake of hunters is protein and something approaching 80 per cent is vegetable, then a small army of root diggers and berry pickers may well have been an advantage to a male.

We can, of course, never know exactly what kind of mating institutions characterized the transitional man-ape; we can only ask the question: In order for the critical developments in the evolution of the brain to take place so quickly, what kind of breeding system must have been in operation? The answer is: One that would rapidly select out the animals with the better brains and pass on their genes to the next generation. And, concomitantly, one that would push to the peripheries of the breeding system animals lacking the qualities of intelligence and control. Some kind of hierarchical system with differential access to females would solve this problem, and seems to me to be the only candidate. If every male had been allowed to contribute equally to the gene pool—as would be the case in a monogamous system—then we might never have made the sapiens bit and been forever stuck as Homo stupidus—promising, with our speechlike grunts and our crude tools, but not really in the top league.

I have considered only the male contribution to brain development here since this is the most obvious. But lest I be accused of prejudice we should look at the female's role. Was she simply a passive mechanism for passing on the genes of the big-brained dominant males?

It could well be, but there is a chance that she actively helped the process along. I have mentioned that the rank of a male's mother may affect his chances of getting into the hierarchy. The son of a high-ranking female can be kept near the center of the group by his mother where the big males will learn to tolerate him—a help when he comes to make his bid for membership. If this is a crucial criterion for membership in the hierarchy— and we are not sure about this—then the qualities that go into being a high-ranking female, insofar as they involve cortical control of sex, may well contribute to the development we have envisaged.

They may also help to account for the gradual loss of hormonal influence over sexual receptivity in the female which led to the loss of the oestrous cycle. The female was no longer subject to periodic sexual mania during which she solicited any male in sight, but gradually came to control her own responses in the same way as the male. It may well be, in fact, that this permanent sexual receptivity in the female was a by-product of the general processes we have been discussing, rather than a result of the pressures introduced by hunting. To answer this question more thoroughly we should have to know what qualities went into being a dominant female. All we can say is that they were not necessarily the same qualities that went into being a dominant male, with the exception, perhaps, of bitchiness and bossiness.

We must be wary of taking only one primate system as our model. Those polygamous primates which live on the arid savannas form "harems" in which several females are permanently attached to a male which monopolizes them throughout the year, despite oestrus and seasonal breeding. Some observers have claimed that the hominids passed through a similar stage of

development, since during the forging time of their existence—
the Pliocene—there was extreme drought, and they must have
adapted to these dry conditions in much the same way as contemporary desert-dwelling baboons. Of course, the creatures we
are discussing were not baboons but man-apes; still, these baboons do rather knock on the head the idea that there could
not have been "stable family groups" within the protohominid
band as long as the females were subject to periodic sex-mania
and breeding was seasonal. There is no doubt, however, that permanent mating of a "human" kind is facilitated by the fact that
the human female, in a sense, comes into "heat" at puberty and
stays there—at a moderate level of sexual excitement—for most
of her life.

There are several forms of breeding hierarchy possible, given
an animal which lacks the oestrous cycle, and we cannot know
which of these prevailed. Indeed, various groups of evolving
hominids may have tried them all. Some may even have tried
monogamy. What matters is not the actual institutional form,
but the differential access to the females.

The fact that permanently receptive females were more or less
permanently attached to dominant males would simply make
life harder for the young males who wanted to get into the
hierarchy, and would increase the demands for better "equilibration"—for greater control and inhibition. It would be unlikely
under these conditions that some males would be absolutely
barred from breeding (although it could well happen), but some
would be *less likely* than others to contribute significantly to the
genetic endowment of the group.

The criteria of dominance would of course differ as the animal
became progressively more "human," but they would be basically
much the same as among the primates. Hence the successful male
would have to be controlled, cunning, cooperative, attractive to
the ladies, good with the children, relaxed, tough, eloquent, skillful, knowledgeable, and proficient in self-defense and hunting.
Depending on the nature of the group, some of these qualities
might have been emphasized more than others.

With the advent of agriculture and the frighteningly rapid
growth of population densities over the last 10,000 years, things

have changed. But the animal coping with these changed conditions is the end product of hundreds of thousands of years of intensive selection in which, if this hypothesis is right, differential access to mates was of crucial importance. And this *must* have left its mark on our behavior.

We should look briefly at the incest taboo to complete our roster of current sexual facts and their evolution. Many observers have put the taboo on incest at the heart of our social development. Animals are incestuous; man is not. This then is the great breakthrough. Many reasons have been given for this, and all assume that the taboo is *imposed*. But it is highly probable that it is, in fact, a natural development.

As far as we can tell from primate evidence, there is, for example, no incest between mother and son. The mother is to her son a "dominant" animal, and mating requires that the female partner be "subdominant." If a young male manages to get into the hierarchy, he may or may not mate with his sisters. On the other hand, the possibility of fathers mating with daughters is quite high. The frequency of occurrence of incest in human society is exactly parallel. This fits our picture of sexual relations evolving in a "dominance" framework.

It follows that with the stabilization of mating relationships equilibration would have been more in demand. Particularly in the case of the growing "boy," it would have been important to control any sexual approaches toward mothers and sisters who were under the control of a dominant male or males, and he also had to inhibit aggressive advances toward the latter. Hence neural mechanisms evolved to this end.

The young hominid met his first and most intensive trial of "controls" in the immediate family circle, but he was learning them as they applied to *all* dominant males and their females. Freud, although perhaps right about some of the evolutionary processes that led to incest taboos, was wrong about locating them exclusively in the nuclear family. The "Oedipus complex" has to do with the relationship of "young subordinate males to older dominant males"—not just sons to fathers.

The sum total of all these processes was to produce a creature capable of control and of guilt—the mechanism that lets the individual know it has broken the rules. As the controlling elements of the brain came to dominate the appetitive elements, the evolving hominid could depend less on "instinct" as a guide to action. D. H. Lawrence, it seems, was wrong: Sex really is in the head.

If "differential access to mates" is the secret of it all, how does this help us to understand our own behavior? It has been argued that man is tenaciously monogamous, but this monogamy, if we are honest, is more apparent than real. It is very rare for men of power, wealth and influence to confine their sexual activities to one woman. Although the majority of males in a population are confined to one woman at a time, those in a position to do so seem to accumulate more. These may be straight "wives," as in overtly polygamous societies, or they may go under other names. A "big man" is one who has access to many females, or is credited with such access, or who controls a large number. They may not be mates, but we know that only a high-prestige man can run even a chaste harem. How far up the pecking order is a man with one wife, two full-time secretaries, 20 typists, and a girl who comes in to do his manicuring? I think of professors with a modest haul of, say, one wife, one secretary, one research assistant, two teaching assistants, several members of a research team and four part-time typists. The gathering unto us of females as a sign of status must surely be deep there in the cunning brain.

Another factor that must be an end product of the processes discussed is the difference between male and female sexual behavior in Homo sapiens. Because the equilibration process was predominantly directed toward the male, we might expect that he is more readily conditionable in matters of sex than the female—that most males are more easily made to feel guilty about sexual matters.

Men are caught between their inherited tendencies to promiscuity and dominance and the necessities of regularized mating; women, between the same promiscuous tendencies and the pulls toward security for self and offspring that can usually be obtained only by at least a show of fidelity. Again, we see a product of the dominance process wherein the status of the male is measured by his control over females.

If this control is challenged, then the "owner's" self-esteem suffers. It is noticeable that it is usually women who are *punished* for unfaithfulness. Thus the other curiosity of male behavior—sexual jealousy—is part and parcel of the scheme.

In any event, the doctrine that male and female differences in sexual behavior are simply the result of the learning of different sex roles needs careful examination in the light of the evolutionary evidence. Also the notion that male-female relationships can be totally explained by "pair bonding" tendencies that never quite evolved properly (Desmond Morris again) should be treated skeptically.

The point here is that human sexual behavior is the product of enormously complex evolutionary processes. It is no good taking fragments of this behavior and trying to "explain" them by *ad hoc* hypotheses, however entertaining. The only theory worth aiming at is one that will account for *all* the basic emotions—dominance, love, guilt, tenderness, parental affection, jealousy, security, lust, fidelity, novelty and many others. Such a theory must take account of the difficult evolutionary problems that we have raised.

There are obviously many confused issues here. I have been able to outline only a fraction of the complexities, and have glossed over many extremely complicated issues and missed others completely. So, if nothing else, perhaps I have put the interested reader on guard against those who seek to exploit the obvious interest of this topic by offering intellectual shortcuts to solutions. As I have said, some things we can never know and it is dishonest to pretend that answers are possible, but other things can be settled with a fair degree of approximation to the truth—given time, patience and hard work.

How Different Are They?

by Stanley F. Yolles

EXPERTS ON behavior hesitate when Henry Higgins asks, "Why can't a woman be more like a man?" Parents who wonder why little girls don't act like boys are assured by one authority that the differences are of "no consequence." A Stanford University professor of psychology now documents what little boys and girls are made of. The details, distilled from some 900 studies, show that boys and girls are indeed quite different. This notion is hardly a news bulletin for parents, but science has documented the obvious generalizations with facts and has also uncovered some fresh answers to the eternal question of Henry Higgins. Here they are as outlined in the book, "The Development of Sex Differences," written in part with National Institute of Mental Health support and edited by Dr. Eleanor E. Maccoby:

Little boys start more fights, make more noise, take more risks, think more independently, are harder to educate and are the more fragile of the sexes. While many more males are conceived, more miscarried fetuses are male. More males than females die in the first year of life and in each decade after that. They are much more likely to stutter, to have reading problems and to suffer emotional quirks of every sort. They lag a year or more behind girls in physical development. By the time they start school, even their hand muscles are markedly less mature.

From the *New York Times Magazine,* February 5, 1967, copyright © 1967 by The New York Times Company

In contrast, little girls are more robust and mature, yet much more dependent, passive, submissive, conforming, unadventurous. They are more interested in people than in things, show more concern for others and are more sensitive to their reactions and are more likely, by far, to remember names and places.

Science has found no difference in I.Q. between boys and girls in childhood, yet their styles of thinking and learning are different. Girls excel in verbal abilities—even before they know they are girls. They talk first, and later on they spell better and write more. Boys outclass them in abstract thinking including math and science. Boys are also more likely to be creative.

How do we explain these basic and early differences? Some experts believe most of these differences are taught to the child. Other experts, such as Dr. David Hamburg, chairman of the department of psychiatry at Stanford, think there may be hormonal and genetic causes. Dr. Hamburg writes that hormones may act on the brain even before birth, or right after, to organize certain circuits into male or female patterns. The evidence for this comes from experiments with the hormonal systems of newborn rats. When male rates are castrated within the first 24 hours after birth, they retain a basic female-type system for regulating hormonal secretions later in life. If castration is delayed until the second 24 hours, only a few males retain the female patterns. By the third day, all male rats have developed a male-type pattern.

In addition, Dr. Hamburg points out that their genetic make-up is different. The female has a chromosomal composition that seems to lend her protection against disease and infection. It protects her against blood-clotting disorders, color-vision defects and one type of rickets.

Scientists at the National Institute of Mental Health who have observed infants right after birth and in the weeks that follow have seen sharp differences too early in life to have been caused by the environment. These differences have been uncovered through ingenious tests. Drs. George Weller and Richard Q. Bell hooked up recording devices to 40 newborns by placing sensors on their skins. By this method they were able to detect the faint electrical activity of the skin called "conductance," a property which turned out to be greater in the female. Since this increases as the baby gets older, it is taken as a sign of maturity. The female infant, therefore, is more mature than the male of the same age. The females also show more sensitivity to contact and to temperature changes on the skin, more proof of their greater maturity in this very early period of life.

Dr. Howard Moss, an institute psychologist who has watched three-week-old and three-month-old infants for seven and eight hours at a time, is impressed with the "striking differences" between boys and girls. Boys sleep less, cry more, demand more attention. "Much more is happening with the male infants," he reports. Some boys, he found, also seem to be much more "inconsolable" than the girls, a sign of lesser maturity.

When children go to school, their differences become magnified. From first grade until well into high school, the girls usually make better grades. One ingenious researcher found that as early as the second grade, little boys think of school as a female institution and, therefore, one which is hostile to them. Our psychologists at the N.I.M.H. asked teachers in Arlington County, Va., to write their impressions of 153 seventh-graders.

According to the teachers, girls are 20 per cent better than boys at sticking to a task. They are more conscientious, compliant, methodical. They are also friendlier to the teacher, and more attentive. And boys are 35 per cent more hostile, domineering, aggressive, also more irritable, boastful, argumentative, quarrelsome. Paradoxically, boys are more introverted—depressed, sad, withdrawn.

Several years ago, educators in Fairfax County, Va., near Washington, D.C., decided to experiment with separate elementary classes for boys and girls.

One teacher said: "I learned things about boys and girls that I had never understood before. I had spent years trying to keep boys from disturbing everyone. This was just wasted effort. I found that boys can still concentrate even when they are noisy. You can learn to work in a boiler factory, if you have to, and that is just what I have done."

Another said: "I always liked girls best until I got a whole classful of them. In the beginning of the experiment, it dawned on me that the girls were not doing their own thinking. Parrot-like, they repeated everything that the teacher had ever said. What are we doing to these girls, I began to wonder, to make them so conforming?"

The results of the experiment were impressive. Both sexes did significantly better in their studies. The boys became much more interested in school. The girls grew more independent and original in their thinking.

Since it is scarcely practical to separate the boys and girls in most of our school systems today, educators might consider what they can do to achieve some of the same results. Principals and teachers can keep the differences in school performance between boys and girls in mind when they deal with problems in the class-room—either of discipline or of underachievement. Devices such as all-boy or all-girl contests, debates, or dramatic and musical clubs might give students the sense of confidence and enthusiasm found in the separate classes.

If schools can capitalize on the differences between boys and girls, parents can do so, too. Parents of a boy can now see that he may be at a disadvantage in early years at school under the twin burden of the girls' better performances and the teachers' disapproval. If parents don't expect their sons' reading or hand-writing to be of the best, it may take some unnecesary pressure off the boys.

The girls' problem is even more complex. Many families feel that education is not so important for a girl as a boy. Today, only one in 10 Ph.D.'s is a woman, a drop from the one in seven of the nineteen-thirties. Teen-age marriages are on the rise, with an accompanying rise in the divorce rate. The question is, are we properly fitting girls for a woman's life as it really is?

After raising a girl to conform and to be subordinate we expect her to face problems that require education, originality, domi-nance and drive. A new study of young married people points out that conformity and submissiveness often lead only to bore-dom in marriage.

Science has found that the brightest girls are those whose inter-ests extend into the masculine range. They like math, motors and abstract problems. The brighter boys also show a sensitivity and responsiveness we call "feminine" although these children are by no means effeminate. The most creative boys for example, are dominant and aggressive, yet show much more sensitivity to their surroundings than other boys.

In my experience, the most successful personalities are those who have the widest range of interests and abilities. I would like to see our boys and girls brought up with as broad and varied an experience as possible, with attention to the many facets of the human mind. This includes insight into the thinking of the opposite sex.

What can parents do to offer this kind of insight to the young child? One psychologist bought his 3-year-old girl a truck when she asked for it, to the consternation of her grandmother. Another brought home an abandoned engine his pretty 12-year-old daughter had longed to tinker with. One father makes a point of answering his girls' questions about science and about his business world, although he has to fight an ingrained tendency against it. He tries to pique them into forming interesting solutions to problems, and to build self-confidence in their mental abilities.

As for the boys, one mother encourages hers to experiment with cooking. She enjoys giving them the benefit of her feminine insight into human behavior and motivation. This insight into the female skills will stand them in good stead professionally as well as in their marriages. It augments rather than reduces their manliness, she argues.

It might be in order to revise our ideas about what the proper sex role is for our boys and girls, and how best to train them for it. Society needs men who are not limited to the so-called tougher masculine characteristics of aggressiveness and dominance. It needs men who are capable of showing the more "feminine" traits of warmth and sensitivity toward the feelings of others. And we need women who are less conforming, more original and daring, women who can think hard and straight.

Henry Higgins, who yearned for more "logic" in women, and Eliza Doolittle, for "a little kindness" in men, surely would agree.

Part 2

MATE CHOICE, COURTSHIP, MARRIAGE

THE FOLLOWING selections include lengthy articles as well as short news items, all of which illustrate the variety of processes and phenomena through which Americans move into marriage. For the sake of contrast, two items refer to the marriage process in India and in Algeria. In considering each of these selections, the reader should refer again to the Introduction, where these processes are analyzed in more systematic fashion.

The first selection, on the vanishing spinster, draws to our attention a fact emphasized at various points in this volume—that in spite of the so-called decline of the family, most people move into marriage early, and move back into it if their marriages are broken up by divorce or death. The American system is a "free marriage market" in which each individual must find his own mate, but where in fact his parents, friends, and kin are likely to help in the process. Since there is no longer a dowry or a bride price, almost everyone can find a mate somewhere in the social system. The evidence is that over the past fifty years an increasingly higher percentage of people enter marriage at least once in their lifetime. In the past, some upper-class women and some well-educated women failed to find mates, usually because they were under strong social pressures not to marry anyone who was not their equal, while men (who in effect created their own social position through their occupational success) were given a wider choice. In our time, however, more women can achieve some occupational success on their own, and thus are worth more on the marriage market. They are given greater independence in seeking out a mate. And they are under much less pressure to stay within their social circle or class if they are unable to find a suitable mate there.

Perhaps equally important is the fact that even in the upper-middle-class home there is no longer a social position for the "spinster aunt," i.e., the unmarried lady who remained to help in the household in various capacities but who for some reason was worth little on the marriage market. In our generation, the young woman who remains unmarried at home to take care of her mother or father is no longer given praise; instead, her behavior is more generally interpreted as neurotic.

The article by J. Kirk Sale and Ben Apfelbaum on teeny-boppers may present an extreme and temporary picture, but the reader can judge its validity for himself by observing the processes going on today among youngsters in any large city. Girls who a generation ago would perhaps not be allowed to wear lipstick are now given the right to date, as well as considerable freedom for sexual exploration. This analysis should be read along with the analysis by Boll, which considers the question of who should arrange marriages, "Cupid or parents."

The American family system has been moving in the direction of greater freedom for the young, including an increasing right to live apart from the parents and even to enter short or long term liaisons which may or may not lead to marriage. In many traditional societies, where most marriages would have been arranged, none of this behavior would have been permitted. Even where marriages were not fully arranged by the elders, the latter did take a very strong hand in the final decision. The American philosophy was permissive in even the early days of the United States, but it is not at all clear whether such a system leads to greater or less happiness or marital conflict. Moreover, the reader might consider the additional philosophical question, whether youngsters who are permitted to enter such liaisons and marriages at early ages are likely to develop their full potential, since so often they become committed not merely to many years of marriage with someone who might have been suitable as a teen-age date but hardly suitable as a spouse; and often saddled as well with the care of a child. It is in any event interesting to speculate just how far the American family pattern will go in permitting this much freedom to adolescents. Most industrial countries are following the American path.

The steady rise in interfaith marriages, which is documented in a later selection, should be interpreted more broadly than theologically, in the light of our analysis in the Introduction. In fact, many bars to marriage have been weakening in the United States: caste, class, religion, age, and ethnic group. In the past, when Negroes married whites, the union was normally between a Negro male who was relatively successful and a white female of a somewhat lower economic position. Thus there was a kind of tradeoff between economic position and caste. At the present time, there is a rise in marriages between Negroes and whites who are of the same class position, but who have in effect moved away from the childhood prejudices of their own groups. In this proc-ess, of couse, the college experience plays a large role.

In interfaith marriages, the percentage of any given religious group who marry out of the faith has been low where the number of co-religionists is large, and high where the number is small. That is to say, when there was a large marriage pool in which to locate a mate of the same religion, the percentage marrying out would be small. But an increasing percentage of Americans have not so much rejected their religion as have decided it does not represent an insuperable bar to marriage with someone of another faith. This has in part occurred because the differences that used to be correlated with religion have lessened consider-ably. For example, fifty years ago one might have supposed that a Catholic boy would also have strong allegiances to his own eth-nic group, whether Irish, Italian, or Spanish, and that many of his social patterns would not be so much Catholic as simply ethnic. Now, however, young men and women of different religious faiths find that what they share is far more important than their religious differences.

The reader should examine the description of the bride price in Algeria and the marriage ceremony in India in order to consider the American system in clearer perspective. While we no longer have neither a dowry system nor have ever had a bride price pattern, American custom does include many informal gifts and exchanges, and in general the bride's family is expected to contribute far more than the husband's.

Case of the
Vanishing Spinster
by Marion K. Sanders

A WOMAN OF rare distinction is Dr. Jocelyn R. Gill, one of a planeload of scientists who observed this summer's total eclipse of the sun from the upper atmosphere. She is—among other things —a Ph.D. and an astronomer. Still more remarkable, in the uxorious climate of our time, she has reached the age of 46 without getting married and is thus one of a vanishing species—the American spinster.

A few years hence, it may be hard to find an American woman who has never been a bride. Right now, of all the nation's females still in their thirties, a whopping 93 per cent have had at least one husband. This is a record figure in our history and in the Western world today. So says the Population Reference Bureau, a nonprofit research organization specializing in demographic lore. In contrast, 28 per cent of Frenchwomen between the ages of 25 and 34 are still unwed, as are 18 per cent of the British and a grim 45 per cent of the Irish.

If this trend continues, future generations of American children will grow up without benefit of maiden aunts and few, if any, of them will be able to identify the scrawny hag who, with cat and

From the *New York Times Magazine,* September 22, 1963, copyright © 1963 by The New York Times Company parrot, adorns the key card in the game of "Old Maid." But while women may rejoice over this remarkable improvement in their marital fortunes, the fact remains that the nation has lost something valuable—perhaps irreplaceable—in the process. Not so long ago, the spinster occupied an honored place in society

Many of the women best remembered in history—from Elizabeth I to the Brontës and our own Jane Addams—were unmarried. Lack of a husband and freedom from the responsibilities of home and family played a demonstrable part in their achievements. Some were esteemed for brawn rather than brains. In the not-too-remote past, there were ticker-tape parades for Amelia Earhart and Gertrude Ederle. Glenna Collett, Helen Wills and Althea Gibson were national heroines. These latter-day Annie Oakleys were all unmarried when they achieved stardom, being presumably too busy with flying, swimming, golf or tennis to take time out for matrimony. Such eccentricity is now out of style—along with the Boyishform brassieres and cropped haircuts of the nineteen-twenties. Modern girl athletes favor ruffled pants and sexy coveralls to demonstrate that, like all right-thinking American females, there is no laurel for which they would shun or postpone a trip to the altar.

Departed, too, is the pattern of dedicated celibacy which produced such battlers' for women's rights and social reform as Grace Abbott, Lillian Wald and Sophonisba Breckinridge. The Grand Old Maids—fondly recalled in labor circles as the Triangle Fire Girls—would find plenty to do if they were still around. One surely would be in the van of the civil-rights struggle, following in the foosteps, perhaps, of Ida B. Wells, the intrepid Negro teacher who mounted a one-woman campaign against lynching in the eighteen-nineties.

Miss Wells eventually acquired a husband, as did several other feminists of her day. Indeed, though they had little time for the domestic virtues themselves, they all worried mightily about child labor, maternal health and the property rights of wives.

Later generations profited by spinster militancy. The doors these pioneers battered down in the professions, the academic world, government and politics are now wide open. The working woman is no longer condemned to what Miss Catharine Beecher a hundred years ago described as "a life of unrequited toil and consequent degradation and vice."

Such noble examples have not, however, made the single state attractive to the average female, and until the early years of the present century this aversion probably made good sense. Unless she married, the average gentlewoman was doomed to become a governess or an unpaid drudge in the home of a male relative. In either case, she was hobbled by numbing standards of propriety. (For the lower-class spinster, the prospects were even more bleak.)

But times have changed. The single woman's economic opportunities have multiplied and she has been almost entirely liberated from the stifling conventions of the past. Why then has the old fear of spinsterhood persisted into this new age of emancipation? Where are the spinsters of yesteryear, and why are they vanishing?

One reason for their disappearance is that the modern American girl has turned into the champion husband-hunter of all time. Haunted—it would seem from the cradle—by the specter of spinsterhood, she gets off to an unprecedentedly early start. Couples have been observed "going steady" in kindergarten and those who are not so linked in their teens are considered freaks.

Former president Charles W. Cole of Amherst saw this curious pubescent monogamy as a conspiracy by the plain girls to prevent the more alluring ones from monopolizing the available boy supply. It has indeed resulted in a more equitable distribution, thus making the belle of the ball—along with the wallflower—virtually obsolete. Such is the determination to avoid spinsterhood that the girl who turns 20 without a spouse and who finds lean pickings in her home territory, will often flee to the greener pastures of New York or Washington—Meccas of upward-striving men, of whom quite a few are still unattached.

Migration—a new element in the marital stakes—helps cut the filial bonds which tied yesterday's young spinster to the family home for life. In the anonymity of a metropolis, she can turn overnight into a dazzling blonde without exciting comment and make uninhibited use of all the other aids to glamour on which American women are said to spend some $2 billion a year.

The competition for marriage partners is likely to be rough in the office and in nearby political and social clubs. Even the Museum of Modern Art—long a favorite mating ground—is said to be pretty well fished out. So she must stalk her prey on vacation cruises and at resorts where the management obligingly equips bachelors with distinctive lapel buttons. If—as is most usual—she is earning only a secretary's salary, she skips many lunches to finance this campaign. And should her spirits flag, she can consult the rich contemporary literature in which the entrapment of the elusive male is blueprinted with a precision that makes Becky Sharp appear a bungling amateur.

In the end, these exertions generally pay off. There is an office shower and after a week-end honeymoon, she is back at her job. Her paycheck then provides a built-in dowry to help furnish the home, thus relieving her parents of what was once an onerous burden.

Indeed—except for the very rich who spend much money and energy on debutante daughters—modern mating involves little work for mother. The ordeal she has escaped was vividly pictured by Samuel Butler in "The Way of All Flesh": "Why, she would rather have three confinements than go through the wear and tear of marrying off a single daughter. Nevertheless, it had got to be done and poor Mrs. Allaby never looked at a young man without an eye to his being a future son-in-law."

Two of the Allaby girls were nearing 30, the borderline of permanent spinsterhood in the Victorian era. Today the peril point hangs more on cosmetics than chronology. No girl can be classed as a chronic spinster so long as she can plausibly celebrate her thirty-ninth birthday, a circumstance which depends largely on the caliber of the beautician and plastic surgeon she can afford.

But for the dwindling few whom marriage eludes, life can often be surprisingly comfortable. Like the buffalo and other declining species, the remaining spinsters are coming to be highly prized. I know a maiden secretary to a steamship executive who wears her graying topknot like a royal crown. She is now 60 and could retire on a hefty pension, but her boss won't hear of it.

"I'll quit myself if she abandons me to those young things," he told me, waving contemptuously at the typing pool outside his door. "The single ones are in the washroom at 4:30 blackening their eyes for the evening's dates. After they marry, they rush home even earlier to whip up fancy casseroles. Then comes baby. They leave and you have to start the whole damn cycle all over again. What this country needs is more spinsters."

Socially, to be sure, the spinster's lot is not enviable. Escorts and vacations are often mentioned as her prime worries. However, the abundance of widows has made many hostesses more relaxed about an extra woman or two at the dinner table, where a nondomestic life and interests may be something of a conversational asset.

I know one unmarried woman of 49 who turns down at least a half-dozen invitations a month. Her job as executive of a civic agency often spills over into evening meetings and conferences— her extracurricular availability being one reason for her five-figure salary. She lives alone in an attractive apartment, owns a weekend cottage which she rents profitably when she goes abroad, dresses elegantly and patronizes a de luxe hairdresser. "I just don't have time to feel lonely," she said.

This, too, was the comment of another spinster of the same vintage who runs a successful dress shop. Pressed to discuss her problem she added, after some hesitation: "Well, sometimes I think I have it too good. When my married friends tell me about all their problems I feel guilty."

In fact, the burden of guilt would probably rest more fairly on the shoulders of America's married women, who have conspicuously failed to reinforce the thinning ranks of spinsters. That doughty pioneer, Susan B. Anthony, would be grieved to know that her sex still accounts for only a tiny percentage of the nation's doctors, lawyers, scientists and members of Congress. And Emma Willard would be amazed to learn that men in large numbers are invading such classic female preserves as school teaching. According to Professor Ethel J. Alpenfels of New York University, they are also grabbing the better-paying jobs. In community after community, she points out, as the older women principals retire, they are replaced by men.

Even the Ivy League women's colleges—those historic spinster citadels—are crumbling, a phenomenon which Miss M. Carey Thomas, Bryn Mawr's long-time president, would never have anticipated. With the retirement this year of Miss Sarah Blanding from Vassar, only four of the seven still have women presidents. Their faculties, too, are changing. In my own undergraduate days at Wellesley, I recall only two male teachers, one of them a limp and temporary substitute for a formidable spinster known to us as "Bible" Smith, who was on a sabbatical. It was startling to learn that this year the Wellesley faculty is 39 per cent male.

Despite the masculine invasion, we are still painfully short of teachers. An upsurge in spinsterhood would help fill the gaps in this and other vital professions and at the same time provide a brake on the population explosion. But since this is unlikely, teachers and guidance counselors are trying hard to persuade their more able students to finish their education and postpone marriage and childbearing until they have won at least a toehold in a vocation. Several colleges have also set up continuing education programs to help married women get back in the national work force. The President's Committee on the Status of Women has focused most of its efforts on the needs of the working wife.

Some of the problems still seem to defy solution. Twenty or thirty years ago there were no garbage-disposals, washer-dryers or mechanized floor waxers to ease the lot of the married career woman. But her home was often graced by the presence of a nanny or a *fräulein,* a cook or an upstairs girl, or—at the least— a treasured "general houseworker." Along with the other spinsters, these, too, have almost vanished. And perhaps they are the most lamented of the lot.

Report from Teeny-Boppersville

by J. Kirk Sale and Ben Apfelbaum

> *The miniskirt is the current*
> *thing, uh-ha;*
> *Teeny-bopper is our new-*
> *born king, uh-ha.**
> —*Sonny and Cher.*

THERE IS no urgency. They move slowly, languidly, along the crowded sidewalks. Bright-colored bell-bottoms, miniskirts, long hair falling straight down the back, a sagging pocketbook swung lazily by its straps, pastel sandals shuffling. Paisley shirts with puffed sleeves and open to the third button, tight cuffless trousers flaring slightly at the ankles, long sideburns flowing into carefully coiffed hair brushing gently on the collar, boots clicking in long, loping strides. Milling and ambling, like a rush-hour crowd in slow motion, they absorb the sights and sounds of the street. From a garishly painted basement cafe, the heavy, shivering, electronic pulse of a band sets an imperceptible rhythm.

"Free admission, come on in, join our show, just starting. . . .

From the *New York Times Magazine,* May 28, 1967, copyright © 1967 by The New York Times Company
* From "The Beat Goes On," by Sonny Bono. Copyright 1967, Cotillion Music, Inc. and Chris-Marc Music.

Yeah, Dylan's dead, I'm hip. . . . My hair isn't short, that's just school rules, look at this. . . . Oh, yeah, she wears her face that she keeps in the jar by the door. . . . Hey, baby, so what's happening?"

A piece of pizza at the corner, eaten slowly and carefully, back against the counter, casually appraising the scene. In the window of the Rienzi, boys in full plumage assessing their reflections, a comb from nowhere patting the bobs in place. Strolling past Googie's and the Tin Angel, then, leisurely, drifting up to the park. Eventually back to the crowded heart, outside the Cafe Wha? and the Cock-'n'-Bull, an orange drink at the newsstand, some new faces, gossip, moving back as the cops push wearily through, then leaning easily, knee bent, against the wall, humming softly with the rhythm of the bands, and the crowds, and the laughter, lots of laughter.

Down in the basement of the Wha? on Macdougal Street, a long and narrow, low-ceilinged cavern, the Raves are into their last set, stark on the blazingly lighted stage, surrounded by huge amplifiers, speakers, microphones and wires. The noise is infectious: both young guitarists on the stage are dancing, shuffling, smiling broadly, and just below them the regulars at the center booths are singing along, yelling to the drummer, pulling on the wires, swaying in their seats, while in the back, against the far wall, two girls, a vinyl miniskirt and a plaid pants suit, are dancing, easily, relaxed, absorbed. The music is unifying and exhilarating, everyone in the room from ticket-taker to tourist is caught up in it, in the good time the band is having, loose, untroubled, free, and when the last electronic chord fades there is a laughing cheer and a sad, sated, little audible sigh that fills the room.

This is a warm spring Saturday night in the center of New York's Greenwich Village, which in the last two years has become the magnet for the newest, and liveliest, subdivision of New York's teen-age world: the teeny-bopper. Along these special eight blocks teeny-boppers from the entire metropolitan area find a world apart, a world dedicated to them and their pleasures, and every evening, every weekend, they fill it; when they can't make the Village scene they dream of it, or wait for the time, or pretend they are *there*. There are teeny-bopper scenes, of course, all across the country—in Chicago's Oldtown, on West Hollywood's Sunset Strip, even in Denver and Philadelphia and Toronto, for the teeny-boppers have sprung up wherever the young congregate and electronic bands pulsate. But the Village is special.

"I feel free to do whatever I want down here. I mean, where I live there's nothing to do, no excitement. Here you can do what you want." That, the statement of a young boy from Queens, is the teeny-bopper testimonial to the Village. "I wanted to be a teacher," says a miniskirted girl from the Bronx, "but I changed my mind. Since I come down here, I have no time for school, I want to come here all the time. I want to live here. . . . I love it down here, it's my kind of people. I'm so comfortable."

"I was a teeny-bopper and I used to come down once a year," said one young New Jersey boy, now a Village regular, "and then every weekend, and soon you like it so much that you don't want to leave at all." The Village magnet is powerful—and the pull is self-perpetuating. One high-school senior, a boy very close to the teeny-bopper world, talks about its attraction to the girls he knows:

"They take a friend and they come crawling into the Village from Forest Hills and Canarsie, dress the way they see in pictures, talk the way they've learned to, and go and sit in the Cock-'n'-Bull with other kids who are exactly like them in every way. And then they all go home and feel proud that they 'hung out in the Village.' They think it's great, and they say to their friends, 'I hung out in the Village—can you top that?' After all, the Village is famous all over the world. I mean, could you go to Paris and say 'I hung out in Borough Park?' "

Barbara, a 16-year-old from the Bronx and a student at Evander Childs High School, is a regular at the Cafe Wha?. Like most, she makes the standard disclaimer, afraid of being put down, hating the imprisonment of the press's label: "Me? I'm not a teeny-bopper; that's that kid over there." We asked her what she does on Saturday morning.

"I get ready to come down here to the Village at night." She laughed, embarrassed.

"And what do you do?"

"Well, first I do all my homework, I do all the things I have to around the house. Then I call my friends and we talk about what we're going to wear—and then we come down the Wha?." ("Down the Wha?," incidentally, is a signal part of the teeny-bopper lexicon.)

"What time do you get here?"

"It starts at 7:30, and we get here at 8:30. We don't want to be the first ones; we have to make our entrance, you know." She laughs at her own frankness. "Then we walk down the aisle, and sometimes if you're lucky you get a wave, you know, from the guys in the group. And then when the set is over, they come down. Then we sit and watch them and wave, and yell, and all that.

"And then we watch the whole show, and after it's over we go out in the lobby. And like last night we were talking with some other kids, and you get to know about them, what they think about the Wha?, you know, and then how old they are, and what *we* think about it. You get to exchange ideas.

"And then at the end, we come back in, the band does its last set, the crazy set, and we're there in the back, singing and joking, and they yell at us to shut up. We sit all the way in the back next to the wall; we can dance there, and crack up and everything." She sighs and smiles and squirms a little.

No easy definition of "teeny-bopper" is possible, for the perimeters of the word change as fast as the Top 10, and as the general press picks it up it is used to describe practically anyone who is not senile. (The word "bopper" itself comes from the old Negro argot "bebopper" of the forties, the bebop jazz enthusiast who dressed oddly and dug the then far-out music.)

But, roughly, the teeny-boppers range from 10 to 19, though the majority are of high-school age, between 14 and 17. They are caught up in the simple fact of being young, scorn the pretense of "acting grownup" or trying to be an adult, and audaciously, aggressively parade their youthfulness. They are intellectually as well as emotionally set against their parents' standards on sex, drugs, music, clothes, behavior, hair and politics. The word "teeny-bopper" at first seemed to refer to girls, but no special term has been coined for the male of the species, so "teeny-bopper" now applies to both sexes.

They are the kids who deliberately involve themselves in more than just a radio-listening way with the current pop-music world, who spend their weekends and summer vacations religiously visiting the cafes where the bands play, who are friendly, or try to be, with the musicians (who are generally of, or close to, their own age), who can tell gossip from truth in the teen magazines and, in fact, make rock 'n' roll the focus of their interest and energy, the theme of their conversations and dreams.

Even in the larger cities, where the teeny-boppers become identifiable as a group, they probably represent no more than a minority of the teen-age population, though a very distinct, involved and articulate minority. Not just any teen-ager with longish hair and a pair of boots is a teeny-bopper. Coexisting with them are the *hippies*—the descendants of the beats, usually the older teens, somewhat scornful of the youthful musicians, more involved with drugs, usually living away from home and perhaps working at odd jobs, tolerant of the teenies but living in a more adult, though thoroughly anti-Establishment, world; the *screamies* —younger children, usually girls, from 9 to 12, who are only beginning to awaken to the world around and have not yet developed any cool about themselves, screaming and fainting at the few big-name concerts they are allowed to go to; and the *squares* —the strait-laced, short-haired, penny-loafer, crew-cut set, football players and A-students.

In a way, the teeny-boppers partake of all these worlds and may have square characteristics along with their hip ones: they may be reading "Silas Marner" and the East Village Other, looking up to both Longfellow and Leary, gossiping about the senior prom as well as last night's party. For teeny-bopperism is a stage, part of a loose evolutionary process of adolescence that connects with other stages. Thus, it is possible for a screamie to become a bopper, or a bopper a hippie—this last is fairly frequent in the Village, where the two worlds overlap—for the categories are loose, and the entries easy.

Although the teeny-boppers resemble earlier teen-age groups in some ways—rebellious, self-centered, questioning—there is a difference of degree so great as to be a difference of kind between them and the flappers of the twenties, the bobby-soxers of the forties or the Presleyites of the fifties. For one thing, they are more obvious, more aggressive, less inhibited, continually play-acting their youthful roles in public, "goofing on" (putting-on-putting-down) the squares and the adults: panhandling the tourists in the Village streets and reveling in their embarrassment, gaily yelling, "Let's go shoot up" in front of policemen and grownups just for the effect, making fun of the blank unsmiling faces in the subways.

But the music they create and listen to tells most about them. The lyrics of today have come a long way from Patti Page's "How Much Is That Doggie in the Window?" Listen to this rather blunt but accurate sentiment from 15-year-old Janis Ian:

> *If you think I'm hating grownups,*
>   *you've got me all wrong.*
> *They're very nice people when they*
>   *stay where they belong.*
> *But I'm the younger generation*
> *And your rules are giving me*
>   *fixations.*
> *I've got those younger generation,*
>   *regurgitating blues.**

And another:

> *Her mother plays on the golf course*
>   *ev'ry day*
> *And her daddy sits at home and plays*
>   *with the maid.*
> *They've found the perfect alibi:*
> *Stay together for the sake of the*
>   *child;*
> *Divorce don't fit*
> *And they're too young to split.*
> *Think they're martyrs but they're*
>   *killing the kid.**

* From "Younger Generation Blues" and "Janey's Blues," copyright 1966, Dialogue Music, Inc.

It's not unusual for the teeny-boppers' music to be written and played by their contemporaries. A group called the Raves, for example, who are very big with the teeny-bop set at the Cafe Wha? and who recently cut a record of their own composition that is moving up on the charts, are led by Michael Jimenez, all of 19, and his brother David, 17. These contemporaries are touchable and talkable to—on the street after their show, in the coffeehouse down the street, at the party on Saturday. It is the everyday quality of these idols that differentiates this generation from those past. Peter Tork of the Monkees, mooned over by girls across the country and probably worth half a million dollars, is right there walking along Macdougal Street and will even stop to talk; Brian Jones of the Rolling Stones, a group nearly as successful and rich as the Beatles, can be seen in the Village restaurants.

John Emelin, a tall, serious young singer of 21, who is a member of a popular new band called Lothar and the Hand People (Lothar is the nickname they have given their theremin, an electronic instrument played by moving the hands along a tubular electrode, hence the "hand people") sums up the attitude of a special group of his generation:

"The difference between 1940 and now is amazing. We don't have a major war, but we have a lot of very strange little ones. We have the memory of an assassination which is still getting fantastic publicity. We have a tremendous race scene that is getting a tremendous amount of publicity. We have a fantastic drug scene that's getting a lot of attention. We have an amazing music scene which was just not happening in the forties the way it's happening now. We have an amazing science scene—fantastic! In the forties they were discovering nylon, or something. We're about to embark for the moon."

What sets the teeny-bopper apart is a special awareness of, and dissatisfaction with, the adult world, and a deliberate attempt to create a separate free-and-easy world through a rough hedonism of music, companionship, emotionalism, sex, drugs and, as the teeny-boppers say, "anything that turns you on, makes you happy."

At the Rienzi, a coffeehouse where boppers and post-boppers

mingle, we asked a boy named David, 17, neatly dressed and with well-groomed hair curling under his ears, about his parents. He snorted, "My father wants me to be rich," and made a face. "My father wants me to grow up to be exactly like him. He's a champion bridge player and he goes down to the bridge club all night. And I say, 'I'm going down to Macdougal Street,' and he says, 'You're just hanging around down there.' So I say, 'I'm just going to be with my friends. *You* go to the bridge club: what do you go *there* for?' Every —— night he goes to the bridge club!" And a young girl echoes: "You rarely find a girl who can talk to her parents. Her parents are always putting her down."

Iris, a pretty high-school senior who has made the Village scene for some years, argues that the big problem is that the teeny-boppers have to lead double lives because they can't get through to their parents. "They say, 'Oh, Mom, I'm going to hang around at the corner,' and they come down here and smoke [that's not tobacco] and have sex, and it's all very teeny. And they go home and they're Miss Goody-Goody again, and comes Friday night, it's 'I'm going to the corner of the park' again. Because they can't say to their parents, 'This is what I am and what I want to do.' So a lot of them lead a kind of double life. How can you go home and when your mother says, 'What, did you do tonight, dear?' say, 'Ma, tonight I smoked grass?' "

This generational gap showed itself one night recently in the Village when a big Lincoln pulled up in front of the Cafe Wha? and a large matron stormed out, went up to the doorman and screamed: "Where's my daughter? Get her up here, you bum! Get her out of this evil place!" She then marched inside and found her daughter talking to a long-haired youth of perhaps 15: "You spend all your time with these disgusting queers?" The daughter took one look and ran off down Macdougal Street. Her mother went tearing after her at a remarkable speed and in a few minutes reappeared, dragging the girl, in tears, back to the car.

An hour later, much to the amusement of the regulars on the street, the daughter was back, strolling casually. She explained: "I ran into the subway and lost the —— bitch."

In reaction to the world of their parents which they think they understand and don't want to be a part of, the teeny-boppers run away into a world of their own where they can be young and revel in their childish enthusiasms without anybody tsk-tsking over their shoulders. They want to be left alone in an arena where they can maintain their own mores and values, however flimsy, which they regard as no worse than their parents'. They ask very little from the outside—except money from home and passing grades from school, both usually given easily—and certainly not meaning or guidance or companionship. These they get from their contemporary heroes in the bands and on the streets, from group experience of emotional music shared at fever pitch, and from being a part of a scene that's "happening."

The dominant note of this world is the amplified twang of an electronic guitar: rock 'n' roll is the lingua franca, musical involvement the passport. Frank Zappa, a member of a new group of talented musicians called the Mothers of Invention, whose wild black curls and black ankle-length coat have made him a Macdougal Street standout, sees a kind of patriotism in this involvement. "The only real loyalty that exists in the American teenager today is to his music. He doesn't give an actual damn about his country or his mother or his Government or his religion. He has more actual patriotism in terms of how he feels about his music than in anything else. And this just has never happened before."

Part of the exhilaration, of course, comes from the incredible noise level at which the music is played, thanks to the complicated electronic gadgetry that has turned a guitar from a sweet accompanying instrument into a blaring siren and a weak teenage tenor into an echo-chamber scream. John Emelin, whose own group's theremin is one of the loudest electronic creations of them all, argues that "it's a lot of noise only in the same way that Indian music is a lot of noise sometimes, or symphonies are a lot of noise. It makes you peak out emotionally."

But the rock 'n' roll world is more than hearing the singers and memorizing the songs—it means buying the records ($250-million worth a year), reading the teen magazines (50 million copies a year), and above all talking, talking about the world of the rock 'n' roll stars. On the streets, in the cafes, over the sausage sandwiches, the conversations are heavily rock-centered: "Hey, d'you see that that Russian guy—what's it? Yevtushenko? —made the Monkees concert in Hawaii?" Or: "You know the Animals where they say, 'Have you ever been so hungry that you had no pride?' Like that's where I'm at now about Eric Clapton, I told you I saw him at the Tin Angel the other night: he's so beautiful." Even gossip and put-downs are couched in these terms: "Oh, no, man, let's stay away from that chick. You know her bag? Like she sits around and watches the Beatles on Ed Sullivan, she just sits there and screams, or sometimes like she'll take pictures of the screen just to have pictures of *them*. She's got this picture of Paul McCartney, it's all distorted, with no focus, and she'll say, 'This is a picture of Paul.' You know, what kind of ——?"

Naturally enough, through this process the culture heroes for the teeny-boppers are in large measure the rock 'n' roll musicians of any stripe—not just the locals who have made good like Lothar and the Hand People and the Mothers of Invention or the famous ones who make the scene like the Rolling Stones and the Animals, but also—and especially—Bob Dylan and, still, the Beatles. Even today when a Beatles song comes on in a Village diner, there is a modified hush, everyone listening with one ear. And Dylan, who was the first to turn many of these kids on to some serious ideas and a glimpse of poetry, represents for many a kind of supreme figure, a kid who dropped out of the parental world, made good, got rich, scored whenever he wanted to, and then dropped out again, a mysterious, beautiful figure proving to the teeny-boppers that they must be on to something great.

In the same way the professional dropouts around the Village, seeable and knowable, are culture heroes: Allen Ginsberg especially ("Oh, what a beautiful life, I mean beautiful"), Timothy Leary and Andy Warhol: there is something about the way they are "goofing on" the square world and yet making a go of it that embodies all the teeny-bop ideals. This "grooving with" the hip dropout spills over to such groups as homosexuals and Negroes who, while they are not themselves teeny-boppers—the Village scene has no more than a handful of Negro teeny-boppers, largely because Negro youths apparently don't need such a scene to declare their freedom from and hostility to the Establishment power structure—represent the kind of sentiment the boppers feel they are into.

If there is hedonism in the music, there is also hedonism in the life that surrounds it. The sights and sounds of rock 'n' roll are enough for most of the teeny-boppers, but there is no question but that the twin revolutions of the adult world in sex and drugs have also filtered down to become a part of their world as well.

We talked to one girl of 18 who had been coming to the Village regularly for four years—she was pretty, shy, and except for her unusual dress could have been any suburban girl—and asked her about sex.

"Well, I'd meet boys, and like, you know, I'd . . . I'd *love* them, not just like them. So I stayed with them. And then the summertime, I stayed down here, I smoked a lot, and. . . . I didn't just go to *anybody;* I really liked these boys. But they used me. Like I'd tell them I liked them and wanted to be with them, and they'd use me and then say, 'Good-by now, that's it.' And I was very hurt. . . ."

"How do you feel about all that now?"

"I don't know. I think it was a good experience. I mean, I'm better now, I learned. I don't think everything I did was right, but I don't feel guilty. I mean it's just a misfortune that it went wrong. I learned about things and how to handle them.

"But even now, I meet boys and the first thing they say is, 'Come on, let's go to bed.' And I want to show the boy that I like him, but now . . . I don't know what to do."

The confusion is natural enough. "My mother knows I wouldn't go with anybody," one girl told us. "Though sometimes I feel that I would. But I know that when it really comes down to things, I'd be scared witless. I feel that if I . . . went with somebody, I couldn't look them in the face afterward, I really couldn't." In addition to the simple fear of the unknowns of sex, most of the teeny-boppers seem to be aware of the other difficulties— the possibilities of pregnancy, venereal disease, emotional turmoil and "a bad reputation." "This may be old-fashioned," says 16-year-old Barbara, "but I think a boy respects you better if the first time you meet him you don't say, 'How about it?', you know?" She laughs at the exaggeration. "I think it's not good, that you should know what you're doing better, when you're 20 or so."

There are enough sad stories of girls who have slept around to indicate that sex is a real—if troublesome—part of the liberality of this world (but whether it is more so than in the corn belt no one knows). "I know this one girl," admits a young teeny, "she was going with this guy in a band, and she went to bed with him. And after that he wouldn't talk to her, and she felt funny. So then pretty soon everybody in the group had her. She's walking around now like she's lost."

The fact is that with the sexual mores of the teeny-boppers the possibilities, and the pitfalls, are much more open than in the past.

Marijuana, too, is more or less routine, though of course it is not confined to the teeny-boppers ("I can get more grass in East Orange than I can down here," said one girl in the Village). By the time they are 16 probably most of the teenies have experimented with marijuana, and quite a number may smoke regularly —"They don't think marijuana is a drug, they think it's normal," one teenie says—and a sizable minority is "into the acid scene," i.e., taking LSD occasionally. But it appears that very few go on to amphetamines—"Stay away from A, man," one boy warns —and almost none to heroin.

Marijuana is obviously a convenient release for some of the teeny-bopper set, most of whom are too young to get a drink legally (their hangouts are all liquor-free and the only thing stronger than Coke is the music) and many of whom profess to be rather repulsed by what they have seen of adult use of alcohol, anyway. ("I came home about 2:30 in the morning when my mother was having a party," one boy told us, "and I saw all these disgusting middle-aged people, all drunk and doing all these foolish disgusting things.") Marijuana is a way, they say, of getting high without being either sloppy or particularly noticeable (losing cool); it is simple and inexpensive; and it serves to heighten rather than diminish the sights and sounds of the scene.

Though marijuana is considered normal enough, the teeny-boppers are keenly aware that possession of it is against the law. "Like, I *know*, man, you can get busted for smoking and sometimes I get up tight when I see these plainclothes guys come with their badges. But I've read all the stuff; I know it can't hurt you—pot, that is—and all that about how it can lead to stronger stuff—well, no one believes that anymore except maybe in Indiana." And they also know the dangers of the stronger drugs—like music, this is a subject on which they seem well-informed—and pretty religiously steer away from them. For though there is indeed a dangerous drug scene in the Village (as elsewhere) and a few of the teenies do get sucked into it— either through some older teen-ager who is pushing drugs for a living or just as a result of youthful experimentation—there is also a powerful built-in correction in the Village: the wasted, empty men you can see around in the darkened doorways who have been hooked. The teeny-boppers can know, perhaps better than their suburban friends, just how evil the addiction scene is.

And so what, in the end, is to be made of this strange new world? What will become of it?

It is really too early to tell. Some of the teeny-boppers will probably simply fade from the scene as they reach 17 and 18— maybe bored, or choosing to go away to college, or settling into a job and its square responsibilities. Some will surely go into the hippie life, find a pad in the East Village, try to live along the Village fringes as long as they can. But whatever happens, it is unlikely that the years of bopperhood will have failed to make their mark.

There is no question about what today's teeny-boppers and those around them believe: "We're on to something new, and wonderful." The singer John Emelin says, "A whole return to a simple philosophy is what's happening. A whole group of kids is now rediscovering the concept of love—and not a romantic love, it's like *agape* or whatever. It's like Christian love without any of the hang-ups of the church scene."

Or, in the words of a 16-year-old boy: "There's one thing the adult generation in this country doesn't dig, man: we are the future generation." "Yeah, I can see our next President with long hair and a beard," said one youngster. Another added,

"Look at us. The society has changed so much since we were 6 years old. Some day you'll see a long-haired cat sitting in Congress saying, 'Fourscore,' right?"

Phil Leone, a 19-year-old drummer with the Raves and very much a part of the subculture of the new generation, says: "Let's put it this way. The teeny-boppers now are going to be the future leaders of the world. And like if they're still thinking the way they are now, it's going to be a beautiful place to live in."

More Coeds Find Less Guilt in Sex

by Jane E. Brody

COLLEGE COEDS today are more likely to enjoy their first experience with sexual intercourse than did the college girls of 20 years ago, a nationwide study has shown.

The same seems to be true for college males, although the change has not been so great as for females.

Dr. Paul H. Gebhard, who described the study's findings yesterday, attributed the increased enjoyment to a reduction of guilt feelings associated with premarital sex and to a growing trend toward sexual equality.

"It is becoming respectable to be an admittedly sexually reponsive female," he said. "The female today is regarded less as a sexual object to be exploited and more as a human being with rights to sexual expression."

Dr. Gebhard, a professor of anthropology, is director of the Institute for Sex Research at Indiana University. The institute, where the late Dr. Alfred C. Kinsey did his pioneering research on sex behavior, conducted the study last summer among a national sample of 1,200 college students. The current findings are being compared with those of a similar study of students in college during the 1940's and early 1950's.

From the *New York Times,* December 30, 1967, copyright © 1967 by The New York Times Company

The data on first premarital coitus were the first of the new study's findings to be processed by computer. Later analyses will deal with such matters as attitudes toward sexual behavior, extent of premarital sex, masturbation, petting and homosexuality.

Speaking at the annual meeting of the American Association for the Advancement of Science at the Americana Hotel, Dr. Gebhard described the first premarital coitus as "a crossing of a Rubicon in life history."

"Once persons begin premarital coitus they seldom recant and remain abstinent until marriage," he observed.

He added that the psychological and social importance of this experience made it "an excellent medium for elucidating changes in sexual behavior and attitudes which have occurred over the last few decades."

One thing that has not changed much, Dr. Gebhard said, is "the enormous difference between how males and females view their initial partner."

"Females surrender their virginity to males they love whereas males are much less emotionally involved," he added.

Fifty to 60 per cent of current college females said their first coitus was with someone they loved and planned to marry, and 20 to 25 per cent said they loved the male although marriage was not anticipated.

But only 11 to 14 per cent of the males said they loved and planned to marry their first sexual partner, and 25 to 30 per cent said they felt some emotional attachment to the girl but did not love her.

Dr. Gebhard noted that there was a small but definite trend toward emotional attachment on the part of the male, but that males still tended to be "opportunistic" about sex. He added that more females today tended to have sexual intercourse with men they loved but did not necessarily plan to marry.

As for female enjoyment of the first coitus, 73 per cent of freshmen, 60 per cent of sophomores, 63 per cent of juniors and 65 per cent of seniors said their experience was pleasurable. This compares with 46, 48, 35 and 46 per cent, respectively, among college women two decades ago.

For junior males, the percentages enjoying their first coitus rose from 74 to 86 and for senior males, from 65 to 89.

Dr. Gebhard commented that the "first coitus is traditionally marred by pain, embarrassment, awkwardness and guilt."

"This is less true of the current college students than of those in the past," he said.

The anthropologist reported further that males were less likely than ever to experience coitus first with a prostitute. The change was from 20 to 25 per cent in the early study to 2 to 7 per cent in the current college population.

Should Parents
or Cupid
Arrange Marriages?

by Eleanor Stoker Boll

AFTER SPENDING the past five years in India, Dr. Marie Finger
Bale of the Methodist Board of Missions recently remarked that
there might be fewer divorces in the United States if we borrowed a little from Indian customs. Divorce is almost unknown
in India, she said, because parents select their children's mates
and continue to control their sons' and daughters' lives after
marriage.

It would be impossible, even if it were desirable, to adopt outright a major feature of a culture so different from our own. Yet
there is no denying that we have become conspicuous for our
marital failures. Our annual divorce rate today is about one for
every four marriages. We might, therefore, take a look at India's
system of arranged marriages. What features of it—if any—
might we adopt?

The Hindu joint-family system is designed to achieve continuation of the family line, including its reputation, status and
property. Families confer in an attempt to mate young people

From the *New York Times Magazine,* December 13, 1959, copyright ©
1959 by The New York Times Company

of similar religion and status, of good health and good character —a responsibility considered too grave for the immature. In making the decision, the parents sometimes "engage" a very young child to another from an acceptable family.

After marriage, family control is maintained by having the young couple live permanently with the bridegroom's parents. His mother strictly supervises their personal lives, social relations and the rearing of their children. She also holds the purse strings; whatever they earn is put into a family kitty, along with other family earnings, and dispensed by the mother for the group as a whole. As the family ages and the parents die, the eldest son and his wife are in a position to assume control over the younger members of the family. Thus there is a continuous process of education for and control of marriage and family living.

Arranged marriages and continued control are not unique in India but have been customary for centuries in various places, including China, Japan and the Arab world. Even though the law today in most areas permits free choice, the old tradition dies slowly because it worked well in accomplishing its purpose— family stability, family protection, family survival.

The case for "arranged marriages" in the United States—or, at least more parental control—is based, first, upon the fact that the marriage age is low here. One out of every three girls in this country who marries for the first time is 18 or under. Our most frequent ages of first marriage today are 18 and 19 for girls and 21 and 22 for boys.

The results do not speak well for the judgment of young people who insist on early marriage and on living as they please. Dr. Judson Landis of the University of California, in a selected sample, found divorce rates six times higher in marriages where both spouses were under 21 when they married than in marriages in which both were 31 or over at the time of marriage. In selected United States states, according to the 1958 United Nations Demographic Yearbook, 22.5 per cent of divorced women were 24 or under and 24 per cent of those divorced had been married less than two years. In fact, one out of every twenty divorced women now remarrying is a teen-ager.

Another argument for more parental say-so about marrying is

the inexperience of our young people—a factor related to our standards of education. More and more young people stay in high school until 18, college until 22—and then go on to professional schools. During this time many want to marry and more of them are doing so every year. Yet what preparation have they had for marriage and parenthood? One is reminded of the 19-year-old girl who knew her boy friend was the right mate for her because they were "mentally compatible"—i.e., they could spend a whole evening discussing Plato's philosophy.

In addition, more than one out of every five Americans change residence every year and many a child moves from neighborhood to neighborhood and school to school five or more times before finishing high school. How can such young people learn the qualities about their associates that are most essential to stable marriage? Do they not, in these circumstances, need all possible parental wisdom and guidance?

A further point in favor of arranged marriages is that our children today live with others from a variety of religious, racial, social and economic backgrounds. The new or different is always appealing, especially during the adolescent's rebellion against traditional family values—precisely at the time when so many Americans choose their mates. Yet a growing number of studies indicate that marriages which cross racial, religious and economic lines yield more broken families than those where the backgrounds are similar.

And when a child's marriage breaks, it is the family that has to bind up the fracture. A case in point is Martha, who at 16 fell in love with a boy of whom her whole family and most of her friends heartily disapproved. The day she turned 18—the age of consent in her state—she eloped with the young man. Three years and two babies later she was back, financially dependent, and in need not only of a divorce but of physical protection as well. For the boy, just as her parents had pointed out, had a violent temper and was threatening to take the children away.

Is it so unreasonable that parents—who have to mend the damage they have warned against—should wish to exercise some control?

A wedding is a ceremony with notably long-lasting consequences. It produces children who have to be reared, children who become the society's future. Dr. Carle C. Zimmerman of Harvard, in a study of the family throughout history, concludes that the strength of a nation closely parallels the solidarity of its family system. Must the "right" of young people to marry whom and when they they please take precedence over the interests of society?

But there is another side of the picture. The arguments against arranged marriage are based on its unsuitableness to our type of society and on the damage it can do to the individual. When marriage is completely dictated by the family, human values are often the last thing to be considered.

In India, for example, young girls have been married to princes and wealthy men regardless of suitability—witness the 14-year-old girl who was wed to a 70-year-old man, bore him three children before his death, and remained a widow from age 19 for the rest of her life. The arranged marriage, going hand in hand with a low status for women, bears most heavily upon the female, who can be and often is miserably exploited. The male has always been harder to control.

Such Indian misadventures could well occur in different form here, even though parents hew less rigorously to the family line. Consider the kind of marriages that might be arranged by Old World parents resentful of New World ways and anxious to keep their children within their own cultural patterns; by status-seeking parents who would gladly sacrifice any child for improved social position; by parents who consider marriage itself such a mark of accomplishment that they shame their children into early wedlock; or by parents who for their own purposes seek to keep their young people from marrying. Such parental pressures occur frequently enough even under our present system of free choice.

Furthermore, if our young people know their prospective mates only superficially—as the supporters of arranged marriage point out—do the parents know them any better? The casualness of our relationships, and the restless moving about from which it stems, both in turn derive from a pace of cultural change that is something new in history.

In these circumstances, it is at least questionable whether one generation's way of dealing with its problems will work for the next. Many an American teen-ager today has already achieved, through better education and choice of friends, a social level higher than that of his parents; could his parents make a wise marriage choice for him? Another aspect of this same social mobility makes it well-nigh impossible to impose a system of arranged marriages on our society. When our young people can get jobs of their own and support themselves, they can marry whether their parents like it or not.

Among the major curses of our society is the thinness of family emotional relationships. Indeed, this is what drives many of our children into early marriage. One wonders if parents who have done poorly in their own marriages are likely to be more successful in guiding those of their children.

Moreover, as the opponents of arranged marriage point out, there is the all-important question of love. The lack of love has obvious and unhealthy effects on human beings—there is even an affliction called marasmus, which causes infants who do not experience love simply to waste away. Quite apart from its own enchantment, the experience of loving and being loved is probably essential to good mental hygiene.

Love is a minor consideration in countries given to arranged marriage, where mates often do not even see one another before the wedding, and where any spontaneous romance between young people is looked upon with suspicion.

Americans, in contrast, have developed a kind of marriage based on romantic affection between two people. This may indeed be an uncertain foundation for marriage. Nevertheless, when matched with congeniality and common values, it can produce the finest type of family life and the healthiest atmosphere for rearing children. And happy families, so the studies say, create more happy families in the next generation.

What, then, is an intelligent balance between these two views of marriage? After years spent in studying modern American marriage at the William T. Carter Foundation, we have come to believe that more control over the marriage of young people should be exerted by law, by parents, by the general public and by educators.

First, we could, and probably should, make it more difficult for the very young to marry in the face of family protest. Most states demand that a boy be 21 before he can marry without parental consent, but in five states he can do so at 18. For girls, the age of consent is 18 in thirty-three states, and 16 in two. While laws alone will never solve the problem of hasty marriages, our laws seem intent on encouraging them.

Parents themselves could become a major controlling force, were they to begin consciously conditioning their children toward good marriages at a very early age. Though they may not formally "engage" young children as the Hindus do, they can effect similar results in several ways.

One is to teach children attitudes toward marriage as a responsibility to the family line, past and future, and not as an orgy of romantic satisfaction between two individuals. Parents can also instill feelings of such pride in the basic values inherent in their own race, religion and social class that their offspring will not be intrigued by other values which, in marriage, will cause conflict.

Parents should seek to select almost from a child's birth, and particularly during adolescence, the companions with whom he associates in neighborhood, in school and in recreation. Children *can* learn to prefer mates approved by parents if other possibilities are kept to a minimum. Furthermore, parents should discuss their own marriage sincerely and realistically with their children, who are sure to take the reasons for its relative success or failure very much to heart.

Parents who try to guide their children into good marriages need, and deserve, the support of public opinion. At present, they get too little of it. For one reason, we are devoted to the ideal that all people are created equal and that there should be no discrimination in association. But we neglect to point out to young people that in marriage, the most intimate and important relationship in life, discordance of values has been seen to lead to failure. Again, as a romantic-minded people, we tend to look askance at any parental interference with young love. We side with the starry-eyed. Even in school courses on marriage and family living, many teachers tend to undercut parents by discussing marriage as a union between two people who should learn to be personally compatible.

According to Dr. A. H. Hobbes, the most popular textbooks

for such courses emphasize romance and individuality, playing down marriage's crucial role in creating the next generation. When parents oppose a marriage, children often seek advice from others. Apparently, they do not have to look far.

Control over mate selection *alone* is no answer to the problem of divorce. Along with control, young people must receive from early childhood an attitude toward marriage so thoughtful and serious that they will *seek* their parents' counsel. True, some parents are selfish and some are unwise. But by and large, no one knows us better—or wishes us so well.

Study Finds Steady Rise in Interfaith Marriages

A STEADILY CLIMBING rate of interfaith marriage in the United States is having its most serious impact on Roman Catholics and Jews, whose marriages to those outside their faiths carry a high risk of divorce and present a source of conflict in the rearing of children, according to a new study of intermarriage.

There are indications, the study finds, that the rate of divorce among interfaith couples is more influenced by a lack of religious identification of the non-Catholic partner than by a clash of religious values and beliefs.

The findings are disclosed in a published report ("Marriage Counseling: Psychology-Ideology," published by Charles Thomas, Springfield, Ill.) by Dr. Victor Sanua, associate professor of psychology at Yeshiva University's Wurzweiler School of Social Work. It encompasses 41 studies on interfaith marriage made during the last 35 years.

From the *New York Times,* December 24, 1967, copyright © 1967 by The New York Times Company

Continued Rise Seen

Dr. Sanua said that "with few exceptions, all studies indicate that the rate of intermarriage is on the rise and is expected to continue upward."

"In some parts of the country, as many as 50 per cent of Catholics and Protestants marry outside their faith," the study reports. "The figure for Jews in the United States is about 17 per cent." Dr. Sanua said that "while data show that intermarriage may affect the three religious groups differently, the more serious repercussions occur among Catholics and Jews."

Various surveys have demonstrated that interfaith marriages will take place mainly in a large metropolis with a mobile population and the absence of home and family influence. Exact figures on the rate are rarely available, however, because most states forbid their marriage license bureaus to ask for an applicant's religion.

"All studies show that the intermarried have a higher risk of divorce than do those who marry within their own religion," Dr. Sanua said in his report. "While there is some evidence that the risk of divorce increases if the husband is Catholic and the wife Protestant, it was discovered that those unwilling to identify with any religion had the highest divorce rate."

Conclusions drawn from an Iowa study made by Iowa State University, the only state that requests religious preference on marriage and divorce records, indicate the rate of broken marriages was influenced more by the lack of religious identification of the non-Catholic partner than by a clash of religious values and beliefs.

Pressure for Jews

Information gathered in the report also points out that Jews who marry outside their faith see their relatives less regularly and also carry an additional burden—along with Catholics—of having to cope with greater pressure from church and family than do Protestants.

Moreover, Dr. Sanua said, strong religious ties among either or both parents of an intermarried couple present a source of conflict in the raising of children in general and in their religious training in particular.

The report disclosed that promises made prior to marriage under the ante-nuptial agreement insisted upon by the Roman Catholic Church are sometimes reneged by the Protestant and Jewish parents. One survey cited disclosed that in half of the cases involving Catholic-Protestant marriages the children were raised as Protestants.

Various solutions to these problems, such as bringing up the children in the separate religious beliefs of their parents, letting the child decide upon his own religion, conversion of one of the parents or the creation of a "religious vacuum" in the house, are seen as confusing to the child, making him insecure.

Incidence in Washington

Dr. Sanua reached the conclusion that the future growth of the Jewish population in the United States is seriously affected by the increasing degree of interfaith marriage. Among the Jews living in and around Washington, D.C., for example, almost 15 per cent marry outside their faith.

Rabbi Malcolm Stern of the Central Conference of American Rabbis discounted the significance of such statistical studies, stating that they were atypical rather than typical. Cautioning against "unnecessary alarm" over what seems to be a sharp rise in marriages between Jews and non-Jews, Rabbi Stern said that there were fewer such marriages today than during the early period of Jewish settlement in this country, from 1654 to 1840.

Rabbi Stern said that by 1840 there were 15,000 Jewish settlers in the United States mostly on the Eastern Seaboard. From 1654 to 1840 there were 942 Jewish marriages and of these 150, or about 15 per cent, were between Jews and Christians.

This percentage, he said, is matched today only on the college campuses. "Although the university figures are cause for concern, one must also consider, as part of the total picture, the sharp increase in Jewish conversions from 12 between 1654 and 1840 to the current figure of 3,500."

A study last year, by Dr. Eric Rosenthal of Queens College, found that a 30 per cent rate of interfaith marriages among third-generation college educated American-Jewish males was more than twice that of the third generation as a whole.

Dr. Sanua's report concurred with this, cautioning that with the exception of religious Jewish students, college youth surveyed showed a growing acceptance of intermarriage.

High Price of Brides in Algeria Assailed by Would-Be Husbands

ALGIERS

EMANCIPATION OF Algeria's white-veiled women, which many here thought would be accelerated by the country's independence, has made little headway in the face of unyielding tradition and lack of economic opportunity.

Most married women, even on the sidewalks of downtown Algiers, still wear handkerchief-size veils and wrap themselves in yards of white cotton cloth. Young women are still the object of hard bargaining between parents and prospective husbands.

The price of brides has recently come under lively discussion here, mainly in the letters column of the official daily, El Moudjahid. A letter from one lonely young man expressing indignation over the price asked of bridegrooms—despite four years of Algerian independence and revolutionary slogans of progress—set off a flood of sympathetic responses from both men and women.

Citing personal experiences, young men told of having been asked by prospective fathers-in-law to pay from $100 to $1,000 or more. Parents of marriageable daughters often want "la dot" to include an automobile, television set and well-furnished apartment as well, they said.

From the *New York Times,* May 7, 1967, copyright © 1967 by The New York Times Company

"You would think we were in a cattle market," wrote one irritated swain.

"When you love a girl and ask her parents for her hand, they want everything you've got," wrote another.

"How do you expect a bachelor making $100 a month to marry an Algerian girl whose parents demand an enormous price?" asked still another. "It's becoming a luxury to marry an Algerian."

Women retorted that marrying foreigners was not the answer, because, as three readers from an Algiers suburb explained, foreign women "get up at noon, expect to be waited on by their mother-in-law, wear miniskirts and like to flirt."

The newspaper's columnist took the occasion to lecture parents that "selling one's daughter to the highest bidder without concern for her happiness is a medieval practice."

In the port of Djidjelli, east of here, the imam, or religious elder, got citizens to agree to a $100 limit on bride prices.

This week the President of the Superior Islamic Council, Sheik el Abbas, reminded Algerians that bride prices were supposed to be symbolic, on the order of one dollar. Even a flower or a piece of jewelry would suffice, he said.

Paying a high price for a wife often means a man regards her less as a partner than as an expensive article he has purchased, like an automobile, the Sheik said in a declaration to El Moudjahid.

"Men should not agree to pay to have the woman they love," he asserted.

Indian Wedding Merges Old and New

by Sydney H. Schanberg

NEW DELHI

A YOUNG research metallurgist who works for International Business Machines in Fishkill, N. Y., was married in New Delhi the other night in an ancient Hindu ceremony in which the dhoti-clad priest invoked the deities of earth, air, fire and water.

It was not a marriage of West and East, as the contrast of I.B.M. and the Hindu priest might suggest, but rather a marriage of modern India and traditional India.

The 29-year-old bridegroom, Rajendra Dhir, had won his Bachelor of Science degree in Bombay, but had then gone abroad —first to Canada and finally to the United States—to seek, and find, success.

After four years away, Mr. Dhir traveled the 8,000 miles home for a family visit. To his surprise—partly because of a matrimonial advertisement placed in the New Delhi newspapers by his eldest sister without his knowledge—he found himself quickly engaged to an Indian girl who had been traditionally reared and who had moved in circles so close to home that she had never even seen the southern part of India. They are spending their honeymoon there.

From the *New York Times,* July 16, 1969, copyright © 1969 by The New York Times Company

Matrimonial ads placed by the families of potential brides and bridegrooms are a relatively new phenomenon on the Indian social scene, having cropped up only in the last decade or two. Even more recent are the growing number of ads placed by the families of young men who, like Mr. Dhir, have gone to Western countries to make a better living but return to India briefly to claim an Indian bride, get married in the traditional religious rites and then hurry back with her to the foreign home.

These ads usually require the woman be "beautiful" and "educated," generally mention the man's salary and sometimes break with custom by saying "caste no bar." (Although the caste system has been outlawed for decades, it is still a powerful force, especially in seeking a marriage partner.) The ads also offer such lures to a potentially homesick bride as "she will be able to come to India every year if desired."

On the day before his wedding, Mr. Dhir—with only a touch of 20th-century embarrassment about his family's advertising for a wife—discussed quite freely the process by which he had selected his bride, Renu Singh, who is 21 years old and just graduated from Delhi University with a Bachelor of Arts degree in economics.

"I felt quite strange. You can't decide something like this in a short time," he said to describe his initial reaction when he arrived here and learned that several potential wives were waiting to be inspected.

The shock apparently wore off soon, as his emotions—amid the familiar Hindu background—accepted his family's role in his marriage. His was, in fact, more modern than most Hindu marriages, in which the families make all the arrangements and the bridegroom does not get to look at his bride until the wedding day.

At least he would interview the eligibles and make the final decision. "I talked to six or seven of them," he said. "But it didn't click. When I met Renu, something clicked. That's the only answer I can give."

Her mother and father had not literally answered the newspaper ad, but they were old friends of Mr. Dhir's family, knew about the ad and were also looking for a husband for their demure, attractive daughter.

"I had never taken her out," said Mr. Dhir, who is slightly chubby, bespectacled, very serious and very outgoing. He continued:

"But I had met Renu before. I knew her and knew her family. She was approved by my family. It has to be mutual. Also, my father told me our horoscopes matched, so that was okay."

"And we assume that a girl from that social setup will have a normal, healthy background."

Miss Singh's father, V. J. Singh, is director of the Delhi Planning Commission. Mr. Dhir's father, K. L. Dhir, is a doctor with a clinic in Gwalior, about 200 miles south of Delhi. There is a heavy emphasis on college and graduate education in both families.

Rajendra, who is called "Raj" at I.B.M., won a master's degree in metallurgy at the University of Toronto and is working part-time now for his doctorate at Brooklyn Polytechnic Institute. A recent raise at I.B.M. put his salary at more than $13,000 a year.

After he made up his mind about Miss Singh, he took her out a few times—another departure from Indian tradition—to tell her about the United States.

"When you're taking a girl to a strange country, you've got to tell her what to expect," he explained. "It's not fair otherwise."

Mrs. Kamala Passi, the sister who placed the matrimonial ad, was asked why she had not told him in advance. Before she had a chance to answer, the eldest brother in the family, Prem, an ophthalmologist, said, laughing: "We thought he might run away. As soon as he landed, we wanted to push the girls on him so he'd have to select one of the bunch. There wasn't much time. He said he wanted to go back on July 30."

Mr. Dhir said he saw flaws in both the wide-open American tradition of choosing mates and the family-arranged tradition of India, but said he was at a loss to suggest a perfect method.

The outdoor Hindu marriage ceremony juxtaposed the old and the new in this country's changing culture. Miss Singh's father was dressed in a Western business suit, but wore sandals, without socks. Mr. Dhir also wore a Western suit, but his head was swathed in a turban decorated with tinsel and flowers.

An electric fan cooled the wedding party—the priest and his assistant wearing dhotis, or long loincloths, the bride in an elegant sari and the bridegroom in his business suit—as they sat on their haunches under a jasmine-covered wedding canopy through the elaborate two-hour ceremony at a social club here.

Mr. Dhir, as is the custom in his Khatri, or martial, caste, rode part of the way to the wedding on a horse. Then he switched to a blue 1959 Plymouth, which arrived at the social club preceded by a peppy marching band.

Since much of the ceremony was chanted in Sanskrit, the priest translated it into Hindi and English from time to time as an aid to those not familiar with the ancient language. A flow of Sanskrit would be abruptly broken by phrases like "permission from the father" and "bank balance"—bringing gleeful chuckles from the guests.

Part 3

HUSBANDS AND WIVES

AMERICAN COUPLES make a much heavier emotional than financial investment in their marriages. They are likely to bring little property but considerable love to the union. Perhaps they would be better adjusted if they expected a lesser emotional return, since such emotional investments seem peculiarly liable to disaster. Any relationship between two people is likely to be fragile, and American marriages are no exception. Because the variation of husband-wife adjustment is so great, the following selections cannot hope to analyze all of them.

The first selection deals with one change in marital adjustment, which was discussed earlier in the Introduction: the growing expectation on the part of wives that they should derive great enjoyment from sexual relations in marriage, and, of course, the corresponding responsibility which the husband must assume to make sure that his wife is not frustrated. As noted earlier, it is possible that even though married couples a hundred years ago may have enjoyed sex far less, sex was not generally viewed as a problem capable of solution. At present, wives who cannot achieve an orgasm feel that they are either cheated or that they themselves have failed in some way; and husbands may feel that they are incompetent because they are unable to solve the problem for them. Many couples look to psycho-sexual therapy as a possible answer.

Although the mother is typically viewed as the pivot of the American family—and in television as well as in popular literature the husband is often viewed as a kind of outsider—Professor Mead's article offers an analysis of the wide range of roles the modern father must assume. She compares the American system with a large number of primitive societies. In some of them, the mother's brother takes a very strong role as disciplinarian and the person who will teach the sister's son how to carry out various tasks. Because of the conflicting social philosophies that are now espoused by different social circles and classes in our society, there is less agreement now than formerly about a husband's tasks. In some families, he may play a traditional role, entering family matters only rarely and remaining distant, austere, and authoritarian. In other families, the husband may be a "pal" to his children, and share in a nearly egalitarian fashion the chores of housekeeping.

European social commentators have often argued that the American family system is a "matriarchy," since women have so much freedom by comparison with most European family systems. Such commentaries are found less often now, since European marriage systems are moving in the same direction as the American, especially in regard to the participation by the husband in many traditional household tasks. As was noted in the Introduction, just how the adjustment is made in the allocation of tasks within and outside the home is likely to be a function of many variables, though the chief factor is likely to be the resources that husband and wife bring to the marriage. These may be age, aggressiveness, education, income or wealth, or include such variables as the age of the children or which spouse loves the other more. In one of the articles in this section, it is interesting to speculate whether the purchase of a home means that the husband will have a heavier investment in the marriage, since he cannot easily escape this financial obligation, and is thus much more committed to a suburban way of life; or whether it is instead the wife who is tied down by the house, since she no longer has the mobility she might be able to command if she were living in a city apartment.

Much has been made of the differences in family patterns between Negroes and whites in the United States, and these are explored in C. Eric Lincoln's article. In considering his analyses, it should be kept in mind that the differences do not totally disappear, but are considerably reduced if we compare Negroes and whites within the same class. For example, if we look at lower-class whites, we shall also find that there is a high separation, divorce, and desertion rate, so that a far higher percentage of households are headed by a mother than is observed in other social classes. In speculating on the consequences of the absent father for the Negro family, it should be kept in mind that such households are more often to be found in slums, where the racial discrimination in American life accentuates the deprivations of the children whose father has left the home.

It is especially here that efforts to improve the economic standing of the lower classes are of great importance. The social system that produced the lower-class Negro male, and the economic system in which he tries to survive, both combine to make it difficult for him to fulfill the obligations of husband and father. His job is likely to be temporary and poorly paid. When he attempts to raise his family on such a slender economic base, he is likely to fail. Negro women are much more likely to be able to obtain jobs. Consequently, the man is likely to find the role as husband and father singularly unrewarding.

Wives in Quest of the "Colored Lights"

by Donald Janson

ATLANTIC CITY

THE SUBJECT of sex played a larger role in the program of the American Medical Association convention here last week than in past years. One thing doctors were apprised of was a growing frustration among wives.

Robert R. Bell, a Temple University sociologist, reported to the 12,000 doctors assembled here that a fourth of 196 wives surveyed complained that sexual intercourse came too infrequently in their marriages.

Dr. Bell drew some far-reaching conclusions.

"The social and psychological sexual liberation of the modern woman has led some to shed many past restrictions and inhibitions," he said, "and emerge in their marriages with greater sexual interest than their husbands."

What this may mean for "the near future," he felt is that marriages will be wracked by more and more problems centering on wifely dissatisfaction.

He conceded that this was "an ironic switch from the patri-

From the *New York Times,* June 25, 1967, copyright © 1967 by The New York Times Company

archal past," when the wife was relegated to a passive, compliant role intended to serve the desires of a dominant mate.

19th-Century Attitude

Past professional attitudes were offered to illustrate the contrast. Throughout the 19th century moral and "scientific" views frowned upon the thought that women might find sex pleasurable.

William Acton, in a standard text on the reproductive system, wrote that "the belief that women had a sexual appetite was a vile aspersion." William Hammond, a surgeon-general of the United States, recorded the official view that "nine-tenths of the time decent women felt not the slightest pleasure in intercourse." Many published poets, physicians and moralists shared the contention that female sexual satisfaction was achieved only by the "depraved" prostitute.

Today it is next to impossible to find any reputable writers voicing the old double-standard values. Now the pendulum has swung so far the other way, Dr. Bell noted, that writers not only take female sex "rights" for granted, but frequently romanticize sexual intercourse sufficiently to guarantee disappointment.

"If a woman has been assured that she will . . . see colored lights, feel like a breaking wave, or helplessly utter inarticulate cries," writes Morton M. Hunt, "she is apt to consider herself or her husband at fault when these promised wonders do not appear."

The better educated wife, Dr. Bell finds, is the one who is finding fault with the sexual capacity of her husband. The problems for husbands will increase because more and more wives are gaining an education and coveting their right to sexual joy in marriage.

The male is taxed, Dr. Bell noted, because, as Kinsey found, men reach their sexual peak in their late teens, many years before women do.

The difficulty is compounded, the sociologist adds, because in addition to declining male desire during the years of marriage there is the problem of biological restriction on frequency that applies only to the man.

The Bell survey on the emancipated woman was conducted among college graduates, all married and living with their husbands. The 196 averaged 26 years of age and four years of marriage.

Dr. Bell contrasted the results with those of similar studies a quarter century and a half century ago. Female desire for greater sexual satisfaction in the 1940's was increasing but in the 1920's "very few gave any indication of a desire for sex that was greater than that of the husband."

Dr. James L. Mathis, a psychiatrist at the University of Oklahoma Medical Center, held a news conference on the matter with Dr. Bell.

"A marriage is no longer seen as a union for the pleasure of the male in exchange for the support of the female," Dr. Mathis said.

Many men are reluctant to accept the new order, he said, creating a troublesome conflict that should "make it mandatory that the practicing physician concern himself with marital problems far more than in the past." He suggested that medical schools act to meet the crisis by providing courses on the subject.

The Job of
the Children's
Mother's Husband

by Margaret Mead

AFTER A decade of attacks on Mom, the guns are being shifted
to Father. Not Pop or Dad—he's all right. But Father, the
solemn public label for the paternal parent or, to put it another
way, the children's mother's husband.

On every side Father encounters fusillades, and significantly
the attacks are contradictory and irrational, as they were on
mothers in the Nineteen Forties. Fathers are criticized both for
neglecting their children and for spending too much time in the
nursery; for being wedded to the rat race in business and for putting their families ahead of their careers; for a lack of interest
in their sons and for forcing their sons into following in their
footsteps.

Similarly in the Forties, mothers simultaneously were berated
for having spoiled and babied their sons, who were found unready
for army life at 18, and exhorted to spend every living minute
with their children.

The latest blast on the subject was contained in a few remarks

From the *New York Times Magazine,* May 10, 1959, copyright © 1959
by The New York Times Company

attributed to a young anthropologist who insisted that Father must make up his mind to being "odd man out, coexisting as a third party." If he consents to this gracefully, and limits his role to that of an "objective, friendly, informal solver of interpersonal problems," he may never become "obsolete or expendable."

Caught on one side or the other of this barrage—damned if he does and damned if he doesn't—the young father may well feel exposed and confused, wondering what his role really should be in such a rapidly shifting world. A little history may help.

From our pioneer days, we have preserved the myth of a self-sufficient farm household in which Father farmed, hunted, built and was home all day to keep the boys' and girls' minds on their chores and their schooling; a home in which the division of labor between Father and Mother was clear but both were strong and self-reliant, and if Father was away when the Indians attacked, Mother could defend the children. To the same general period of mythology belong the widowed mothers who reared their children on the farms or in the growing cities, where they took in washing while their sons delivered newspapers and rose to be millionaires.

These two American myths contradict each other superficially but not actually: on the farm the father provided a model for the son, who in all probability would not stay on that farm nor depend upon his father's bounty and goodwill, but one day would strike out for himself, leaving the meager acres of the East for the wide plains of the West. The fatherless boy who helped support his mother simply stepped early into his dead father's shoes, as a responsible hardworking man before his time—and he succeeded, and became a folk hero.

Then came a second period of father-images, the fathers of the late nineteenth and early twentieth centuries. If they were rich self-made men, they ruined their sons, who had been born with silver spoons in their mouths and thus could come to no good; if they were men just getting along, they neglected their sons, devoting themselves to making money, while the mothers raised the children; if they were poor, they were thought of as immigrants who, ignorant of the culture, had to accept low-paying jobs for which their sons could not respect them, and who left the whole management of their homes to their wives.

The father who sent his children to expensive schools and his wife to Europe, while he slaved in the heat; the father who never saw his children, who came home from the office when they were fast asleep; the father who was too illiterate and inexperienced to control or appreciate his American-born or city-born children— these were the father figures of the early part of this century.

There were a few other facets to the stereotype. In the hurly-burly of settling a new country, the finer things of life were left to the women while business became a man's career, with money its measure. Women were the custodians of social class, and leisure activities which were masculine also were "common"—fishing and playing poker in one's shirt sleeves and politics.

A good woman had to watch out that her boy didn't follow his father to the corner saloon; if he was to go up in the world— and everyone was to go up in the world—he had to adopt the proprieties which his mother, who traditionally had "taught school," was able to teach him. The politician's maxim, "All that I am and all that I hope to be I owe to my angel mother," was often a literal truth.

Such a mother's son married a woman who, like his mother, would help him control his low, masculine impulses and keep his mind on his career. In each generation, however, the women carried along the image of the masculine side of their fathers, of which their mothers had disapproved, and in daydreams wished they themselves had chosen the Sheik of Araby to marry instead of the successful bank president. Each generation of children was exposed to the contrast: the masculine man who drank, fished and gambled and, by implication, beat his wife and neglected his children; and the emasculated man, Mr. Milquetoast, who did just what his wife wanted him to do—made a business success, bought her a new hat and supported her plans for their children.

Then women went to work, and the single clear sign that a man was really a man—the pay envelope—was clouded over. Sometimes, particularly in depressions when men's whole sense of themselves as responsible heads of families was threatened anyway, women made more than their husbands. The simple division of labor, so clear in the eyes of children, that father went *out,* and mother stayed *in,* disappeared. Men demonstrated their sense of loss of manhood by refusing to give any woman—old, young, pregnant or with a baby in her arms—a seat on a bus.

The worry that American men weren't masculine grew stronger. It persists today in the form of an adolescent's concern about proving his sexual prowess or his ability to perform crudely symbolic acts such as driving a car like a demon or messing about with firearms. Tales from the Korean war of how unprepared young men were to fire guns or to stand up under imprisonment have not improved this picture, but only intensified the game of "chicken" played at all levels of society.

Meanwhile, after World War II, something did happen to men as fathers. The G. I.'s came home to be the best fathers—from the standpoint of their young children—that any civilized society has ever known. In the Australian deserts and the mountains of New Guinea, fathers hold their little babies in their arms and limit their demands on their wives to protect the health of their infant children. But in all the known civilizations of the world, as soon as a society has become complicated with governments and armies, merchants and ships, nobles and serfs, men have no longer cared for small children.

An important man in most such societies was protected from the night cries of his children by many walls between his bed-chamber and the nursery, and an army of women—nurses, pensioners, female relatives—stood between him and even the sight of a diaper. His children were brought to him occasionally, well washed and prettily dressed, to be admired and whisked away again. Such fathers saw very little of their children until they were partly grown, and then more in a disciplinary or didactic relationship than in a companionable and loving one.

But now, for the first time in their history, the United States, North America and parts of Northern Europe and the British Commonwealth are experimenting with a new kind of fatherhood. Now the élite of our societies, the statesmen and scientists, the financiers and entrepreneurs, the judges and the legislators, are helping their servantless wives take care of little children.

This new style in fatherhood crept up on us gradually, with the G. I. Bill, life in trailers, early marriage and the currently fashionable large family. It is a very extreme contrast to anything we have known before, and we don't know yet what the effects are going to be. In the past little boys have learned that child-bearing and child care were for women, while their job was to go out into the world and do things—farm, fight, build, invent, govern. Now for the first time, men are being given a chance to enjoy their children.

There seems to be a real danger that the care of young children will prove both so time-consuming and so fascinating that many men will skimp their careers in order to get more time with their families. In the past, dedicated scientists, artists who starved in garrets and explorers of strange places either postponed having children or left their care to women. We have known for a long time that being a mother of several children was a full-time job, and definitely interfered with a woman's career. Now it looks as if we were turning being a father into a full-time job, too, with all a man's best energies going into the home, and too little left over for work outside.

From the whole sweep of human history, it is possible to trace the growing responsibility of men for their children, and women for the wider world. At the beginning of history—if we may judge by the very simple primitive people living today—women stayed close to home, burdened by their children, while men ranged abroad. The sexes envied each other even then, and men invented ceremonies in which they pretended to bear children, and women borrowed their husbands' head-hunting regalia to pretend they were men.

Then, thousands of years of experimenting with civilization brought us to the kind of world where men had become highly specialized and far removed from their children, while women, although occasionally developing airs to grace a court, or competence in running a plantation or a manor, remained essentially as housebound as their primitive forebears.

Next we experimented with educating women, and permitting them to venture out into a man's world. Now we are experimenting with letting men into woman's world. Both moves involve drastic changes in the relationships between the sexes.

These are upsetting changes, when men feel less like husbands because their wives work outside the home, and women feel less like wives because their husbands do so much work inside the home. They are dangerous changes because we don't know what effects they will have on men's sense of themselves as men, as well as husbands.

In attempting to judge what the consequences of these new styles may be, and especially what kind of fathers this new generation will make, we can examine the traditional ideals for an American father. The ideal American father does not expect his son to follow in his footsteps, to be what he is, but to go on to better things, to get a better education, earn a better salary, have a better career.

True, many fathers have insisted on their sons going to their own colleges, and taking up their occupations, especially when their colleges or their occupations were at the top of the heap. But these are not ideal fathers. The ideal father leaves his son free to choose, cheers him on when he does well, encourages him when his spirits flag, expects him to live his own life—not his father's life.

At the same time, the American father is expected to hold enough of his children's respect so that they will care about having him as an appreciative supporter. The stereotype immigrant father who doesn't know enough about the new culture to recognize his son's success loses his son's allegiance altogether.

The ideal American family is like the American two-party system at its best, in that parents are expected to be strong, yet different, and each is expected to be a responsible part of the whole. So the ideal American father is strong, but does not have to demonstrate his strength by dominating his wife and children, or to live out his own sense of inferiority by pushing his son in the Little Leagues.

The American ideal for strength without domination, encouragement without trying to live through one's children, is a difficult one. It is more difficult when fathers are still supposed to represent the outside world—to know more than mothers about what is going on in the whole field of male achievement, from baseball to international politics, from mending the furnace to explaining a satellite, from running a savings account to explaining the World Bank, from electing the school board to evaluating the U. N. No matter how small a section of the outside world a father commands, it remains his expected role to encourage his son to move out of the home, into the world.

Much of the concern about Father's supposedly diminishing masculinity may not be so much the result of the fluctuations and uncertainties of his new role—as a father—but rather the result of an increased confusion about the difference between being masculine and being a man. Masculinity is that part of a male's behavior which distinguishes him from a female—in his sex relations, in fighting and in sport. Stress on masculinity means stress on *not* being like a woman. But manhood is that part of a male's behavior which makes him a responsible human being, able to control his sexuality, bridle his aggression, protect and provide for his wife and children and make some positive contribution to the world.

If taking care of children is seen as playing a woman's part, being a sucker, being dominated by women, it will be looked at one way. If it is seen as an extension of manhood, as an exercise of strength, imagination and tenderness, it will be looked at the other way.

Interracial Marriage
Is a Sometime Thing
by William Barry Furlong

CHICAGO

THE U.S. SUPREME COURT recently declared invalid the anti-miscegenation laws in Virginia. Stanley Kramer's latest movie, "Guess Who's Coming to Dinner," and Gore Vidal's recent play, "Weekend," deal with interracial couples. The daughter of Dean Rusk, the Secretary of State, has married a Negro, and the daughter of Senator Edward W. Brooke, a Negro whose wife is white, plans to marry a white man.

Clearly interracial marriage is in a kind of vogue, though it is hardly the racial amalgamation that Arnold Toynbee once saw as one of the two routes to world peace (the other, which holds out about the same hope, was world government). More interracial marriages are recorded today than in the past—according to census figures, 2.5 times as many as in the nineteen-thirties. But the figures may be misleading; the increase may be the result of the population growth, of a more widespread willingness to acknowledge an interracial marriage—a willingness that may diminish with the rise of black separatism—or of more thorough record-keeping by the Census Bureau. The 1960 census turned

From the *New York Times Magazine,* June 9, 1968, copyright © 1968 by The New York Times Company up 51,409 Negro-white couples. That was 0.12 per cent of all the married couples in the country. Roughly the same percentage was found in a survey by the Department of Health, Education and Welfare on marriages performed in 32 states in 1963. However, the experts agree that, because of flaws in the reporting technique or less than representative samples, both studies may have underestimated the number of interracial unions.

There is a singularity to each of those marriages, though some are more singular than others. No one couple reflects all the woes and worries of marriage across racial lines, but there are some representative reactions and problems. Here are the thoughts of a few of the people who have been through it:

A white social worker married to a pretty Negro girl: "I think at first there's a feeling of pride for the white person—that you've brought somebody into the world, that you've given her a chance that she wouldn't have had otherwise." Her rejoinder: "Dear, don't you think at first you were trying too hard to impress Negroes with how liberal you were?"

A blonde woman married to a half-Negro truck driver: "At times my mother has said, 'Don't stop in this weekend. So-and-so is coming to visit, and what they don't know won't hurt them.' And when our daughter was born and turned out to be quite light, she said, 'Better not have any more. Don't press your luck.'"

The half-Negro truck driver, whose mother was Italian and whose father was black: "I treated my father like a dog—I resented him so much because he was black. It took me a long time to admit it, but I'm as prejudiced as the next man. Now I'm passing as white; no one at work knows I'm Negro. Why shouldn't I, if that's how life is better for me? I had to spend a lot of time with a psychiatrist before I realized what a great guy my father was. He came from the South with no education, moved into an Italian neighborhood and proved himself, taught himself math and English, moved up to foreman. Now when I go back to the old neighborhood, everybody tells me what a great guy he was. I know that, too, now. But he's dead now, and he'll never know how I love him."

A Negro postal worker just over 40 and a white woman a few years younger might represent the fairly typical interracial couple.

They have been married for 20 years—and isolated for about as long. In the most middling of middle-class circumstances, they live on the second floor of a two-flat house in Hyde Park-Kenwood, an integrated neighborhood near the University of Chicago. It was a step up for him; he grew up in one of those tormented slums in which the sun always seems strained through a brassy haze and the houses are filled with the sweet smell of rotting wood. "I can still remember the stairways," he says. "The smell, the garbage, the way the wood was worn by all those feet all those years." You could almost sense his toes wriggling in his shoes, still feeling the scalloped stairways bleached at the edge by wear. For his wife, the move to Hyde Park-Kenwood was lateral. She came from a middle-class neighborhood on the South Side, an area of six-flats and an occasional bungalow behind a patch of creeping bent where the kids were forbidden to play for fear of "bruising" the grass.

Their early years were spent in worlds apart: she knew no Negroes and he no whites. He won a parochial fame in the ghetto as a high-school athlete and that brought him a football scholarship to college. Then he fell sick and couldn't play, so the college canceled his scholarship. He returned to Chicago just after World War II and went to work in the "car barns," the maintenance sheds for the transit system, at night. On his lunch break each night, he went to a soda fountain where she happened to work and ordered three milk shakes. "Nothing else," she remembers, "just three milk shakes. He always had a book to read. Paperback. He'd just sit there and drink his milk shakes and read his book and never raise his eyes." She thought he didn't notice her.

The sickness had left him underweight, he says, and he thought the milk shakes were a good remedy. He also thought he should be quiet and keep his eyes down; this was white man's territory. But he did notice her: "She was a well-girdled girl. I remember wondering why a girl like that—with the way she looked and the way she moved—why she wore a girdle." In those days and in that neighborhood a teen-age girl wore a girdle not to shape her figure so much as to help preserve her chastity. It was a warning to the bolder young men that they would have a struggle on their hands.

In those days, too, the great migration of poor Negroes from the South was beginning to engulf Chicago. Housing patterns began to shift, and soon the neighborhood around the soda fountain was showing the first faint signs of "changing." "My father wanted me to quit the job," the housewife remembers, "but you know how kids are. The money looked good and I was having fun." The ex-football player changed with the neighborhood: he lifted his eyes a little and began a careful give-and-take with the girl behind the counter. One night she was quite nervous, and he noticed a gang of boys from *his* neighborhood looking at her in a way that he didn't like. "They were smartin' off," he says, "but I could see what was on their minds." He ordered more milk shakes and lingered over them until closing time. Then he stood under a streetlamp and read his book until she came out.

It was half a block to the street-car stop and she would have to wait at least 15 minutes, so he made an excuse to say hello and suggested that they walk to the car stop together. It was very difficult for him, he remembers; he is not an outgoing man. But the gang was waiting down the street in a car and he felt he should protect the girl. The gang made no move when the couple passed. At the street-car stop he made a sudden decision and got on behind her. But then he didn't know whether to pay her fare—does a black boy do that with a white girl?—or to sit beside her. He did neither. When she was getting off she paused —just slowed down, really—beside his seat and said, "Thank you."

Though he lost his job at the car barns because he had not returned to work that night, every night for a week he waited at the soda fountain until closing time because the gang was still hanging around. If the girl left with friends he disappeared into the shadows. If she left alone he fell into step beside her. Soon it became a habit, something he looked forward to; and soon she made it a point to leave alone. The progression thereafter was natural: he paid her fare on the street-car, he sat beside her, and soon he got off and walked her home.

They found, as young people do, that they had a lot in common, and they imagined that the similarities outnumbered the differences. They also found that they were being thrown together by outside pressures. "Somebody saw him walking home with me one night—a Negro with a white girl—and in those days you didn't do that, not in our neighborhood." So the talk began going around, and the more it went around the more defiant she felt. Talk was going around in his neighborhood, too. "Your people get to thinkin' you're a little uppity," he says. The gossip forced them together.

So they got married. Nothing big; in fact, nothing at all—a City Hall wedding. Her family—like the average white one in such circumstances—didn't acknowledge the marriage. They feel she's living in sin because she didn't get married in church; they also feel that she's living in sin with a *nigger*. That disgraced the whole family. "I just dropped off the edge of the earth as far as they were concerned," she says.

Her brothers and sisters married and moved to a newer Chicago neighborhood or to the suburbs. Her mother is living with one of her sisters in the suburbs. "I've never gone out to see her; she's not interested. She's got plenty of other grandchildren, none of them niggers." She read of her father's death in the newspaper. "I went to the church and sat in the back. I thought I could get in and out without anybody seeing me. You know, go a little late, leave a little early."

At first, she and her husband made a decision typical of inter-racial couples: to have no children. "We thought it would be too hard on them," she says. "And we had each other—sort of the two of us against the world." They also faced typical problems of the Negro-white couple. All of their relatives and friends had suddenly disappeared, and it was difficult to find new friends, black or white. They were reluctant to face the humiliation of travel together, even in the North. Both met people at work, but—again, typically—they hid from their co-workers the inter-racial character of their marriage. "The kind of relationships you have at work," she says, "if there's a party and you're a young girl you don't want to show up with a husband who's a black man."

Their solution was night school. "We both had this thing about education, that it would help us. Well, it's not us that has to be educated. It's the rest of the world." They enrolled at a junior college and happily mapped out their whole future together, right through graduate school. "We had some pretty grand plans," she says.

When the second semester began, however, they registered individually, not as man and wife. "It was too hard, everybody staring at us because we sat next to each other and talked as if we *knew* each other." For almost three years, they pretended in class to be strangers. "Then we asked what was happening to us. We were spending half our nights in a place where we felt uncomfortable just saying hello to each other." They dropped out with a handful of credits and not much in the way of pleasant associations.

It took time, but they gradually adjusted to their twilight world. Like most interracial couples, they suffered the inequities visited upon Negroes in search of adequate housing—higher rents and the constant threat of rejection by real-estate salesmen who want to sell or rent only to whites. But they found an apartment in an integrated neighborhood. "It's not as good as Lake Meadows"—a newer high-rise development in which many inter-racial couples live—"but it suits us," he says.

He did well in his job, eventually becoming a supervisor. Some of his progress he probably owes to his Government employment. Dr. Robert E. T. Roberts, a Chicago sociologist who has devoted almost 30 years to the study of interracial marriages, says that in one 36-member group he questioned only eight were employed in private enterprise. Four worked for the Government, 12 were self-employed and 12 were unemployed or retired. Dr. Roberts points out that marriage to a Negro may mean the end of advancement for a white man in the business world, and a girl who is the product of a mixed marriage adds: "A young man with talent and ambition is going to think twice—maybe five or six times—before he marries a Negro girl because he knows that's the end of his high ambitions." In the view of Dr. Roberts, the effect of interracial marriage on business advancement is one of the reasons that the male partner in such a union has historically tended to be the Negro.

The postal worker and his wife built a little nest egg and decided that children might help fill the vague, indefinable gap in their lives. They have two now, one colored, one virtually white.

"I suppose it might be hard in some neighborhoods, being a white woman with a colored baby," she says. "You might not want to take him out walking or go to the park or even go shopping with him, there'd be so many tongues wagging." But it's not so bad in their neighborhood. "You go to the Co-op"— the local supermarket—"and you see a lot of mixtures there. You begin to realize just how many mixed marriages there are, Saturday mornings at the Co-op."

They are reluctant to think too deeply about the future of the children. "It'll be all right for the boy," says the father. "He can choose the black world, whatever that's going to be 10 or 15 years from now. But the girl, she'll be torn." She's light enough to go into the white world, but "she'll *know* she's been brought up a Negro. That makes a difference—it's like a secret you dread having." His somber looks grow heavier. "She's a good little girl; I don't think she'll want to turn her back on her daddy and what he is. But what if she falls in love with a white boy and they want to get married and she doesn't tell him— she'll always be worried about what color children she'll have."

He is not quite defeated, but neither does he have the soaring ambitions of youth. He still loves to read and takes refuge in his books. One wall in the front room of their apartment is lined with books. "I don't have a really *fine* mind," he says with just a touch of firmness in his husky voice. "But I know it's not a mind to be ashamed of."

His wife is, perhaps, more obviously alienated; it is usually the white partner who suffers more. She has lost her family, her friends, the social position and middle-class home in which she grew up—even her religion, though she still goes to church regularly. There is no place she belongs: the white community has banished her to the ghetto, and the ghetto refuses to accept her. "There are two classes of people who can't stand mixed marriages," says the white wife of another Negro. "They are colored women and white men." Negro women resent the loss of one of their men and the implication that white women are superior to them; the white men resent the supposed degradation of white womanhood. Even in her own neighborhood, an integrated area, the postal worker's wife feels left out. The neighborhood is academically oriented, and she says that she never really went to college—"just junior college at night, *nothing.*"

She is back in school at night, not for college credit but for the "culture courses"—art appreciation, music appreciation, drama, literature. This is her separate world: "Nobody knows about me down there. They accept you for what you are." Her husband has noticed a change in her. "She's spruced up a little more, she has something to look forward to every week."

He does not give voice to the fear that she finds people "down there" more attractive than he is. He knows that she has her problems, but he talks about them in general terms: "I imagine there are a lot of housewives out in the suburbs who are trying to find their way, too." He realizes that he's growing inward as she struggles to move outward. But instead of trying to hold things together, he has prepared for the ultimate separation; although he is only in his 40's, he talks of death. When their first child was born, he insured his own life heavily—he knows that if he dies, his wife will not easily find another husband, particularly a white husband. "Not with a black boy for a son, she won't." And he can't quite see her marrying another Negro, as many such white widows do, for fear that it would only add to her problems. He regards her with an enormous fondness and he appreciates how much he's complicated her life. "If I go first," he says, "maybe she'll be able to go back to her church." He pauses. "And maybe even her family."

Some interracial couples insist that they have not experienced the quiet, smoldering desperation that has been the lot of the postal worker and his wife. Edwin C. (Bill) Berry, for instance, contends that the partners in an interracial marriage suffer no indignities except those heaped upon Negroes in general. Berry is a slim, spare man with gray hair, penetrating eyes and an air of muted humor. He has worked for the Urban League in various cities for 31 years, for the last 10 as executive director in Chicago. "I didn't marry a white woman," he says, "I married my wife. Races don't get married; only people do. I didn't marry the white race. I married Betsy Berry and all the problems that come with this particular woman."

Despite his contention that their marriage of 10 years is normal, the Berrys were opposed by in-laws on both sides, and the wedding took place in Milwaukee, not Chicago. When a Chicago newspaper discovered their plans, Berry arranged to have the paper omit any mention of the interracial aspect of their marriage. Instead, the paper printed a picture of Betsy that made the point more subtly.

The Berrys are not uneasy about "the stare," the look that annoys most interracial couples when they appear in public. "If somebody stares at us, I wave and say hello. I don't know if they know me or not." They did not travel together in the South until recently, but they have now visited Atlanta and Miami, and they are not sure that a venture into Mississippi would be altogether intolerable. "We didn't see any signs of hostility that we might not have seen in New York City," he says.

Berry is equally sanguine about the place of the child of an interracial marriage. He and Betsy have no children of their own, but they have raised his son by an earlier marriage. Berry deplores the notion that interracial marriage is necessarily bad for the child. "What's so bad?" he asks. "Look, my boy was a little brown boy. Now there are several ways he can get to be a little brown boy. One way is for brown and brown to marry. Another way is for black and white to marry. So the boy turns out brown. Society doesn't know how he got that way." But certain segments of society—the child's neighborhood, his church and his school—invariably do know how he got that way and direct at him an attention that is not given others.

Berry concedes that he knows of an interracial marriage in which the husband is terribly tormented. "But all his life he wanted to punish himself," Berry says, "and he thought that by marrying a Negro he would *really* be punished." Some psychiatrists agree that an interracial marriage may be motivated by the desire for punishment. One of them calls such a union "the exquisite torment," and Dr. Thomas L. Brayboy, a New York psychiatrist who has treated many partners in interracial marriages, suggests that the ultimate motive is often a feeling of guilt over the white man's treatment of the Negro.

A spirit of rebellion is also common among the partners in

interracial marriages, Dr. Brayboy says. "They make use of the unique opportunity that socially opposed interracial sex offers for acting out their hostility toward parents or society. It was their desire for revenge, not love, that brought them together." Dr. Roberts, who concedes drily that "romantic love occurs occasionally in any society," adds that the Establishment's reaction to interracial courtship and marriage may add a certain urgency to the relationship: "To lose all for love, to voluntarily suffer disgrace and humiliation for a loved one, is very much in keeping with the romantic ideal."

The experts also say that the myth that Negroes offer more satisfaction in sexual relations may encourage some interracial marriages. "Sex—whether in mind or in fact—is certainly a conspicuous factor," says one psychiatrist, "but it works both ways." The belief in greater sexual prowess may impel some whites to marry Negroes, he explains, but it also produces in some white men a fear of inadequacy that is "one of the basic drives underlying racial antagonism in our society." Love, sex, rebellion or the desire for punishment can, of course, be a motive for any kind of marriage. "The primary difference in interracial situations," Dr. Brayboy says, "is that the broader social problem accentuates the neurotic potential."

One might consider a marriage that is both interracial and interreligious to be loaded with neurotic potential. Diane and Steve Cohen, an uncommonly intelligent young couple, illustrate some of the problems and some of the solutions in this kind of union. Diane is the daughter of Earl Dickerson, one of the richest Negroes in America. She and Steve met while studying for their master's degrees at the University of Chicago. Diane had been married—to a Negro—and had a son, Steven, now 10 years old. Steve, her present husband, is an Orthodox Jew. "It wasn't that Diane was a Negro that upset my family," he says. "They would have been upset by my marrying anybody who wasn't Jewish." Diane became a convert to Judaism and she and Steve are raising their son, Joshua, as a Jew. Diane's first son is being raised as a Christian.

One of their first problems after their marriage five and a

half years ago was the attitude of Steve's father who had many
stereotypes about Negroes. "He'd ask us to dinner and have
watermelon *just* for me," says Diane with more wonder than
rancor. "Or he'd ask—seriously—if I ate anything besides fried
chicken."

"He liked to believe—as I suppose most fathers would in
the same circumstances—that, as the white relative in the union,
he was bringing a little bit the better to the situation," says Steve.
"Then, bit by bit, he discovered that Diane's father has many
of the things that most people covet in life—great wealth and
high status in the community. Eventually, I noticed that he was
bragging just a little bit that his son was married to the daughter
of Earl Dickerson."

Joshua, it turned out, has his own insight into color. One day
when he was 3 years old, an insurance man visiting the family
asked Joshua what color he was. Joshua didn't hesitate. "Beige,"
he said. And so the world looks to Joshua Cohen. His mother is
beige and a Negro; his father is beige and a white man. There
are no simple blacks and whites to Joshua.

The Cohen family is not only black and white but also Christian
and Jewish. Young Steve Cohen, the non-Jew in the family, might
be expected to have some difficulty in identifying. One day while
he was out playing touch football in the neighborhood, one of
the other youngsters dropped a forward pass. The leader of his
team became enraged and shouted the worst names he knew:
"You dirty Jew! You filthy kike!"

One of the kids happened to remember Steve Cohen. "Say,"
he said, "you're not *Jewish,* are you?"

"At that moment," says the elder Steve Cohen, "he was. He
had complete identification with his family."

The history of opposition to interracial unions stretches back
to Biblical times. In Numbers XII, 1, there is a suggestion of
the ferment raised against Moses for his interracial marriage:
"And Miriam and Aaron spake against Moses because of the
Ethiopian woman whom he had married." In "Othello," Iago
foreshadows the antagonism of Desdemona's family to her marriage to the Moor, described as "thick-lips," when he warns her
father:

> *Even now, now, very now,*
>   *an old black ram*
> *Is tupping your white ewe.*
>   *Arise, arise!*
> *Awake the snorting*
>   *citizens with the bell,*
> *Or else the devil will make*
>   *a grandsire of you.*

Thus, while marriage between the races and social opposition to it are not new, there have been changes. Dr. Roberts, who in his investigations has interviewed more than 500 interracial couples, some of whom were married as early as 1882, sees a social evolution.

In earlier times, encounters between the races were most likely to take place at work, he says, whereas today they are likely to occur in schools or social movements. Just before and after the turn of the century these encounters tended to bring together Negro men and white immigrant girls. They were thrown together in menial jobs in the mansions of the rich or in businesses that demanded unskilled help. Dr. Roberts has uncovered "at least a dozen" interracial marriages that developed in a hotel in Milwaukee where Negro men worked as porters and waiters and white immigrant girls worked as pantrygirls and chambermaids. The girls frequently came from cultures in northern Europe in which there was no conspicuous prejudice against the Negro, and they were so new to this country that they didn't understand how deep was the antagonism between the races in the United States. Immigration was restricted in the nineteen-twenties, reducing the number of foreign girls who might marry Negro men. After World War I there was a tendency for white girls to take the jobs once held by Negro men—waiting on tables in restaurants, for example—and for Negro girls to take the jobs once held by white immigrant girls. Thus the opportunity for encounters between the Negro male and white immigrant female was reduced.

During World War II, American Negroes met foreign white girls who lacked the strong prejudices of their counterparts in the United States. When the soldiers came home, society began to change: leisure time was increased and television arrived, bringing with it a new prominence for entertainers, many of whom—Sammy Davis Jr., Harry Belafonte, Lena Horne, Pearl Bailey and Eartha Kitt, among them—married across racial lines. There were other changes as well.

"In the nineteen-twenties and before," Dr. Roberts says, "you rarely—I might almost say you never—saw a marriage between a Negro and a Jew." This was because endogamy—the custom or requirement of marrying only within one's tribe, caste or social system—is strongest among Jews. After World War II, there was a lessening of endogamy among Jews and there were more opportunities for social encounters between Negroes and Jews or other potential "high-status" whites as more Negroes entered college. The number of Jewish-Negro marriages increased.

Dr. Roberts says that an influx of Negroes into colleges in the postwar period created interracial unions entirely different from those of the late Victorian era. He believes that the percentage of interracial marriages involving partners who have had some college education has increased 10 or 15 times over the level of the nineteen-twenties. In a study of 22 interracial couples in New York, the median schooling was 16.5 years—somewhat above the average for married people in general.

"Before World War I," says Dr. Roberts, "children of interracial marriage were likely to know as many white people as Negroes. Then in the nineteen-thirties I found they were likely to know Negroes only—they seemed to know Negroes 99 per cent of the time. Now it's changing back—the kids are likely to know whites about as often as Negroes."

Before World War I, interracial couples frequently lived in predominantly white neighborhoods, if only because the vast Negro ghettos had not been formed. In 1910, for instance, only two per cent of the population of Chicago was Negro and some 24 per cent of the Negro population of the city lived in neighborhoods that were 95 per cent white. But the ghettos began forming swiftly after World War I, and by 1929 interracial couples were being forced more and more deeply into the ghettos.

In recent years, interracial couples have been moving out of the ghettos into integrated neighborhoods—sometimes even into the suburbs. Not long ago, Dr. Roberts made a search of two large ghetto areas in Chicago and found among almost a quarter-million people only 15 interracial marriages. "In Hyde Park-Kenwood, you might find five or ten marriages in a single block," he says.

The interracial marriage has tended to involve a Negro man much more often than a white man. Of the first 188 couples Dr. Roberts interviewed, 147, or 78 per cent, involved Negro husbands. There were, as we have seen, economic reasons (the penalties fell more heavily on the white man) and social reasons (encounters were more likely between Negro men and white women). But as the social situation changed, so did the economic structure.

The white husband in an interracial marriage today enjoys a choice of occupations not available in the past. It is unlikely that any such man will become head of A.T.&T. or I.B.M., but he might rise high in government or academic life; he might enter the professions or find a rewarding niche in those fast-expanding areas in which his marital status would not be a matter of vast concern—in the entertainment industry, for instance, or in editorial work.

Dr. Roberts contends that the percentage of white men entering interracial marriages is increasing, and the figures of the Census Bureau support him. The bureau's 1950 figures indicate that 44 per cent of the husbands in interracial marriages were white; its 1960 figures indicate that slightly more than half the husbands were white.

Yet another change that affects the interracial couple is the rise of the black-separatist movement. The Black Power advocates are beginning to bring some pressure on the many "public-status" Negroes who are married to white women—such men as Bill Berry, James Farmer, once national director of CORE, and Senator Brooke of Massachusetts—in an effort to cut them off from the civil rights movement.

In a San Francisco speech in April, Cassius Clay, after explaining that he did not wish to offend the integrated couples in his audience, said: "We believe mixed marriages should be prohibited."

None of the major speakers at the innumerable Black Power rallies in Harlem these days ever appear with their white wives, and the subject of interracial marriage is rarely mentioned at the meetings. There seems to be a tacit agreement among black separatists that nothing will be said about those who married whites before the movement became popular. Nonetheless, some of the militants—notably LeRoi Jones, the playwright—have divorced their white wives and married Negroes, and the leaders seem to realize that they would jeopardize their positions by dating or marrying white women.

It has become popular in some parts of the black community to observe that the modern Negro who is attracted to white girls is forced to "sneak around like the old master snuck around" in the South when he hoped to dally in the slave quarters. The number of visible Negro-white relationships in Harlem has diminished, and the bonds between black men and black women have grown stronger. It used to be said that Negro mothers told their daughters that black men would do nothing for them, and black girls now say they were forced to go to white men because Negro men couldn't or wouldn't protect them. As the black woman turns back to the black man, she is putting great pressure on him to shun the white woman. Black Power militants are even taking the process one step further: they are ignoring average Negro girls in favor of those who have "gone natural"—who wear their hair African-style and prefer African print dresses and jewelry. H. Rap Brown's wife "went natural" about a month after she began dating him, and others have followed.

In a less formal way, the Black Power adherents are offering a challenge to the offspring of interracial marriages. "It comes up all the time in conversation," says the attractive young daughter of a white mother and a Negro father. She is brown-skinned but dates young men of both races. "It would be a shame to cut out one entire race," she says with a smile. "Think of all the fun I'd miss."

But her militant friends deplore her lack of commitment. "Oh, so you're going 'unblack,' too," said one such friend not long ago. "No," she replied. "But if I do what you want or what the other side wants, I'm going to have to deny the existence of my mother or my father. I'm not going to do that, for you or anybody else." Her attitude, she says, "is to pick issues. I won't pick sides."

Purchasing a House: A Matriarchal Move?

by Judy Klemesrud

THE MOTHER who wants to move her family from a city apartment to a house in the country may well be thinking of green grass, fresh air and the good of the children.

But the move from an apartment to a house also indicates a switch from male to female domination of the family. This is one conclusion of a nationwide psychological study released today. The study also says:

Males resist moving and romanticize their present environments.

A woman's favorite rooms in a house are the master bedroom-bathroom combination, while men prefer the foyer and the kitchen.

A vacation house is strictly a male province, and women often regard it as "nothing but trouble."

The study, based on a survey of 2,514 families, is called "The Motivations Toward Homes and Housing." It was made by Raymond Loewy-William Snaith, Inc., industrial designers, for the Project Home Committee, the working name of a group of 28 manufacturers serving the housing industry.

From the *New York Times,* September 5, 1967, copyright © 1967 by The New York Times Company

The findings are contained in a 323-page report that cost $200,000 and took three years to compile. It is intended to help the manufacturers develop effective advertising campaigns.

"The biggest surprise to me was the lack of agreement between husbands and wives these days," William Snaith, president of the company that did the study, said recently in an interview in his office at 425 Park Avenue. "About the only time they really agree is when they're newlyweds."

The husband starts getting the short shrift as soon as the first child arrives, he added. "Immediately the wife becomes child centered, and is no longer dominated by that big beautiful male creature who meant so much."

Mr. Snaith said the female was the prime motivating force in the family's decision to buy a house. She originates the notion for home ownership, he said, presumably because she thinks it would be a more convenient place to raise children and perform her duties as a homemaker.

Males generally resist moving, especially if they are apartment dwellers, he said. "A man likes being close to work, and he relishes the privacy and anonymity this kind of living gives him."

When a male does give in and buys a house, it is usually for the sake of his wife and children, the report says. This is one of the first steps in the switch from male to female domination of the home.

Mr. Snaith, who is an architect, artist, author, designer, decorator and yachtsman, said another of the study's surprises was that women prefer the master bedroom to the kitchen.

"It [the bedroom] is a symbol of marriage security, the room where she retreats when she wants to be alone. It is the room where she sees herself as a pampered, desirable female."

The husband is partial to the foyer, he said, because it is the place where he greets his guests, and the place where they get their first impressions of him as a host and bon vivant.

The husband is also fond of the kitchen, because he loves to cook on occasion, Mr. Snaith said. "But he won't cook alone—he has to have people watching him, with his fancy tools and big white hat."

The woman, on the other hand, he said, tends to think of the kitchen as a sort of Siberia, where she has been exiled while her family is sitting in the living room enjoying themselves.

According to the study, the biggest divergence between husband and wife occurs in the 35-to-54 age group, when their children are in school and their income now justifies the purchase of a better home.

"About this time the wife begins to lose the sex appeal she once had, and the husband—especially if he is in the higher-income groups—begins to stray," Mr. Snaith said.

Sometimes a house can help hold a marriage together, he said, "because men become attached to things—like lawns, gardens, trees and bushes that they've worked on for years."

The vacation house, Mr. Snaith said, is one place where the male is definitely dominant, largely because he thinks of himself as a rugged, outdoor he-man when he is staying there.

Mr. Snaith, who is 59 years old, resides with his wife, Elizabeth, in a house in Weston, Conn. He insisted that it was male-dominated.

The Absent Father Haunts the Negro Family

by C. Eric Lincoln

UNDER PRESSURE of law, public opinion and Negro militancy, progress in civil rights has reached the point where many Americans assume that the practical end of discrimination is only a matter of time. But even the end of formal discrimination falls short of the distant goal: full integration of the Negro into American life. Nor can true integration be achieved until the nation— and the Negro—solves a crucial and immediate problem: how to "Americanize" the fragile, fractured Negro family.

The Negro in America was never a "black Anglo-Saxon," though sometimes he tried to be. He was never simply "another ethnic group" to be assimilated into the mainstream. His family structure is unique in American society.

The U.S. family is primarily patriarchal. The husband and father is the chief breadwinner, carrying the responsibility for his wife and children. Even in families where husband and wife supposedly share equally in making decisions, our society regards the male as "more equal." The law defines this relationship; custom

From the *New York Times Magazine,* November 28, 1965, copyright © 1965 by The New York Times Company.

supports and rewards it. But the majority of Negro families do not follow the U.S. custom and are appropriately penalized. Because women have assumed primary responsibility as head of the family, the matriarchal Negro household is at a distinct disadvantage in competing for its rightful share of benefits offered by American society.

About 25 per cent of Negro families are headed by women who have no husbands. These are families where the male is absent because of divorce, separation or desertion, and do not include families with illegitimate children which have never included a male parent.

The easy explanation of the shattered Negro family puts the blame on the Negro male, caricatured as shiftless and lazy. A more socially acceptable reason attributes the matriarchal family structure to superaggressive females. In fact, the blame rests on the horrors of a slave society which stripped the Negro male of his masculinity and condemned him to a eunuch-like existence in a culture which venerates masculine primacy.

There are no discontinuities in history. Negroes today (like any other people) are largely the product of yesterday. And American slavery, the "yesterday" of the American Negro, ended only 100 years ago. For 250 years before emancipation, slavery ordered the lives, the thinking and the behavior of white people in one way, and of Negroes in quite another.

American slavery was a different institution from contemporary slavery in South America, Portugal, Africa, or from ancient slavery in Greece and Rome. It developed its own institutionalized values uniquely designed to promote its own ends. Its peculiar impingement upon the Negro in America inescapably conditioned his values, his behavior and his future.

When Negroes were slaves, neither the law nor the slave owners recognized marriage between slaves. Males of prime physical condition were mated with females, like so many cattle. Children were left with the mother, giving the Negro mother an early, exclusive interest in the family and forcing upon her full responsibility for its care. In those instances where a male and female were permitted to live together longer than necessary for procreation, the Negro father (he could hardly be called a husband) had absolutely no control over his family or its fortunes. Children were seized and sold. Often the father himself was sold away from his family, never to see them again.

The psychology of castration was viciously applied in other ways, too. No Negro man was given a title of respect, a practice which continues in much of the rural South today. A Negro man was simply "Sam," "Jim," or frequently "boy," no matter what his age. He was never "Mister." If he was "living with a woman" —the nearest thing to marriage—he was known as "Hattie's Sam" or "Mandy's Jim," again denying him a position as head of the family. And if the white man wanted Hattie or Mandy for himself, the Negro male had to step aside; interference as a "husband" meant severe punishment and, not infrequently, death.

When the Negro was freed from bondage all the laws Congress could muster were not effective in wholly transferring him from the category of slave to the category of citizen.

The slaves were freed without any provision for their economic or social well-being. They were almost totally uneducated, for to have educated a slave was a criminal offense. They had no money and no homes. And they were concentrated in a politically and economically distressed society hostile to their presence as freedmen. Even those who made their way to the North quickly found themselves unwelcome, for as indigents with low skills they threatened to glut the unskilled labor market and become a burden on the tax-paying citizenry.

Because of her peculiar relationship to the white woman as a servant, and because she was frequently the white man's mistress, the Negro woman occasionally flouted the rules of segregation. Her impunity was by no means absolute, but because she often reigned supreme in the white man's kitchen and nursery she could, in times of crisis, "talk to the man" and get concessions that made life a little more bearable for herself and her children.

The practice of sending the Negro woman to do business with the white man became quickly established in the Negro-white pattern of relations. In the ruptured economy of the postwar South, Negro women were frequently paid more than their menfolk and they could ordinarily find jobs in domestic service while their men walked the streets looking for work.

"Freedom" did not improve the image of the Negro male or give him a sense of security as head of the family. He remained a semi-slave, and his slavery was rooted in the centuries he had spent in America.

If you want to understand his hatreds, his resentments, his castration as a husband and father, look back 100 years. And if you ask why in 100 years he has not overcome the past, it is because the past has never died: every day, every hour of that 100 years of semi-freedom has had to be rewon day by day from the prejudice which still promotes, openly or covertly, the old ways of slavery. The Negro did not earn rewards for being manly, courageous or assertive, but for being accommodating—for fulfilling the stereotype of what he has been forced to be.

We may note, in the interest of keeping perspective, that some stable Negro families with male heads existed before and after slavery. Before the Civil War, some free Negroes in the South and the North maintained family structures and customs as closely analogous to those in the prevailing white culture as circumstances would permit. A few upper-class Negro families, mostly along the Atlantic Coast, have an unbroken tradition of more than 100 years of social stability and cultural progress. And in the Deep South a handful of Negro families that date to slavery, or the first decades after emancipation, testify to the Negro's determined attempt to overcome the scars of thralldom.

The symptoms of the Negro family's enduring sickness are everywhere evident today.

The Negro crime rate is higher by far than the national average. The rate of illegitimacy is higher—regardless of the inconsistency of reporting procedures—and may be as high as 25 per cent. Negro drug addiction, especially among juveniles, is much higher than among whites—dramatic evidence of the attempt to escape the rigors of living in a society which for them bears little promise of a better future. The percentage of Negro high-school dropouts, again far above the national average, reflects the same sense of Negro hopelessness.

This is social sickness of epidemic proportions, and it spreads with the steady deterioration of the Negro family.

As the basic unit of socialization for the young, the family needs the presence of both parents if children are to learn the values and expectations of society. But socialization is a continuing experience which affects not only children, but parents as well. A "family man" is much less likely to lapse into criminal activity than one without ties and responsibilities.

The absent father has not been, until recently, a particularly disturbing factor among Negroes themselves (except for educated Negroes who were particularly sensitive to the white man's blanket charge of racial immorality). Any male in the average Negro family might function as a father-figure: uncles, older brothers, grandfathers, even cousins. Similarly a grandmother or aunt was frequently "mama" to a brood of children not biologically her own.

Television has been one factor in sensitizing the Negro child to the fact that his family is different. Another increasingly important factor is the integrated school. In their association with white children from complete families, Negro kids learn early that something is different about their households. This awareness is sharpened even further by white teachers who have Negro pupils for the first time. As a Negro teacher in a newly integrated school explained it: "My white colleagues get *so* frustrated when they ask little brown Johnny, 'What does your father do?' and Johnny says he doesn't know. Then they ask, 'Well, Johnny, what does your father look like? Is he big and tall?' and Johnny says he doesn't know. And finally they say, 'Well, all right, Johnny, what is your father's name?' And Johnny says he doesn't know."

The divorce rate among Negro families is 5.1 per cent, compared to 3.8 per cent among whites. But divorces are expensive, and the rate of desertion—the poor man's divorce—is even higher. In many cases, the psychological strain of being a member of a family he cannot support because of unemployment or lack of skills is too much for the Negro husband, and he simply disappears. More often he "deserts" so that his family may become eligible for relief payments, since the family is often better off on relief than depending on the uncertainties of a job. In any event, only a minority of Negro children will complete high school in a two-parent home.

Among middle-class Negroes the battered male ego is frequently a factor in divorce or separation. The Negro professional is in actual or vicarious contact with the American mainstream. He knows his white counterpart is the chief breadwinner and head of the family in *his* home, and the Negro is acutely sensitive to the possibility of his own failings in these respects.

As tangible goods accumulate, and increasingly important decisions are made, most Negro men become restive and uncomfortable if they are married to women who outearn them, and who assume the prerogatives of family leadership as a corollary to their earning power. In Atlanta, for example, I asked a young Negro woman, a teacher, "Who is head of the family at your house?" She thought for a moment, then answered: "Well, Jack is now, but when I get my raise, I'll be head, because I'll be making $27 more than he will."

The problem is considerably more formidable than such naiveté, I assure you. The Negro female has had the responsibility of the Negro family for so many generations that she accepts it, or assumes it, as second nature. Many older women have forgotten why the responsibility devolved upon the Negro woman in the first place, or why it later became institutionalized. And young Negro women do not think it is absurd to reduce the relationship to a matter of money, since many of them probably grew up in families where the only income was earned by their mothers; their fathers may not have been part of their lives at all.

Even in middle-class Negro families where the husband earns more than his wife, the real cement holding the marriage may be status and "appearances" rather than a more fundamental attachment. The Negro wife who grew up in a matriarchal home finds it difficult to assent to male leadership in the family; the Negro husband with a similar family history may be overanxiously insistent on male prerogatives in order to align his family in what he conceives to be the American tradition.

I know a prominent professor in Atlanta who has taught there for 15 years while his wife works as a teacher in her hometown several hundred miles away. They see each other at Christmas and for a brief period at the end of his summer term. This respectable arrangement obviates, or at least postpones, the problem of who will be head of the family—at the price of maintaining a one-parent household.

The task of giving the Negro husband and father a status in keeping with the larger society requires a basic change in established patterns of Negro education, training and employment.

More Negro women go to college than men, just the reverse of the white educational pattern. Six per cent of all female professionals are Negroes, while just a shadow over 1 per cent of all male professionals are Negroes. Negro females do better in school too, probably reflecting the low incentive of the Negro male who frequently feels that even if he graduates, he still won't be getting anywhere.

The long tradition of educating the girls in the Negro family is rooted in the system of segregated employment which limited sharply the Negro male's prospects of finding a job commensurate with college training. In the typical Negro family the boys leave school and go to work early, frequently pooling their earnings for the education of their sisters. The process inevitably produces a pronounced imbalance in the ratio of educated women to educated men, reinforcing the disproportionate power and prestige of the Negro woman in the family.

Having to "marry down," if she marries at all, is a common experience of the Negro woman and one which perpetuates the matriarchal pattern while fostering dissatisfaction, desertion and divorce. For that reason, certain Negro colleges are famous as hunting grounds for eligible men, and the tuition of many an indigent medical school student has been paid by the doting parents of aspiring daughters.

The ratio of Negro college men to women is changing slowly as employment opportunities for Negro men are broadened. In time, the existing disparity as a distinctive feature of Negro life may disappear, but not until Negroes can try for success in fields closed to them for so long, and not until the incentives of Negro youth can be sharply increased.

The problem of education is, of course, interwoven with the question of jobs. Since 1930, the ratio of Negro unemployment to white unemployment has hovered steadily at about two to one.

The working husband of any race is usually the key to family stability; when the husband loses his job it represents the point at which the family may begin to deteriorate. His loss of self-esteem, the inability to support his family, dependence upon some social agency or the wife's earnings—all these factors generally presage more difficult problems to come. In the case of the Negro family, with its historic weaknesses and the tentative nature of male leadership, a prolonged period of unemployment can be disastrous. The family may break up completely and in the long run society has to pay.

The problem is far larger than the individual Negro family; it is bigger than the limited resources of the Negro lower class, which is most affected. The Johnson Administration, using the pioneering report on the Negro family by Daniel P. Moynihan as a point of departure, has recognized the dimensions of the crisis and inaugurated the most comprehensive series of social rehabilitation programs ever designed by the Federal establishment.

Even that will not be enough. The Government can make available better schools, better housing and better opportunities for employment. It can enforce the laws protecting the franchise and the right to public accommodations. But the Government cannot establish a pattern of family relationships which will foster the values needed to make all this meaningful and effective. Only the Negro can save his family. The substantive help of law and the Government is essential, of course, but the incentive, the motivation which can transform the Negro predicament into a shining achievement of the Great Society must come from within the group.

The white man destroyed the Negro family and kept it weak by preserving the psychology of slavery, thinly disguised as racial discrimination and prejudice. But the white man cannot give back the values he took away.

For years, myopic but well-meaning whites have been challenging the Negro to pull himself up by his own bootstraps, even though the Negro didn't have either boots or straps. The white man was looking at his own boots and imagining the Negro owned a pair, too. The "straps" of the Negro's family problem are not encouraging, but he must work with what he has.

Negro Wives Find Need to Take Job

by Eileen Shanahan

WASHINGTON

THREE OUT OF four Negro wives have to work if their family income is to rise above the $10,000-a-year mark. In white families, fewer than one wife out of every two must work to bring the family income to that level.

These were two of the findings of a survey of the contribution of working wives to family income published today by the Department of Labor. The study dealt only with intact families, in which husband and wife were living together.

Proportionally, more Negro women work at every income level.

For the population as a whole, fewer than one wife in three works when the family's income is in the $5,000 to $7,000 range. But among Negro couples in that income bracket, more than one wife out of every two works at paid employment.

Negro women also make a somewhat proportionally larger contribution to the family's total income. For white families, the wife's paycheck averages 23.6 per cent of total family income; for Negroes, it is 25.1 per cent.

With one exception the percentage of wives who work at paid

From the *New York Times,* May 21, 1967, copyright © 1967 by The New York Times Company jobs increases steadily, regardless of race, as family income goes up.

Sharp Drop Noted

At the top of the income heap—$15,000 or more—the percentage of wives who are working starts to go down, and it goes down sharply at the $25,000-plus level.

In the population as a whole, the highest proportion of working wives is found at the $12,000-$15,000 level of family income, where one wife out of every two works. In the $15,000-$25,000 bracket, 44 per cent work. But in families whose income exceeds $25,000, only one wife in four works.

There is no income category for the population as a whole in which more than one out of two wives work. But for Negro couples, more than one in two wives works in every income class beginning with the $5,000 to $7,000 bracket.

For all couples in the population, exactly one in three wives work, but for Negro couples, almost one in every two works.

For all of the nation's 42 million families in which there is both a husband and a wife, the median income, as of 1965, the date of the study, was $7,265. For the three million Negro families with husband and wife living together, the median income was $4,425. By median is meant that half earned more, half less.

For all families, the median income was $6,592 when the wife did not work and $8,597 when she did.

For Negro families, the median income was $3,650 when the wife did not work and $5,429 when she did.

Part 4

PARENTS
AND CHILDREN

EVEN WHEN we take into account the widespread parent-youth conflict of our time, it is safe to say that far more parents are pleased with their children over the long haul than are spouses with one another. Most parents fail to socialize their children to the degree they would like, but they are not likely on that account to be very disappointed in the final adult who emerges. Perhaps this is because so much of socialization is actually carried out by neighbors, kin, the school, and the larger society—all of which press the growing child to become a socially acceptable person. The cynic may also claim that they are simply biased in favor of their own children, as they are not in favor of their own spouses.

In the selections that follow, various aspects of socialization are explored. In the first selection, the problem of the perfect child is discussed—especially the contrast between the kind of "nice child" that so many parents and teachers want with the kind of child that psychologists believe to be healthy. In the second, Katharine Davis Fishman deals with class differences in child rearing, making a comparison between English and American patterns. In various social commentaries of our day, middle-class mothers are ridiculed because they hover over their children, and try to make them docile, unaggressive, neat, clean, and in general slaves of conformity. Yet, the social and psychological data suggest that middle-class patterns of child rearing are likely to create a more secure child, one better able to innovate and explore life for himself. This article should be compared with the findings on the achievements of the firstborn and only children. A great number of studies have suggested that the drive to achieve is much greater in the firstborn child if he is male. Comparable data for female children do not yield the same clear results. The firstborn child is likely to be given more attention, to hear more adult language, to be somewhat more dependent emotionally on others, and to be held to somewhat higher standards. At the same time, he is likely to feel somewhat more secure in exploring new ways of doing things.

In the next two selections, by Christopher Jencks and Bennett Berger, the contemporary patterns of socialization are linked to the larger social problems of parent-youth conflict, political rebellion, and the much discussed immaturity of the American male. Whether these links can be accepted as validated by the evidence is open to question, and the reader should consider these analyses somewhat skeptically. For example, the failure of the American school is often laid at the door of John Dewey, just as the disrespect among adolescents is laid at the door of Dr. Spock. Yet, few American schools were ever patterned after Dewey's prescriptions, and most parents did not follow Dr. Spock's advice. Parents do not easily change their way simply because they have read a book that advises them to do so. The factors that have increased parent-youth conflict in our time are many and varied, and the socialization within the family is only one major variable among them.

The "Perfect" Child

by Eda J. LeShan

GRANDMA HAD BROUGHT 4-year-old Lauri a walking-talking doll for her birthday. Lauri, her parents and grandparents watched in wonder as the doll walked across the floor in jerky steps, a mechanical voice from within saying, "Hello, I love you, hello, I love you, hello, I love you."

"Now *that's* what I call a perfect child!" exclaimed Lauri's mother.

As a not at all objective bystander, I found this scene thoroughly nightmarish. It seemed to me to embody the most terrifying and outrageous aspirations held for children in a pseudo-scientific, technological age. Specifically, it expressed the wishes of frightened, uncertain parents for comfortable, predictable, reassuring child behavior.

Whatever most of us may be manifesting outwardly, the inner wish for children to behave like mechanical dolls seems to me to be real and widespread. And, I am afraid that at least some of the discomfort with unsettling, all-too-human children is felt by those who for the last half century have devoted their time and professional talents to the study and understanding of children.

During those 50 years, it seemed possible, for the first time in history, to create the perfect child; since this subtle premise has remained unfulfilled, many of us dwell on our failure to become

From the *New York Times Magazine,* August 27, 1967, copyright © 1967 by The New York Times Company perfect parents—instead of realizing that we shouldn't have set such a goal in the first place.

Attitudes toward child raising changed from decade to decade in this period, reflecting whatever knowledge or insights we thought we had arrived at. This has undoubtedly been true throughout history, but during the last 50 years, these attitudes have had the prestige of "Science" behind them. Because of this, we have tended to forget that even in an age possessing scientific methods for observation and evaluation one day's theories are often the next day's castoffs.

When one decade's attitudes are compared with those of say, three decades before, the changes are, of course, striking. Martha Wolfenstein, writing in the 1951 Journal of Social Issues, provided an example of this from her study of the 1914-1945 editions of Infant Care, the publication of The Children's Bureau reflecting the best thinking in this period.

By the nineteen-forties, the baby was described by Infant Care as being interested in the world around him and eager to explore it; play was natural and it was obligatory that a mother play with her child. The 1914 edition of Infant Care represented the infant as a creature of strong and dangerous impulses. It advised mothers to wage a ceaseless battle against the child's sinful nature. Playing with the baby was regarded as dangerous; it produced unwholesome pleasure and ruined a baby's nerves: "The rule that parents should not play with the baby may seem hard, but it is without doubt a safe one. . . . The dangerousness of play is related to that of the ever-present sensual pleasures which must be constantly guarded against."

While I was attending the 74th Annual Convention of the American Psychological Association in New York, it occurred to me that styles in what we consider to be the Perfect Child have changed as often as clothes in the world of fashion. I looked up the convention programs for the 54th meeting in 1946 and the 64th meeting in 1956. Both were concerned with different aspects of child-raising from those discussed at this 74th meeting. Both stressed the emotional problems of young children, and the effects on personality of parental behavior. By 1956, mothers were taking something of a beating—psychosomatic illnesses in children, for example, were being identified quite strongly with "maternal rejection and hostility." Children were viewed essentially as the innocent victims of poor mothering. At the 1966 meeting, there was less interest in this, far more in problems of learning and programed instruction.

When I began to attend these meetings, about 20 years ago, the aim of child psychology was to create children who would be free from anxiety—who, with the aid of insightful and psychologically sophisticated parents and teachers, would be helped to feel unconditionally loved and accepted. The dream of that era was to help children gain insight into their needs and feelings, to eliminate guilt and shame from their life experience and thereby make it possible for them to be "well adjusted." An outstanding feature of our concept of the Perfect Child in those days was that the child would have the ability to express his feelings—and since, in the preceding Puritanical and Victorian times it was the less lovely feelings of anger and hostility that could *not* be expressed, what we really meant by "expressing feelings" was the expression of the very kind that had been so long repressed.

Parents of the nineteen-forties frequently seemed to be most complacent when their children were angry. We accepted temper tantrums, being mean to the baby, telling Mommie she was horrible, as indications of what a good job we were doing. It made us slightly uncomfortable when our children were unselfish, kind, thoughtful and serene; if we were helping our children to live more comfortably with the baser instincts we were now aware of, we were a little uneasy and suspicious if our children didn't cooperate. A few years later, as the psychiatrist Fritz Redl said, we had been so concerned with psychology, that we had not bothered to really examine what we meant by health. We had become adept at labeling and describing the disturbed child, but would have been uneasy and puzzled if we had tried to say what we meant by a mentally balanced child.

In 1943 "The Rights of Infants" by Dr. Margaret Ribble discussed the emotional problems that might result from early traumas, such as frustration associated with nursing. Also during the period from 1940-1950, Drs. Thomas French and Franz Alexander were influencing specialists and parents in their thinking about the emotional factors in childhood illnesses, and again the stress was on the ways in which adults create disturbances by not meeting the emotional needs of the young child.

A 1949 book, "New Ways in Discipline" by Dorothy Baruch epitomized the thinking of this decade. Mrs. Baruch wrote warmly and practically about ways to apply our new information to child raising—all we had to do was help children understand why they misbehaved; they needed to be aided with their inner feelings, not punished.

Mrs. Baruch described the difference between a modern mother and one who lived 25 years earlier. The mother of the earlier generation had less to think about when she disciplined her child; if he turned on a gas jet he got spanked, his mother felt that she had made him afraid of gas jets, and that was that. The modern mother, in the same situation, was forced to examine the effects of such discipline; would her child be afraid of the gas jet or of his mother? Would he be learning to behave out of fear rather than understanding?

Mrs. Baruch's book gave hundreds of examples of the "hidden meaning" behind a child's actions and urged parents to respond to those meanings rather than to the behavior itself. A child might disobey because he wanted more attention: he might knock over a lamp because he was really jealous of the new baby; he might refuse to go to sleep because he didn't want his mother to have time alone with Daddy. "Emotional hunger lies at the root of disciplinary problems," the reader was told, and the challenge to parents was to help a child verbalize the inner meaning of what he was doing: "Let the poison out . . . The hurts and fears and angers must be released and drained."

In the nineteen-fifties the emphasis began to shift from preoccupation with insight. Now the Perfect Child was the one who adjusted to his group. The distinguishing characteristic of such a child was that he was hardly noticeable in classroom or recreational club. The child who chose to be alone, the restless agitator or troublemaker, the child who seemed different and an outsider, was the source of our concern. We were uncomfortable with the "bookworm," the "social isolate," the "rugged individualist." In a parent discussion group in 1954, one mother expressed feelings common then to many parents when she said, "I don't want Dennis to be too smart. I want him to be just average and be popular and have a good time."

Dr. David Riesman, in a 1951 article entitled, "How Different May One Be?" mentioned a child who was a gifted musician, but whose mother said, "I don't let him practice much because I want to keep him a normal boy." Dr. Riesman added, "Thousands of parents throw away their children's special gifts . . . in return for gifts of social adjustment to a particular group at a particular time and place."

Other objectors began to be heard. Dr. Harold Taylor, then president of Sarah Lawrence College, said in 1958 that colleges were just getting the first generation of "understood children." He explained, "In the absence of a strong line of parental authority, the child has little to rebel against, and in a world in which he is not ordered around but told to choose his way, he may stifle in an atmosphere of kindly over-approval."

By the nineteen-sixties we discovered that being "well-adjusted" often meant just being kind of "blah." We began to be concerned about the inherent dangers in too much conformity to group pressures. In addition there was Sputnik, the scientific race for the moon, the suddenly overcrowded colleges and the necessity for higher education as a prerequisite for almost any kind of work. "Adjustment be damned," we now seemed to be saying to our children. "Be as individualistic as you like, but for heaven's sake, *be smart!*" We became most concerned with how to make children's brains function as efficiently as our new and greatly cherished computers.

Today's concept of the Perfect Child has as its core the wish for a no-nonsense child who grows up as quickly as possible, with or without his emotional quirks: One who can be manipulated in such a way that he will read and write at 2, solve calculus problems at 10 and be graduated from an Ivy League college at 18. Parents have spent hundreds of thousands of dollars on a $19.95 kit "guaranteed" to make the preschool child learn to read and write. "Give Your Child A Superior Mind," by Siegfried and Theresa Engleman, says that if its instructions are carefully followed, a child will read 150 words a minute, add, subtract, multiply and divide, understand fractions and simple algebra, before he is 5.

Slowly, in the last half of this decade, there is beginning to emerge an awareness that however much we may think we know about human beings, we must not use this knowledge to manipulate, control or predict what will be essential or useful or good in the development of any specific person.

If we have learned anything from the past, it ought to be that what is most precious about human beings is their refusal to be categorized and pigeonholed. We are each of us partly a product of our own entirely unique arrangement and assortment of genes and chromosomes, with all this implies about inborn constitutional differences; we are also the product of a myriad of combinations and possibilities of interactions with our environment, with all that this implies about social change and our unique relationships with other people—and beyond all this, no school of psychological thought or investigation has yet come along that should allow us to dare to decide what perfection might be for any person or group.

It is time we devote our energies to creating a climate in which every growing person has the opportunity for fulfilling himself, whatever he may discover that self to be. What is wanted is an environment so rich in resources, challenges and opportunities that formulas for self realization disappear and each child is helped toward a sense of meaningfulness without regard to standardized goals.

In Praise of the Middle-Class Mother

by Katharine Davis Fishman

FOR ALMOST TWO years, a team of researchers tape-recorded interviews with 700 mothers of 4-year-olds in Nottingham, England, in an attempt to discover the effects of class differences on child rearing. Their findings were published in this country last week as "Four Years Old in an Urban Community" (Aldine) by John and Elizabeth Newson of the Child Development Research Unit at the University of Nottingham. Guided by a basic questionnaire, the Newsons and their staff asked each mother how she handled such problems as feeding, toilet training, fighting and discipline. All responses were grouped according to the father's occupation: professional-managerial and white collar representing the middle class, and skilled, semi-skilled and unskilled comprising the working class.

The conscientious middle-class mother, too often deflated by child-care experts, will be relieved by the Newsons' findings. In contrasting her approach with that of the working-class parent, they may give her a new respect for her own reasoning and help her to see herself as someone who is lovingly and intelligently bringing up her children. The authors make no flat judgments;

From the *New York Times Magazine,* November 3, 1968, copyright © 1968 by The New York Times Company indeed, they show a sympathy and understanding for the average mother, whatever her class, that is remarkable these days.

The Newsons first noted that the 4-year-old is not a "lay figure passively waiting for Child Upbringing to be practiced on him, but an active personality in his own right, whose determination to make his mark on his parents' awareness is nearly as great as theirs to socialize him."

How a mother handles the needs and demands of this fascinating creature is partly a matter of environment, partly a matter of philosophy. The authors observe that it is easy to be relaxed about toilet training, for instance, when one owns a washing machine.

Working-class mothers try to ignore their children's squabbles and insist they fight their own battles; middle-class mothers arbitrate or isolate. But working-class families usually share a back yard with their neighbors and they dread falling out with other parents over some children's dispute. Moreover, the child usually has no room of his own. If mother brings him inside, he is under her feet. Middle-class mothers are more tolerant of noise and mess, but they have more space, fewer children and perhaps some domestic help.

Middle-class mothers are stricter about meals and bedtimes. Many working-class families, the Newsons point out, don't have formal meals. Father works on the night shift and they can't all fit around the table anyway. So the youngsters take a slice of bread when they feel like it. Working-class children often share their beds with siblings or even with parents. "He sleeps with me," said an unemployed laborer's wife. "When he's sleepy, he'll pick up my purse and my fags and matches and say 'ta-ta,' and that's it. So's I'll go to bed with him, you see."

Beyond merely physical factors, more deep-seated differences of attitude and emotion divide middle- and working-class mothers. The working-class mother thinks the value of play is in teaching children the law of the jungle; the professional-class mother thinks play is worthwhile only when the children get on well together.

A clergyman's wife explained: "If it's a *bad* squabble in which people are fighting and shouting, then I separate them. They have a corner each until everyone's quietened down. And when we've said we're sorry, we go into it and work out what it was all about. And then we try and put it right."

A foreman's wife said: "It's just a waste of time to interfere, I think. It's only a childish argument when all's said and done. 'Jane's got my dolly' or 'Linda's got my something else.' 'Oh, go and sort it out for yourselves,' I say."

Middle-class parents feel a strong educative duty. They "expect to *provide* suitable company, just as they provide food, clothing and education." Well-informed about the importance of messy play, they cheerfully furnish paints and clay and gloat over Nigel's blobs and scrawls; the working-class mother thinks painting is worthwhile only if it produces a recognizable tree.

As a packer's wife said: "He had a box of paints at Christmas. Well, everywhere was covered, and he was in it as well. He didn't actually *color* anything, he just scribbled over the whole page. Well, I didn't think he was getting much out of that. I put them out of the way."

Professional-class parents are more willing to play with a child on *his* level (the you-be-the-engine-I'll-be-the-caboose sort of game) because it develops his imagination and verbal facility. A working-class mother, if she has the temperament, may join in for fun, but she will apologize, as did one chauffeur's wife, "if anyone saw me! I'm as bad as the kids sometimes!"

Four is a peak age for fantasy companions, invisible dogs that make cocoa, fictitious little girls who get underfoot. "She imagines this friend at the door, Susan," a storekeeper's wife related. "We have to say hello to Susan. She often comes to tea. You have to laugh sometimes. But we don't laugh now, mind, because we know she really means it."

And a salesman's wife said: "We have Noddy and Billa and Gunny. When we go out and come in we have to be sure to let Noddy through the door before we close it and sometimes we've had to go back to the gate and let him in because she insists we've left Noddy outside."

If mother is middle-class, she's delighted to see Veronica's imagination developing and gaily sets an extra place for tea. If she's working-class, she worries about Jimmy's mental health. A machine operator's wife, whose daughter had many ectoplasmic friends, unwittingly pinpointed the difference: "I remember telling the doctor's wife down the road about them. It worried me because she used to carry on and on and *on* about them. And the doctor's wife said that her children never had them and she wished they would."

Indeed, the encouragement of imagination and talk takes precedence in a middle-class home. Mother may be strict about which fork the children use, but as a university teacher's wife observes, "Talking I *like* at mealtimes; that's one of the times we talk *most*. It's a sort of meeting time, when we all find out what the others have been doing during the morning. That's what mealtimes are *for*." Only when her eardrums are shattered would she agree with the truck driver's wife who opines, "Well, you don't like them rattling on, do you? I say, 'Oh, shurrup and gerrit down yer!'"

In matters pertaining to sex, the gulf between the classes becomes a chasm. The Newsons write: "On every issue of physical or sexual modesty as it affects the 4-year-old, differences can be demonstrated between social classes which are both consistent and sizable: indeed, these differences are so striking that it has been suggested that attitudes towards sexual modesty might be a better index of social class affiliation than the more conventional 'occupation of father'!" One in five 4-year-old children of all classes know where babies come from; in professional and managerial families the figure rises to almost one in two, and in unskilled families it goes down to 15 per cent. Moreover, three-quarters of all unskilled laborers' wives state their intention to evade or prevaricate should their child *ask* where babies come from. The middle-class mother, the Newsons suggest, is just as keen as her working-class counterpart to preserve the child's sexual innocence, but the former hopes to neutralize her child's curiosity by bringing everything out in the open, while the latter prefers to suppress it.

Perhaps the most significant difference of all between the philosophies of middle- and working-class mothers is in the area of discipline and control. The Newsons first note that the authoritarianism of the 19th and early 20th centuries is no longer considered acceptable, but "this is not to say that parents do not want their children to respect their authority and to comply with their wishes; but it does mean that they hope for voluntary and rational cooperation, as opposed to automatic obedience and servile docility.

"I don't believe in all these books which tell you, 'Don't smack,'" says a working-class wife. "If you're going to *talk* the child out of it, you're going to spend half your day standing there *talking* to them. I think it does them good to have a smack if they've done something wrong, I think it lasts longer than simply talking to them."

On the other hand, the middle-class mother "tries to get through to the child with a determinedly cool voice of reason. Anyone who has experience of children of this age will know that appeals to the reason of a furious 4-year-old are often rather poorly rewarded; but it is typical of middle-class mothers to treat their children from a very early age *as if* they were capable of being persuaded by rational argument; and, because this line of action is rooted in attitudes and ideals about life to which they are deeply committed, they persist even when the initial success rate is very low."

The slap is easier on the child, observe the Newsons, because it gets him off the hook and also makes mother an instant villain. But the "explanation of principle involves him in a lasting commitment. . . . The most effective conscience, which is comfortable neither to acquire nor to possess, is likely to be achieved by the process of cumulative verbal reasoning which we have described."

The principle of reciprocity guides the middle-class mother in dealing with her child. If Victoria gets cheeky, mother objects mainly to her rudeness: "I wouldn't speak to *you* like that, don't do so to me." In the working class, it's a question of authority: "I'm gaffer [boss] in this house, milady." When Charles is asked to set the table and says he's busy, his middle-class mother reflects that she herself is often busy when Charles calls for help. Again, when a working-class mother accidentally breaks her child's toy, she will replace it promptly, but feels an apology would undermine her authority. The middle-class mother may not replace the toy but apologizes copiously, hoping to set an example of civilized behavior. (Middle-class parents love to teach by example.)

The Newsons offer some interesting speculation on the results of each approach. "The working-class child is significantly less often rewarded for making verbal excuses, while the middle-class child finds this a rather potent means of getting his own way.

"Given experiences such as these, it follows that for the working-class child, protests are more likely to become increasingly a matter of form only, the expression of rebelliousness against an authority which he has little hope of converting to his own view by the time-honored democratic process of discussion and compromise, and which, because it is inflexible, invites eventual rejection rather than offering a possibility of coming to terms. For the middle-class child, on the other hand, there is every incentive for refining the ingenuity with which he states his case, encouraged as he is by the knowledge that it will be duly weighed and taken into consideration in deciding the outcome of a situation; and this will help him to cooperate with authority, and eventually to internalize its values, rather than turning his back on it altogether."

This turning the back on society worries the Newsons. They feel that the lack of discussion and verbalization can lead to a total mistrust of authority in later life, building a gulf between Them and Us.

Another area of difference is that of permissiveness vs. restrictiveness. The Newsons remark that, "The social classes tend to part company not so much on the issue of whether to be permissive or restrictive as upon which issues demand restrictiveness and which permissiveness." They offer two sharp examples, to illustrate this point:

"Mrs. B. is a laborer's wife. She lets Ronnie play in the street with whomever he finds there, shouts at him if he refuses to fight his own battles, insists that he obeys her because if he doesn't he'll get a slap, and cuddles him to sleep with a dummy [pacifier], which Mrs. A. would never dream of doing, when he comes in at 9; jumping on his bed and genital play both merit a smack, and his mother insists in the face of his questioning that babies come from the sweet-shop."

"Mrs. A. is a professional-class wife. She keeps a close super-visory eye on Edmund, vets his friends discreetly, makes him stay in the garden if he fights with neighboring children, insists that he obeys her for reasons which she carefully explains to him, and puts him to bed at 7 o'clock; however, he may jump on his bed and use finger-paints, is ignored if he plays with his penis, and has been told where babies come from."

In conclusion, the Newsons note the prevalence in current child-care literature of what one expert has called "the fun morality." The middle-class parent, influenced by that literature, wants to "be a friend to her child" and "have fun with him," and most of the time, she is and does. But egalitarianism often brings con-fusion. The parents "retain, at the back of the mind, an image of the 'good' child who, while obviously bright and alert, at the same time defers to parental wishes." The methods they use, however, are more suited to raising a free spirit. Moreover, the child's naughtiness is particularly disturbing because it "involves a rejection of the parent's proffered friendship." When the child misbehaves, his mother has to become somewhat authoritarian whether she likes it or not.

Throughout the study one is struck by the similarities between the English and the Americans in both the attitudes and the prob-lems related to raising children. Despite small environmental dif-ferences—English children seem to have more physical freedom than Americans (at least in New York), the apartment-play-ground life is non-existent, and nursery schools are more common here—there are more similarities than disparities.

The Newsons, who previously completed a similar study of 1-year-olds and are looking forward to another when these 700 Nottingham youngsters turn 7, do not draw any conclusions. They do wonder, however, whether since "working-class parents lag always a few years behind their middle-class counterparts as trends in child rearing change," they will meet them one day on the way back. There has been much recent yearning for the virtues of "old-fashioned up-bringing," which is the kind practiced by the working-class Nottingham parents and there are signs that the child-rearing pendulum is swinging that way again. After reading the Newsons' observations, however, many parents may decide that the current middle-class approach should not be scrapped lightly.

Parents Linked to Adult Success

by John A. Osmundsen

A CALIFORNIA PSYCHOLOGIST has found evidence that the way parents treat their children may have a lot to do with their chances of rising to eminence.

Factors in parental treatment that may favor a child's prospects for getting on in the world, according to William D. Altus in the Jan. 7 issue of Science, include:

¶ Strictness in contrast to relaxed permissiveness.

¶ Stress on the attainment of certain standards of performance between the ages of 6 and 8 years.

¶ Training in independence and mastery.

¶ A warm personal regard by both parents, who are ambitious for the child but not too dominating.

¶ A strong positive attitude toward education.

Dr. Altus, a professor at the Santa Barbara campus of the University of California, drew those conclusions from a survey he has made of studies of the relation between the order of birth and achievement. He cited more than 10 such studies, the earliest done in England in 1874.

From the *New York Times,* January 8, 1955, copyright © 1955 by The New York Times Company

Birth Order a Factor

Those studies indicated, he wrote, that "in England and in the United States, there appears to be an indubitable relation of birth order to the achievement of eminence, however it has been defined, [and] the dice are loaded in favor of the firstborn."

That is, those studies revealed without exception that eldest children were superior achievers in significantly greater numbers than their brothers and sisters.

The youngest children in some studies ranked second in achievement to the eldest; the in-between ones were most frequently lowest. An only child—a special case of being firstborn —appeared to be ablest of all.

In addition, Dr. Altus wrote, the studies indicated that the sex of the other children in the family affected the first-born's performance; he or she did better in the company of brothers rather than sisters.

Finally, family size seemed to be involved. The first-born with three siblings, one study indicated, rated highest on a certain aptitude test of all birth ranks among those who came from families of two, three, four and five children.

By comparison, those with two older siblings scored the lowest of all those ranks.

In an effort to explain these findings, Dr. Altus went to studies concerning relationships between birth order and personality.

According to such studies, eldest children were found to have a better developed conscience, were more cooperative and curious, and depended more upon adult standards than later-born children, the California psychologist wrote.

Those qualities, he said, might be accounted for by differential parental treatment accorded children born at different times in the growth of the family.

Moreover, the qualities attributed to the first-born child would tend to enhance his adjustment to school and performance there, Dr. Altus wrote. This could explain why colleges attract such a high proportion of first-born.

Why more first-born children do not achieve their prospects

for superior achievement than is actually the case may have a two-fold explanation, the California psychologist observed.

First, Dr. Altus wrote, not many parents have all the necessary qualities for promoting their children's abilities.

Second, being first-born is not enough. Several studies indicated that the advantage that eldest children have in achieving eminence holds primarily in populations that are "quite bright."

In other words, even if you are the eldest child in your family and your parents treat you in just the right way, to make it to the top, you are going to have to be pretty smart to begin with.

Is It All
Dr. Spock's Fault?

by Christopher Jencks

RESPECT FOR authority has never been an official American virtue. Our folk heroes include Puritan religious refugees who defied the Church of England, political revolutionaries who defied the British Government, and men we would now call psychological misfits who fled civilized America to make their own rule as frontiersmen. Our constitutional form of government placed unprecedented restraints on the authority of the state. Competition between denominations had the same effect on the traditional authority of the church, since potentially rebellious parishioners could always leave a congregation whose demands they found burdensome. Even the informal authority that communities had traditionally exercised over their members was undermined by geographic mobility—today the typical American family stays in the same place only five years.

But every society must curb individualism in certain ways and induce men to submit to certain kinds of discipline. The family and the school have been America's principal institutions for doing this. Until fairly recently the American family was avowedly hierarchic: Men exercised power over women, and adults

From the *New York Times Magazine,* March 3, 1968, copyright © 1968 by The New York Times Company

exercised power over the young. Those who had less power were expected to show respect for those who had more, to obey orders, to inhibit their feelings of resentment and to work hard to meet the demands placed upon them. It is true that even in the eighteen-thirties a European visitor like Alexis de Tocqueville was struck by the fact that American parents seemed more permissive and American children less obedient and less docile than their European counterparts. Nonetheless, earlier generations of children were generally kept in their place ("seen and not heard"), at least compared with children today.

American schools traditionally played a role rather similar to that of the family. One of their avowed purposes in the 19th and early 20th centuries was to teach children "to behave"—in particular to make them accept the impersonal discipline imposed first by a teacher and then by a textbook. While these efforts were not uniformly successful, especially when contrasted with Europe, neither were they totally without effect. The adults who emerged from these schools were by no means all pliant, subordinate bank clerks and secretaries, but neither were they all rebellious would-be cowboys. The genius of Ame can institutions has been to find a place and a use for both these conflicting attitudes toward authority, making room for both innovators and consolidators, entrepreneurs and "sound men," rebellious dreamers and stern adjudicators.

Modern capitalism (like modern Socialism and Communism) relies on highly complex organizations. These can function only if most workers do what they are told most of the time. They must do it even when they feel the task is difficult, disagreeable or pointless, and they must do it with only minimal supervision. They must, in short, act precisely as parents used to urge their children to act and as teachers tried to make their pupils act. Yet capitalism also requires dissidents who will cut loose and go into business for themselves when their boss will not do something that obviously needs to be done. Without such men every organization would sooner or later cease to serve the public and simply perpetuate itself—as, indeed, some have.

The American political system requires similar rebels who will continually argue the case against the status quo, formulate alternatives and try to create a constituency committed to those alternatives. When this kind of skepticism and resistance to established authority ceases, democracy becomes a mere facade for preserving the status quo—as, again, some radicals think it has. Yet at the same time every political system also needs dutiful civil servants who will carry out whatever program their political superiors inaugurate. If every civil servant had strong convictions of his own and then blocked anything which did not conform to these convictions, politics would become meaningless.

America has been built on a mixture of discipline and rebellion, but the balance between them has constantly shifted over the years. During the nineteen-forties and fifties the antiauthoritarian side of the American tradition lay politically dormant. Politicians and voters were mainly concerned with national security and prosperity. Conservatives expressed some alarm when pursuit of these objectives led to the growth and centralization of government power, and liberals expressed similar alarm when it led to the growth and centralization of corporate power, but almost nobody opposed either trend in any serious way.

The nineteen-sixties, on the other hand, have seen a spectacular revival of the antiauthoritarian tradition. The most visible spokesmen for this revival are black militants and student radicals, but it has also affected many less outspoken liberals and conservatives—especially those under 30. It is important to ask why this questioning is taking place, for only if we know its roots have we much chance of predicting its consequences. This article offers only tentative speculations, but that is all anyone has to offer at the moment.

The sources of the current unrest are many, but changes in the traditional structure of the American family strike me as playing a crucial role. The traditional, relatively hierarchical pattern of family relationships is being replaced by a new and far more egalitarian one, especially among the middle classes. This revolution began in the late 19th and early 20th centuries with the feminists' attack on masculine dominance. That battle was never entirely won, but relations between the sexes are certainly more equal today than they were in the 19th century. World War I and the Model A Ford encouraged a parallel change in the relation between parents and their adolescent children. This too is a continuing guerrilla war, but since the nineteen-twenties there has been little doubt that adolescents have been gradually gaining ground. During the nineteen-thirties this emancipation process began to have a dramatic effect on parents' relations with younger children as well.

Like most revolutions this one had its origins in a failure of nerve and loss of self-confidence among those who held power (in this case, adults). The origin of the crisis was probably the accelerating rate of social change. During the 19th century most parents had been able to assume that there were certain fixed standards of "civilized," "respectable" behavior to which every child should conform. These were the rules on which they themselves had been raised and (they assumed) their parents before them. In reality, of course, child-rearing practices have never been entirely stable. But until the past generation changes were fairly slow and hard to pinpoint. A mother who upheld these standards was therefore not asserting her personal authority over her children; she was enforcing rules which, if not inscribed on golden tablets, were at least widely supported by her friends, her neighbors, her ancestors, her clergyman, and so forth.

By the nineteen-thirties the rate of social change and the amount of communication between dissimilar subcultures had increased to the point where no cosmopolitan parent could any longer cling to particular standards of behavior simply because "everyone" accepted them or because things had "always" been that way. Developments which would once have taken two or three generations now took one. Self-conscious choices were inescapable. Most urbane, educated parents knew they had been raised for a world very different from the one they lived in, and they at least suspected that their children would grow old in a world they could barely imagine. In such a context it was hard to be sure about anything, least of all whether children were better off on scheduled or demand feeding.

The anxiety accompanying these choices was heightened by the popularization in this same era of psychoanalysis. Millions of parents came to believe that they were responsible for whatever went wrong with their children's lives, that almost any parental act could have permanent traumatic consequences for a child, and that if they insisted on what had once been regarded as minimal standards they could easily turn their children into repressed neurotics. Many parents responded by trying to make as few choices as possible for their children, forcing the children to make more choices and (they hoped) take more responsibility for the consequences.

The task of channeling parental anxiety into a new system of child rearing fell to Dr. Benjamin Spock and his colleagues. Spock never urged complete permissiveness, but he did insist that a child's immediate needs had the same legitimacy and intensity as those of adults, that it was important for children to control their environment, and that authority should be rational and flexible rather than arbitrary and absolute. While this view is still by no means universally accepted, it has dominated upper-middle-class child rearing since the nineteen-forties. Two features of this new style deserve particular attention in trying to understand contemporary America: the role of children in formulating the rules which govern their behavior, and the use of disapproval rather than actual punishment to keep children in line.

The idea that children can be implicated in the formulation of rules governing their behavior is certainly not entirely new. Parents have always tried to explain why certain rules existed, and by getting the child to acknowledge a rule's rationality they have in effect made him a partner in its preservation, if not its enforcement. But it is still fair to say that progressive-minded parents were more concerned with persuading their children that rules were legitimate and for their own good in the nineteen-forties and fifties than in earlier times. Such parents were also more willing to listen to their children's counterarguments. Children were encouraged to see themselves as equals who could use rationality to curb their parents' power, just as the parents used it to curb the children.

This ideal was, it is true, frequently violated. The child who asked his frazzled mother "Why?" 15 times in the same day sooner or later exhausted her patience and evoked the expected answer: "Because I say so." But forcing a "modern" mother to admit that her authority rested on superior power rather than reason made her feel guilty, and her children were quick to take advantage of this. By refusing to join the consensus which gave legitimacy to a particular request or rule, children could wear their parents down and eventually force them to retreat and reformulate their demands in a way that the children would accept. Child rearing in such families often became a process of overt negotiation. The fact of negotiation did not, of course, mean that the two parties were completely equal, but it was a long step in that direction. In a sense, Dr. Spock did for the young what the Wagner Act had done a few years earlier for the labor movement.

The upper-middle-class family's emphasis on consensus, rationality and relative equality was accompanied by new forms of discipline. If Johnny misbehaved he was made to feel that he was rejecting his parents and undermining the bonds of love which held the family together. For small children, this kind of fear and guilt seems to have been terrifying. As children grew older, however, they learned that their parents were vulnerable to the same tactics. A mother could keep a child in line by making him feel guilty and unlovable, but the child could do precisely the same thing to his mother. The result was a system of mutual deterrence.

When the products of these permissive, upper-middle-class homes entered school, they usually encountered teachers with more traditional standards of behavior and methods of control. A handful of progressive schools tried to recreate the atmosphere of a well-run permissive family, but these schools were almost all private. In the public schools rules were still rules, and teachers seem to have felt less self-doubt when enforcing rules made by the administration than parents felt when trying to carry out the mandates of either their neighbors or Dr. Spock. The child who asked "Why?" all day in school was almost always silenced or at least subdued. Few schools even pretended to offer any answer but "Because we say so" (or "Because the book says so").

Yet even in the schools there was some change. More and more young teachers were anxious to win their pupils' love, reluctant to impose their will through physical punishment or intimidation, interested in dialogue rather than monologue, and hence more subject to both individual and collective pressure from their students. This was particularly true of the better suburban schools. So, while most schools continued to give children a foretaste of the "real"—i.e., nonfamilial—world, the flavor became more muted than in earlier times.

The first product of these semipermissive homes and schools reached maturity in the nineteen-fifties. They—perhaps I should say "we," for this is my own generation—found that adult society was organized along very different lines from the families in which we had been raised, and that most employers were more like the teachers we had learned to hate than the teachers we had come to love.

Our reactions to this discovery were mixed. We were not sufficiently numerous to reinforce one another's prejudices, so we mostly assumed that our discontents were the result of personal maladjustments rather than societal ones. Even when we suspected that established institutions were unnecessarily hierarchic, authoritarian and repressive, it seldom occurred to us that they could be changed. The older generation which dominated America during the Eisenhower years had been so scarred by the nineteen-thirties and forties that it assumed fundamental change could only make America more totalitarian, not less, and its fatalism affected us too. Most of us therefore accepted the general principle that adult society could not be as egalitarian as our families had tried to be, and that we would have to subject ourselves to various kinds of remote, arbitrary authority.

Fatalistic as we were about reconstructing the adult world, we seldom threw ourselves into that world with much enthusiasm. Some of us took corporate or Government jobs, but few of us expected to get much satisfaction from them. They were simply a device for making a living. Those of us who wrote off the 9-to-5 portion of our lives pinned most of our hopes on creating a comfortable and comforting family life which embodied the ideals we had picked up in our own childhoods.

Others among us were slightly less pessimistic, and decided that while a corporate job would be intolerable we might find a habitable niche in one of the professions. Yet even this portion of my generation seldom saw its profession as an instrument for remaking the world.

Our professions were "just a job," preferable to a managerial career only because they gave us more day-to-day freedom and subjected us to less direct supervision and pressure from above. While many of us had an abstract sympathy with liberal causes, we seldom let this affect our work in conspicuous ways. Most of us were even willing to let our professional knowledge and skills be used to strengthen the very hierarchic structures we disliked. Those of us who did scientific work, for example, had little compunction about working for the military as long as our personal independence was unaffected.

I do not want to exaggerate the extent of these attitudes among people reaching adulthood in the nineteen-fifties. Indeed, World War II may have played a larger role than permissive ideology in shaping my generation. The war took millions of fathers away from their wives and children for long periods of time. This meant that the children in question did not encounter an impersonal, remote "law-giver," such as the American father had traditionally been, until they reached school. Even more important, mothers in these circumstances became more dependent on their children for emotional support, security and company.

Normally, a mother whose child rejects her can turn to her husband for reassurance; if the father is gone, she must make her peace with the child as best she can. This gives the child far more power than he usually has when dealing with two parents at once. (Where the two parents are in conflict, of course, a child may have more power when both are around and can be played off against each other than when one is away and the child has no potential ally.)

Nonetheless, neither permissive ideology nor the war affected my generation during its earliest and presumably most formative years, and we must be viewed as a transitional group. Children born in the nineteen-forties were more clearly the products of the new ethos. Especially on leading college campuses in the sixties, the upper-middle-class children who set the tone are mostly products of permissive homes. Even those students whose parents had sought to preserve their traditional authority over their children had been affected by the national mood. All but the most self-confident of their parents had been troubled and ambivalent about imposing their will on the young, and had been vulnerable to pressures of the "Mrs. Smith lets Johnny stay up as late as he likes" variety. Thus they learned that rules were, in fact, malleable under pressure, and that even apparently conservative authority figures could be made to yield.

Once the children of permissiveness arrived on campus in large numbers, they established their own cliques and way of life. Like all student subcultures, these were almost immune to adult control. Once established, such a milieu not only reinforced the prejudices of children from permissive homes but attracted—and to some extent resocialized—rebels from other backgrounds. Instead of one Greenwich Village in New York, populated by a handful of rebels from traditional homes, America developed scores of campus Villages, populated by young people whose values were shaped by the ideals espoused by their liberal parents. As the proportion of young people entering college grew, and the proportion going to work at 16 or 18 shrank, the new values flourished as never before.

Like young people in all eras, the present generation discovered what Kenneth Keniston calls the institutionalization of hypocrisy. No group of adults (or adolescents, for that matter) applies its ideals equally to all people and all areas of activity. Permissive parents, for example, often refuse to extend their generally libertarian values to sex. Many parents with strong ethical views are reluctant to apply the same standards to business relationships as to personal ones. Many who believe every American citizen has a right to elect the legislators and officials who exercise power over him are untroubled by the fact that America unilaterally determines the fate of hundreds of millions of foreigners who have no voice whatever in choosing American policymakers. The young have responded to such contradictions by growing cynical about America's professed ideals, even though these ideals are in most cases also their own.

Another difference between the old and the young is that many of the young have extended their parents' ideals about family life to society as a whole. This is not just a matter of rejecting traditional status distinctions or insisting that those who have power must respect the needs and feelings of those who lack it. That has been a recurrent theme in America for many generations, only marginally reinforced by recent changes in family structure. The really startling thing about the young is that so many of them have turned against the whole idea of industrial society and have tried to revive a complex of older ideals associated with the word "community."

Community can mean as many things as there are men using the term. Nonetheless, certain common themes recur over and over in talking about it with today's students.

First, community means that nobody is expendable. Everyone has some kind of function, makes some kind of contribution to the group, and is accepted as a full member of the group for that reason. This means that every member of the community has a commitment to every other, regardless of whether he likes or dislikes him, just as every member of a family has a commitment to every other member, no matter how much bad blood there may be between them.

The liberal idea of voluntary association, especially voluntary association of like with like, has little place in this vision, for it allows too many "misfits" to fall through the cracks. The meritocratic idea that jobs should be ranked in terms of difficulty, and rewards given on the basis of where a man stands in the hierarchy, is also alien to this vision of community.

A second aspect of community as envisaged by the young is that everyone knows everyone else fairly well, so that even nonfamilial relationships involve "the whole man" rather than being confined to narrowly stylized roles. An employer sees his employes not just as subordinates but as neighbors. A seller sees a buyer not just as a source of cash but as a friend. A policeman who pick up a drunk deals with him not just as a violator of the law but, perhaps, as a fishing partner or a fellow P.T.A. member. Because all relations are multifaceted—indeed, the ideal is that they should be total—there are very few impersonal, legalistic or "businesslike" encounters between people.

This has its dangers. A man who is, let us say, a "good" lawyer but a "bad" friend gets little business in such a society and makes little contribution. A student who does brilliant work in physics but is a poor neighbor does not get admitted to a selective graduate department, which makes the department pleasanter but may leave humanity more ignorant. And a policeman who finds a man he dislikes drunk in the street presumably gives him a kick and walks on rather than feeling obliged to act out his legally defined role and treat this particular drunk like every other.

If this vision of community sounds like an extended family, that is no accident. If it sounds unworkable for a society of 200 million people, that is no accident either. The young men and women who hold these ideas are not much taken with societies of 200 million people, which is one reason they talk continually about decentralization. Indeed, the young radical who suggested that Students for a Democratic Society should change its name to Students for a Small Society was speaking only half in jest.

Given their dreams of an egalitarian, familistic world, the young men and women who came of age in the early nineteen-sixties were naturally quite appalled by the reality of American life. These young people were increasingly allergic to the idea of becoming organization men or organization wives, for example. Yet the hard fact was that new jobs for college graduates were almost all being created by large hierarchical organizations, either public or private. (The major exceptions to this were universities, which were creating openings for Ph.D.'s at a great rate, were subjecting these Ph.D.'s to relatively little supervision, and were, in most cases, allowing them a collective veto over those aspects of university policy which affected their own lives. Many rebellious young people therefore concluded that the only possible career for them would be an academic one.)

Yet, unlike my generation, the undergraduates of the nineteen-sixties did not all retreat into quiescence. For them, private problems *did* become public issues. One key reason for this was the election of John F. Kennedy in 1960.

Kennedy was by no means similar to these young people in either style or temperament. He was an élitist whose greatest triumph (the Cuban missile crisis) involved a dozen men deciding whether 300 million others should live or die. One can hardly imagine a better symbol of the kind of hierarchical, authoritarian system the young were in revolt against—though most of them certainly applauded this particular coup.

Yet Kennedy shared the youthful conviction that some change was necessary, and he managed to persuade a great many people, young and old, that it was also possible. The Kennedy years were not a time of significant political achievement, but they were a time of hope, and that hope was communicated to the young. The future did not look bright to everyone, but at least it looked open. The missile crisis provided one kind of symbol, but the Peace Corps provided another and, a few years later, so did the atomic-test-ban treaty. Equipped with 20-20 hindsight, many now laugh at the naiveté of those who took these gestures seriously, but at the time they were widely seen as tokens of more and better things to come.

Another factor in breaking through the fatalism of the nineteen-fifties was the civil-rights movement. This was mainly a response to changes in the mood of the black lower classes on the one hand and the Federal courts on the other. It had almost nothing to do with the child-rearing revolution I have been describing. Nonetheless, the movement captured the imagination of many white undergraduates. It gave them something to do, and when they did it they often achieved tangible results. It was an extraordinarily decentralized movement, in which local action played an enormous role. (There was a Woolworth's within picketing distance of nearly every campus.)

Students' discovery that they could affect the seemingly remote and unshakable political system by both persuasion and civil disobedience transformed many of them, reinforcing their childhood discovery that their seemingly powerful parents could be pushed around by these same means. It is true that the achievements of this era were modest in comparison with the total problem. The movement produced only reforms, not a revolution. Nonetheless, the sense of movement was real and enormously important, as was the sense that individual citizens could affect the course of this movement by personal effort. History does not vouchsafe many people such potency, but when it does it usually takes a generation to restore order and recreate the general passivity which is normal in all political systems.

The net result of all this was that while large numbers of young people thought America a dreadful mess, many also thought it could be reconstructed along lines consonant with the values they had grown up believing in. Some of these young people became full-time political activists, but most entered the professions or went to work for the more glamorous agencies of the Federal Government. Most of them described themselves as liberals or radicals, but some of the young conservatives who rallied to the banner of Barry Goldwater were equally anti-authoritarian and dissatisfied with the status quo.

The difference between the two groups was that those on the left were usually concerned with the problems of the least competent and least privileged, while those on the right paid more attention to the problems of the most competent and most privileged. The right therefore tended, almost despite itself, to create centralized, authoritarian political organizations in which those who had advantages could maximize them. The left, on the other hand, created anarchic organizations in which the least competent members often neutralized the most competent.

The Vietnam war has certainly not given the liberal-minded, open-hearted children of permissiveness any further grounds for supposing that they can affect the political events which most concern them. But it has reinforced their feeling that hierarchical systems of government which rely on *expertise* and technology to solve problems are fundamentally destructive. Some who draw this conclusion have become revolutionaries, demanding a complete reorganization of American life along nonhierarchical lines. (How this might be accomplished is unclear.) Many others, of whom the hippies are the visible fringe, have no interest in revolution or any other "political" solution. They think salvation is individual, and, like their predecessors in the nineteen-fifties, they have "gone limp" politically. But, unlike their predecessors in the nineteen-fifties, many of them refuse even to go through the motions of conformity to rules they think absurd. Whereas members of my generation followed careers that bored them and sought solace in family life or alcohol, some of our successors have no careers at all. They simply drop in and out of the labor force in order to support themselves. Their solace, if any, is found in sex and drugs rather than drink.

Neither the political nor the psychological dropouts are yet anything like a majority. Most children, even from egalitarian and permissive homes, still climb through school and college into the established institutions of adult society, rather than trying to create alternatives. Yet their acquiescence should not be mistaken for support. The majority may have only a passing interest in LSD and may not respond to the New Left's demands for participatory democracy, but that does not mean they have any enthusiasm for the institutions their parents have created. They are a kind of fifth column within these institutions, unwilling to struggle very hard to preserve them and perhaps even available to support alternatives, should these come into existence.

What does this imply for the future? First, it suggests that the current unrest of the young is not just a response to external events like the war in Vietnam or racial injustice. These events are real enough, but they evoke very different responses in people of more traditional temperament: rallying round the flag, support for established authority (rather than insurgency), repression (rather than acquiescence or compromise). Vietnam and Watts are symbols for the young and the alienated, but their elimination, even if it proved possible, would probably not make dissenters into passionate advocates of American institutions and social arrangements. As long as children are raised in increasingly permissive ways, and as long as the values developed in permissive families are reinforced by ever-longer immersion in adolescent subcultures, while adult life remains regimented and hierarchical for all but the most fortunate few, disenchantment will persist and probably grow even more intense.

This estrangement is unlikely to have much political effect in the near future. Recent events make an American victory in Vietnam seem unlikely even in the long run. If victory is impossible, the alternatives seem to be a larger land war in Asia, perhaps involving the use of nuclear weapons, or else a "compromise," probably involving an eventual take-over by the National

Liberation Front. A settlement along the latter lines, while certainly preferable to the former, seems certain to produce a bitter reaction among American conservatives, just as Versailles and Panmunjom did in earlier times. Such a reaction would, most likely, be reinforced by continuing summer riots and "crime in the streets."

These appalling probabilities are not certainties; they could be averted with luck and leadership. But, if they materialize, America's "postwar"—i.e., post-Vietnam—politics are likely to be dominated by a combination "Red scare" and "black scare." The results would probably be irresistible pressure for a "return to normalcy," repression of past and potential radicals, and attempts to strengthen established authority against both external and internal enemies.

While many of the young people I have been talking about would greet such a development with sorrow, they are not likely to be either sufficiently numerous or sufficiently well-organized to prevent it. My guess is that it will take at least a decade, and possibly two, before they are in a position to dominate American politics—and by then they may well have internalized the very standards and assumptions they now question or reject.

The fundamental challenge to the status quo posed by the recent revolution in child rearing may turn out not to be political but economic. I suggested at the beginning of this article that the viability of any social system depends on its ability to establish political and economic institutions which both serve the public and fit the character and temperament of those who staff them. A bureaucratic system which is tolerably efficient when staffed by conscientious Scandinavians or Prussians, for example, can be a complete disaster when staffed by self-indulgent Italians or cynical Latin Americans. Similarly, a capitalist system which worked tolerably well when it attracted America's ablest and most public-spirited citizens could deteriorate into an unmanageable system of self-serving feudal baronies if its staff was less competent or entirely self-serving.

The rising distaste for managerial careers among the ablest and most altruistic students at leading colleges is therefore an ominous portent. If the trend continues, the established machinery of business and government may be handed over by default to individuals who have neither the skill nor the wisdom to make the machinery serve the public interest. Those who could and should take a leading role in reshaping American life along more humane and civilized lines may simply slip quietly into the professions, where their influence will usually be marginal, even if their lives are comfortable. Some, indeed, may drop out of the economic system entirely.

It is too early to say whether this gloomy possibility will become a reality. One crucial variable in determining the outcome will be politics. If the nineteen-seventies turn out to be a conservative rerun of the nineteen-twenties or fifties, as seems possible, the egalitarian, familistic, antiauthoritarian youngsters I have been describing are likely to grow bitter, cynical and privatistic.

This has happened before, of course, both with the young people who nourished great hopes for progressivism before World War I and lost hope after Wilson's defeat, and with those who hitched their wagon to the star of radicalism during the nineteen-thirties and were defeated after World War II. The difference, I think, is that a far larger proportion of today's younger generation seems estranged from the American system than was the case in those earlier times. Unless that system does much more than it so far has to accommodate these young people's values and co-opt their talents, it could easily go into a decline similar to that which has undermined every previous civilization in history.

The New Stage of American Man—Almost Endless Adolescence

by Bennett M. Berger

When I was an undergraduate 20 years ago, I was chairman of one of the radical student groups at my college and an active official in the regional intercollegiate association of that group. I marched in my share of picket lines, published an article attacking my college president for anti-Semitism, was sung to by the sirens of the local Communist party and even, in a burst of creativity, wrote what in this age of instant classics I suppose qualifies as a classic militant's love song. I called it, "You and I and the Mimeograph Machine" and dedicated it to all the youthful romances born amidst the technology of moral protest.

Later, when I got older and became a sociologist, I resisted becoming a "political sociologist," by which in this context I mean what a lot of the militants mean: a former activist who traded his credentials as a conscious moral and political agent in

From the *New York Times Magazine*, November 2, 1969, copyright © 1969 by The New York Times Company *exchange for the rewards of* expertise *about political behavior. Though the remarks about student militance which follow may be analytic, I yield nothing to the young in the way of moral credentials.*

In trying to throw some sociological light on the nature and character of student unrest, I am not going to comfort the militants by saying that students protest because this is a racist, plastic society or because the curriculum is irrelevant or because the university has sold its soul to the military-industrial complex or because the university is a machine in which students are treated as raw material—when, indeed, their uptight teachers take time from their research to treat them as anything at all. On the other hand, I am not going to comfort their critics by saying that students rebel for kicks or because their upbringing was too permissive or because they are filled with a seething self-hatred or because they are symbolically murdering their fathers in a recurrent ritual melodrama of generational conflict.

What I will try to do is show how certain conditions generic to the direction of our present societal development have helped to bring about the present situation among youth and in the universities. I will also hazard a prediction as to the effects of these conditions during the next decade. An understanding of the problem will not make the solution any easier, for knowledge is power, but it can at least arm us against panaceas.

THE PROBLEM of student unrest is rooted in the prolongation of adolescence in industrialized countries. But it should be understood that "adolescence" is only minimally a biological category; there are only a very few years between the onset of puberty and the achievement of the growth and strength it takes to do a man's or woman's work. As we know, however, culture has a habit of violating nature. Proto-adolescent behavior now begins even before puberty (which itself is occurring earlier) with the action —and the orientation—we call "preadolescent," while at the other end, technological, economic and social developments conspire to prolong the dependence of the young, to exclude them from many of the privileges and responsibilities of adult life, and therefore to *juvenilize* * them.

The casual evidence in support of this deep institutionalization of adolescence is diffuse and quite remarkable. It includes such spectacles as 6-foot, 200-pound "boys" who in another time and place might be founders of dynasties and world-conquerors (like Alexander of Macedon) cavorting on the fraternity house lawn hurling orange peels and bags of water at each other, while tolerant local police, who chucklingly *approve,* direct traffic around the battlefield. It includes the preservation of childlike cadence and intonation in voices otherwise physically mature. It includes the common—and growing—practice (even in official university documents) of opposing the word "student" to the word "adult" —as if students were by definition not adults, even as the median age of university students rises with the increase of the graduate student population.

Adolescence, then, is not the relatively fleeting "transitional stage" of textbook and popular lore but a substantial segment of life which may last 15 or 20 years, and if the meaning of adolescence is extended only slightly, it can last longer than that. I have in mind the age-graded norms and restrictions in those professions which require long years of advanced training, and in which the system of sponsorship makes the advancement of one's career dependent upon being somebody's "boy" perhaps well on toward one's middle-age—a fact not uncharacteristic of university faculties.

Much of the discussion of "youth culture" in recent years reflects the prolongation of adolescence, since it is not surprising that a period of life which may last from age 12 to age 35 might develop its own cultural style, its own traditions and its own sources of motivation, satisfaction—and dissatisfaction. There is thus an enormous stratum of persons caught in the tension between their experience of peak physical strength and sexual energy

---

* "Juvenilize": a verb I have devised to describe a process through which "childish" behavior is induced or prolonged in persons who, in terms of their organic development, are capable of participating in adult affairs. If the process exists, there ought to be a verb to describe it.

on the one hand, and their public definition as culturally "immature" on the other.

This tension is exacerbated by a contradictory tendency: while modern industrial conditions promote juvenilization and the prolongation of dependence, they also create an "older," more experienced youthful cohort. They have more and earlier experience with sex and drugs; they are far better educated than their parents were; urban life sophisticates them more quickly; television brings into their homes worlds of experience that would otherwise remain alien to them. Young people, then, are faced not only with the ambiguity of the adolescent role itself and its prolongation but with forces and conditions that, at least in some ways, make for *earlier* maturity. The youthful population is a potentially explosive stratum because this society is ill-equipped to accommodate it within the status system.

Erik Erikson's well-known theory of the "psycho-social moratorium" of adolescence takes the facts of adolescent prolongation and transforms them into a triumph of civilization. By emphasizing the increased time provided for young persons to postpone commitments, to try on social roles and to play the game called "the search for identity," Erikson suggests that the moratorium on lasting adult responsibilities contributes to the development and elaboration of personal individuality. I have no wish to quarrel with Erikson's general thesis here; I have done so elsewhere. Instead, I want to emphasize a fact that is seemingly contradictory to Erikson's observations about the moratorium on adult commitments. Namely, there have actually been increasing and clearly documented pressures on young people for earlier and earlier occupational planning and choice. "Benjamin," ask that famous Graduate's parents repeatedly, "what are you going to *do?*" And the question is echoed by millions of prosperous American parents who, despite their affluence, cannot assure the future economic position of their heirs.

Logically, of course, prolonged identity play and early occupational choice cannot be encouraged at the same time; the fact is, they are. And like other ambiguous values (and most moral values are ambiguous, or can be made so), this pair permit dif-

ferent groups of youngsters to rationalize or justify the kinds
of adaptations that differing circumstances in fact constrain them
to make. The public attention generated by protesting youth in
recent years (hippies, the New Left, black militants) obscures
the fact that the majority of young people are still apparently
able to tolerate the tensions of prolonged adolescence, to adjust
to the adolescent role (primarily, student), to take some satisfaction from the gains it provides in irresponsibility (i.e., "freedom") and to sail smoothly through high school into college
where they choose the majors, get the grades and eventually the
certifications for the occupations which they want, which want
them and which higher education is equipped to provide them—
degrees in education, business, engineering, dentistry and so on.

For others, however, the search for identity (quote, unquote)
functions as a substitute for an occupational orientation; it gives
them something "serious" to do while coping with their problems
of sex, education, family and career. In college most of these
people tend to major in the humanities or social sciences (particularly sociology) where they may take 10 years or more between the time they enter as freshmen, drop out, return, graduate
and go on to pursue graduate degrees or give up on them entirely.
I will return to this matter, but for the moment I want to make
two general points: (1) that the contradictions create understandable tensions in the young and feed their appetite to discover
"hypocrisy" in their elders; (2) that this condition is largely
beyond the control of the universities; it is generated by the
exigencies of a "post-industrial" society which uses institutions of
higher education as warehouses for the temporary storage of a
population it knows not what else to do with.

The situation has become critical over the past 10 years because the enormous numbers of the young (even small percentages of which yield formidable numbers of troops for worthy
causes) and their concentration (in schools and cities) have
promoted easy communication and a sense of group solidarity
among them. Numbers, concentration and communication regarding common grievances have made increasingly viable, in almost
precisely the way in which Karl Marx described the development

of class consciousness among workers, the creation and maintenance of "deviant subcultures" of youth.

This youthful population is "available" for recruitment to moral
causes because their marginal, ambiguous position in the social
structure renders them sensitive to moral inconsistencies (note
their talent for perceiving "hypocrisy"), because the major framework of their experience ("education") emphasizes "ideal" aspects
of the culture and because their exclusion from adult responsibilities means that they are generally unrestrained by the institutional ties and commitments which normally function as a brake
upon purely moral feeling; they also have the time for it.

The two great public issues of the decade (the Vietnam war
and the rights of despised minorities) have been especially suited
to enlist the militant predispositions of the young precisely because these issues are clearly moral issues. To take a strong
"position" on these issues requires no great *expertise* or familiarity
with arcane facts. And the moral fervor involved in taking such
a position nicely reflects our traditional age-graded culture to
the extent that it identifies virtue with "idealism," unspoiledness
and innocence, precisely the qualities adults like to associate with
the young.

It is almost as if the young, in the unconscious division of
labor which occurs in all societies, were delegated the role of
"moral organ" of society—what with all the grown-ups being
too busy running the bureaucracies of the world (with their in-
evitable compromises, deals, gives and takes) to concern themselves with "ideals." This even makes a sort of good structural
sense because the unanchored character of the young (that is,
their relative unfetteredness to family, community and career)
fits them to perform their "ideal" functions—in the same sense
and for the same reason that Plato denied normal family life to
his philosopher-kings and the Roman Catholic Church denies it
to their priests.

It is the combination of moral sensitivity and alienation that
accounts both for the extreme juvenophile postures of moral
critics like Edgar Friedenberg, Paul Goodman and John Seeley
(which sometimes reach the belief that the young are simply

better people than the old or middle-aged, and hence even a belief in juvenocracy) and the fear of and hostility toward militant youth by writers epitomized by Lewis Feuer in his new book on student movements. In the latter view, the idealism of the young becomes corrupt, violent, terroristic and destructive precisely because, alienated, detached from institutions, youth are not "responsible"—that is, not accountable for the consequences of their moral zealotry upon the groups and organizations affected by it.

So one is tempted to say that society may just have to accept youth's irresponsibility if it values their moral contributions. But evidence suggests that adult society is in general sympathetic neither to their moral proddings nor toward granting the young any greater responsibility in public affairs. Research by English sociologist Frank Musgrove clearly documents that adults are unwilling to grant real responsibilities any earlier to the young, and there is good reason to believe the same is true in the United States, as is suggested by the repeated failures of the movement to lower the voting age to 18. And as for the "idealism" of youth, when it goes beyond the innocent virtues of praising honesty, being loyal, true and brave and helping old ladies across the street, to serious moral involvements promoting their own group interests ("student power") or those of the domestic or "third world" dispossessed, the shine of their "idealism" is likely to tarnish rather quickly.

Moreover, the moral activism of youth *is* sometimes vulnerable to attack on several counts. The "morality" of a political action, for example, is weakened when it has a self-congratulatory character (and the tendency to produce a holier-than-thou vanity in the actor). It also loses something when it does not involve substantial risk of personal interests of freedom (as it unambiguously *does* with the young only in the case of draft resisters). In the end, along with the society's prolongation of adolescence and encouragement of "the search for identity," continuing praise of the young for their "idealism" (except when it becomes serious) and continuing appeals to them to behave "responsibly"— in the face of repeated refusal to grant them real responsibilities (except in war)—are understandable as parts of the cultural armory supporting the process of juvenilization.

Colleges, universities and their environs are the places apparently designated by society as the primary locations where this armory is to be expended. It is clear that the schools, particularly institutions of higher learning, are increasingly being asked by society to perform a kind of holding operation for it. The major propaganda campaign to encourage students not to drop out of high school is significant less for the jobs which staying that last year or two in high school will qualify one for than it is for the reduced pressure it creates on labor markets unable to absorb unskilled 16- and 17-year-olds. The military institutions, through the draft, help store (and train) much of the working-class young, and the colleges and universities prepare many of the heirs of the middle classes for careers in business, the professions and the semiprofessions. But higher education also gets the lion's share of the identity seekers: those sensitive children of the affluent, less interested in preparing themselves for occupations which the universities are competent to prepare them for than in transcending or trading in the stigmata of their bourgeois backgrounds (work ethic, money-grubbing, status-seeking) for a more "meaningful" life.

It is these students who are heavily represented among the student activists and among whom the cry for "relevance" is heard most insistently. Does it seem odd that this cry should be coming from those students who are *least* interested in the curricula whose relevance is palpable, at least with respect to occupations? Not if one observes that many of these students are, in a sense, classically "intellectuals"—that is, oriented toward statuses or positions for which the universities (as well as other major institutions) have seldom been able or competent to provide certification.

The statuses such students want are those to which one appoints oneself or which one drifts into: artist, critic, writer, intellectual, journalist, revolutionist, philosopher. And these statuses have been undermined for two generations or more by technical and bureaucratic élites whose training has become increasingly specialized and "scientific." In this context the cry for relevance is a protest against technical, value-neutral education whose product (salable skills or the posture of uncommitment) contributes nothing to the search by these students for "identity" and "meaningful experience."

Adding final insult to the injury of the threatened replacement of traditional humanistic intellectuals by technical élites is the ironic transformation of some of their traditional curricula (social sciences particularly) into instruments useful to the "power structure" or "the establishment" in pursuing its own ends. It makes no sense to call a curriculum "irrelevant" and then to turn right around and accuse its chief practitioners of "selling out"; the powerful do not squander their money so easily. The ironic point, then, is not that these curricula are "irrelevant" but that they are far *too* relevant to the support of interests to which the left is opposed.

The villains here are the methodological orthodoxies of the social sciences: their commitment to objectivity, detachment and the "separation" between facts and values. In the view of radical students, these orthodoxies rationalize the official diffidence of social scientists regarding the social consequences of their research, a diffidence which (conveniently—and profitably—for social scientists, goes the argument) promotes the interests of the established and the powerful. This is far from the whole truth, of course. There is plenty of research, supported by establishments, whose results offer the establishment little comfort. But like other "nonpartisan" or value-neutral practices and procedures, the methodological orthodoxies of the social sciences do tend in general to support established interests, simply because the powerful, in command of greater resources and facilities, are better able to make use of "facts" than the weak, and because avoidance of ideological controversy tends to perpetuate the inequities of the status quo.

But the demands for a more activist and "committed" social science and for social scientists to function as advocates for oppressed and subordinated groups may not be the best way of correcting the inequities. A thorough *doctrinal* politicization of social science in the university is likely to mean the total loss of whatever little insulation remains against the ideological controversies rending the larger society; and the probable result would be that the university, instead of being more liberal than the society as a whole, would more accurately reflect the still-burgeoning reactionary mood of the country.

For students who tend to be "around" a university for a long time—the 10-year period mentioned earlier is not uncommon—the university tends to become a kind of "home territory," the place where they really live. They experience the university less as an élite training institution than as a political community in which "members" have a kind of quasi-"citizenship" which, if one believes in democratic process, means a right to a legitimate political voice in its government.*

This conception of the university is quite discrepant with the conception held by most faculty members and administrators. To most faculty members the university is the élite training institution to which students who are both willing and able come to absorb intellectual disciplines—"ologies"—taught by skilled and certified professionals whose competences are defined ·by and limited to those certifications. But which way one sees the university—as a political community or as an élite training institution—is not purely a matter of ideological preference.

The fact seems to be that where training and certification and performance in politically neutral skills are clearest, the more conservative view is virtually unchallenged. This is true not only for dentistry and mathematics but for athletics, too. Presumably many militant blacks are not for any kind of a quota system with respect to varsity teams, and presumably football players in the huddle do not demand a voice in the decisions that shape their lives. But where what one's education confers upon one is a smattering of "high culture" or "civilized manners" or the detached sensibility and ethics of a science whose benefits, like other wealth, are not equitably distributed—in short, where the main result of liberal education is *Weltanschauung*—it indeed has "political" consequences.

---

* Much remains to be clarified about the nature of "membership" in academic communities. So much cant has gone down in the name of "community" that I often feel about this word much like that Nazi who has gone down in history as having said, "When I hear the word 'culture,' I reach for my revolver."

These consequences were not controversial so long as the culture of the university was fairly homogeneous and so long as the "aliens" it admitted were eager to absorb that culture. They have become controversial in recent years because the democratization of higher education has revealed the "class" character of academic culture and because of the appearance on the campus of students who do not share and/or do not aspire to that culture. These newcomers have arrived in sufficiently large numbers to mount a serious challenge to the hegemony of traditional academic culture.

Despite their many differences, the new militant "ethnic" students and their supporters among "white radicals," "street people," hippies and other young people on the left have in common their anti-academicism, which is the campus version of the anti-establishment outlook. This is true notwithstanding the fact that the academy has been the most liberal sector of establishment thought and the most sympathetic to at least some of the aspirations of dissident students. Partly, of course, their hostility to the academy is rooted in the fact that the university is where they're at, the institutional location in which they have to work through their prolonged adolescence and the problems associated with it. But beyond this, there is real conflict between the traditional criteria of academic performance and what dissident students demand from academic life.

Research suggests that most of the white radical students have grown up in a milieu where "intellectual" matters were discussed, where books were probably present in their homes, where middle-class manners and style were their birthright, and where, therefore, they learned how to "talk"—that is, where they developed the sort of verbal facility enabling them to do well enough in high school and to seem like promising "college material" if only because they look and sound much like college students have always looked and sounded. With the ascendence of the view that everybody has a right to a higher education (along with the fact that there's no place else to send well-born adolescents), most of them wind up in colleges and universities.

Some of them, despite their verbal facility, are not really bright; many others, despite their ability to get good college grades, strongly resist "conforming" to many of the requirements for professional certification which they demean as mere "socialization." Confronted by academic demands for rigor in their thinking, for sufficient discipline to master a systematic body of knowledge, for evidence that they can maintain a line of logical thinking beyond one or two propositions, and bring evidence systematically to bear upon a problem, many of them are found seriously wanting—some because they are not bright enough, others because they think it a point of honor to resist the intellectual demands made on them.

When their numbers are large enough to enable them to turn to each other for mutual support, it is not surprising that they should collectively turn against the system of criteria which derogates them and, in a manner not unanalogous to the "reaction formation" of slum delinquents who develop a subculture in opposition to middle-class school norms which judge them inadequate, develop an anti-academic viewpoint which defines abstraction, logical order, detachment, objectivity and systematic thinking as the cognitive armory of a repressive society, productive of alienation, personal rigidity and truncated capacity for feeling.

Preoccupied as most of these students are with "identity problems" and moral protest, it is again not surprising that many of them should be less interested in the mastery of academic disciplines, even if they have the ability, than in pursuing what they are likely to call "gut-issues" or nitty-gritty. The kinds of problems they apparently are interested in studying can be inferred from the examination of almost any "Free University" brochure, and what these add up to is a sort of extension division for the underground: practical, topical "rap sessions" on Vietnam, civil rights, encounter groups, pottery, psychedelics, macrobiotics, Eastern religion, rock music and so on.

In the conflict with the established interests of science and scholarship in the university, radical students do win significant victories. New courses do get approved; experimental curricula do get tried out; students do get appointed to important committees; greater weight is attached to teaching in the appointment and promotion of faculty members. But large numbers of these radical students, exhausted by conflict and depressed by negative criticism, drop out of school. In dropping out, however, they do not immediately disappear into the labor market. They tend to remain in the university community, employed occasionally or part time in dead-end jobs, living in furnished rooms or communal houses near the university, and most important for my purposes here, still participating in the marginal student culture which they know so well.

Their participation in this culture is made possible to some extent by the fact that their youth protects them from the degrading consequences of being poor and having no regular or "approved" status in the community. Part of the age-grading system which postpones adulthood is the temporary protection of the young against the stigmata which, for older people, are normally attached to poverty. But over time, this group of "nonstudents" can be regarded as downward mobile, and thereby hangs an interesting prospect.

The United States has no major tradition of large-scale downward mobility. The only major image of intergenerational decline is associated with decadent aristocratic families in ruined Southern mansions. Given the general tendency for downwardly mobile groups to resent the system which derogates them, and given the fact that the channels of upward mobility today are largely through higher education, the hostility to the university of these radical, middle-class "nonstudents" is probably maintained even after they leave it. The irony is that in dropping out, the hippie and New Left children of the middle classes provide opportunity for the upward mobility of the new black and other ambitious "disadvantaged" students.

The blacks and other ethnic militants are presently using higher education in a manner different from that in which their predecessors from the lower class used it. For earlier ethnics, the university served as a channel of mobility for *individuals* from the talented poor; today, it is sought as a means of collective mobility. There are two aspects to this movement. There is the emphasis on ethnic studies programs designed to provide the members of the respective ethnic groups with a sense of pride in their history and culture, and there are the demands that the university play a more active role in ameliorating suffering in the ghettos, not merely through programs of research which exploit the cooperation of ghetto residents without helping them measurably, but by taking the university off the campus, bringing it to them, in their terms, on their turf, for their own purposes.

In the struggle to achieve the ends of the militants, black and white, the traditional university is very vulnerable because the militants have great leverage. Just as the blacks can conceivably turn the urban core into a guerrilla battleground, militant students can bring the universities to the proverbial grinding halt. Continual rallies, classroom disruptions, picket lines, building seizures, student intimidation and general paranoia (to say nothing of the almost continual meetings by faculty and administration committees to cope with the crises and the continual corridor and coffee room gossip by knots of faculty members) can bring the teaching and other academic functions of the university to a virtual standstill.

This prospect raises seriously for the first time the question of whether the traditional university, as we know it, is an expendable institution. And another question, as well: Is it possible that a decision has been made somewhere that it is better to risk the destruction of the university by confining the unrest to the campus than to allow it to spill over into more critical institutions? Pickets, sit-ins, building seizures and non-negotiable demands are one thing on the campuses. Imagine them at C.B.S. on Madison Avenue: no TV until S.D.S. gets equal time; at the Stock Exchange: the ticker tape does not roll until corporation X gets rid of its South African holdings; at the headquarters of the Bank of America: no depositors get through the doors until interest-free loans are made to renovate the ghettos. There would be machine guns in the streets in no time at all!

In 1969, despite the tear gas and the National Guard, it is still hard to imagine tanks and machine guns used against student radicals so long as their militance is confined to the campus. Because if they do close the universities down, exactly who would miss them? The most practical functions the university performs and its activities which are most directly relevant to the national economy (engineering, science, law, medicine, etc.) could be transferred to the private sector. The beginnings of such a transfer are apparent already in the educational functions carried on by private foundations, institutes and industrial corporations.

And if the departments of English and history and political science and sociology and art and so on closed tight shut tomorrow, who would miss them? Aside from the implication of some social science departments in the military-industrial complex, the studies in humanities and social science departments are civilized luxuries with very few sources of government or business support. The student radicals have little sympathy for them and there is probably even less sympathy for them among the students' severest critics. These days, even conservative legislators, in the same breath that they denounce student militance, will quickly add, "Of course, this doesn't mean that there isn't plenty wrong with the university; there is." And if the student revolution can be bought off by substituting Bob Dylan for Dylan Thomas, Mc-Luhan for Freud, Marcuse for Plato, rock for Bach, black culture for Greek culture, rap sessions for formal examinations, how many will care? Who needs high culture anyway? For the radicals it's an instrument of class oppression, and their oppressors, at least in America, have never been too keen on it anyway, except as a tax dodge.

Short of machine guns in the streets and outright revolution, what one can expect to see over the next decade in academic life is greater adaptation by the university to the new kinds of students it must serve and to the new publics whose anticipated support or hostility it must take into account in its planning. By the new students I mean ghetto youth, middle-class white radicals and the identity seekers. By the new publics I mean those millions of citizens whose taxes support the great state universities but who never thought of the university as "theirs" until its politicization encouraged ambitious politicians to call this fact to their attention. Having once been reminded (by Governor Reagan and others), the voters are not likely to forget it soon.

If it comes about, this adaptation is likely to occur in a manner not dissimilar to that in which the major political parties have adapted to third-party movements in the larger political community: by isolating the *most* radical through the adoption of some of their programs and demands, while at the same time adopting severe and punitive policies toward the more intransigent and violence-prone who are still unsatisfied.

For ghetto youth, then, there will be more ethnic studies programs and compensatory admissions and grading policies and practices and more energetic recruiting of ethnic students and faculty. But there will be less indecision or tolerance in the handling of sit-ins, seizures and other disruptions. For the radicals (ethnic as well as middle-class white), there will be greater emphasis on programs granting academic credit for extension-type activities such as tutoring of ghetto children, neighborhood seminars on consumer savvy and community organization. For the identity seekers there will be more encounter groups, more classes emphasizing "openness and honesty" in dialogue, more experiments with less structured curricula and residential communities, more "retreats," more student-initiated courses on subjects which engage their sense of "relevance" to their interests, from sex to drugs to rock. For all, there will be further loosening of the *in loco parentis* restrictions which hardly anybody in the university believes in anymore, and a little more student power (at least influence) on faculty and administrative committees. All this, combined with a more effective public-relations campaign explaining the mission of the university and its problems in coping with the consequences of prolonged adolescence, may just bring about a semblance of peace on the campus. But without peace in Vietnam, it will be an uneasy peace at best.

There will be opposition. Academic conservatives will see in these new programs the prospect of the dilution or outright abandonment of traditional standards of scholarship. The legitimation of ethnicity, the amelioration of suffering by the poor and the search for identity by the young may all be noble endeavors, they will say, but the major functions of the university are the creation and transmission of systematic bodies of abstract knowledge. Political conservatives will see in these programs harbingers of social changes which they oppose. Militant students imply more leaders and troops for restive ghettos; "the search for identity" and the self-exploratory activities the phrase suggests are redolent of the "liberalism," "permissiveness" and self-indulgence offensive

218 • *Bennett M. Berger*

to the traditional Protestant ethic which "made this country great."

Yet academic conservatives might well be reminded that the university is facing radically transformed constituencies, that academic disciplines which are well institutionalized and "traditional" today were themselves academically born in the blood of earlier periods of such transformations and that they were initially opposed by still more "traditional" fields. Political conservatives might well be reminded that student unrest was not invented by outside agitators, that its source is in social conditions conservatives affirm and that it is not repressible short of military measures. The alternatives to the adaptable university involve blood on the quad and an expendable university.

Part 5

FAMILY PROBLEMS

SINCE THE Introduction discusses an extremely wide range of problems, from overpopulation to inadequate socialization, the selections in this section are limited to only two of these problems. The American family generates many problems of its own, and creates problems for the larger society; but the larger society puts great strains and pressures on the family, as well. This is notably true in divorce. Hugh Carter's article presents some of the basic descriptive facts about divorce, and Morton Hunt attempts to analyze some of the causes of divorce, while focusing far more upon the problem of adjustment after divorce has been accomplished. Since a high percentage of the population is involved in divorce in one way or another, as either spouse or child or as the new spouse of a divorcee, the analysis is relevant to a large segment of the population. Hunt suggests the possibility of accepting divorce fully as one kind of solution for marital problems, but one in which many people need help, both in arranging the divorce and in making their adjustment afterward.

In the last three selections in this section, attention is paid to a major social problem that is created by the continuing high birthrate in the American family system. This rate is much lower than in underdeveloped nations, but the available ecological and demographic evidence now suggests that our population is already too large for our available resources. Of course we can feed our population, but many resources cannot be expanded, such as the water supply, minerals, space, recreation areas and parks, etc. Since we are still unable to face, much less solve, the problem of pollution and garbage disposal, and a rich country produces more of both than a poor country, the result of existing family patterns is to reduce steadily the quality of American life for the future.

Eight Myths About Divorce—and the Facts

by Hugh Carter

THIS YEAR, close to 400,000 couples will be divorced in the United States. The figure is one that many people find alarming, but much of the talk about the divorce problem in America seems to be based on misunderstandings or fallacies. Here are some of the most frequently encountered myths about divorce:

1. The divorce rate is going up rapidly.

The figures do not support this. For more than 20 years nothing drastic has happened to the divorce rate except for a brief, sharp increase caused by the war, followed by a decline. In 1946—when many war marriages ended—the rate was 4.3 per 1,000 of the population, an all-time high. In that year, more than 600,000 couples were divorced. For the next five years the rate fell, reaching 2.5 in 1951. In 1960 the rate was 2.2 per 1,000 of the population, identical with the 1941 rate. Provisional figures point to no drastic change in the rate through 1963. It is true that the rate is higher now than it was 40 years ago; it stood at 1.5 in 1923.

From the *New York Times Magazine,* May 3, 1964, copyright © 1964 by The New York Times Company

2. The divorce rate is about the same in all parts of the United States.

Actually, the rate in the Western states is 3.4 per 1,000 of population—almost four times as high as the rate in the Northeastern states of 0.9. The remainder of the country is in an intermediate position, the rate being 2.1 in the North Central states and 2.8 in the South.

It is true that the rates are affected to some extent by migratory divorce—establishing residence in a state in order to obtain a divorce. Then, too, since most divorcing persons are young adults, the divorce rate depends, in part, on the age distribution of the population. Where there is a heavy concentration of young adults, the divorce rate tends to increase. There are also marked differences in divorce laws and in the strictness with which judicial authorities interpret the laws. However, the differences among the four regions are greater than could be explained by these factors.

There is a good deal of speculation that because the West is a new region its people have a relaxed attitude toward divorce. On the other hand, the South, which has the second highest rate, cannot be considered a new region. The truth is that we really do not know the reason for the regional differences in divorce rates.

3. Most divorces are granted in Reno and similar places.

The evidence indicates that migratory divorces are only a small fraction of the total. *All* Nevada divorces equal less than 3 per cent of the national total. The figures probably seem high because of the great amount of publicity attending them. The majority of divorcing persons cannot afford to establish residence in another state to obtain a divorce. This seems to be true also of divorces for American citizens in Mexico and other foreign countries. From time to time there is a great deal of publicity about divorce mills, but the number of cases involved is small compared with the national total.

4. The third year of marriage is the hardest.

A first glance at divorce statistics may seem to support this myth. In some divorce tables the largest number of divorces is shown after three years of marriage. (In other tables the peak comes after two years, or after one year).

However, the facts are more complicated than appears at first glance. Frequently, because of marital discord, a couple separates, but without serious thought of divorce. Months, or even years, may pass before the beginning of legal action.

After a decision is made for divorce, the plaintiff, usually the wife, consults a lawyer. He, in turn, must inquire into the pertinent facts. If the grounds appear adequate, he prepares the case and has it entered on the appropriate court docket. In due time, the case is heard and the decree granted. All these steps require time—from several months to several years.

An analysis of the statistics and related facts leads one to conclude that the first year of marriage is the hardest, even though the peak in divorces may come after three (or two) years. It also appears from the statistics that each year of marriage is less likely to end in divorce than the immediately preceding year.

5. Having children will prevent divorce.

Latest published statistics show that more than one-half of divorcing couples have children.

Two opposing views are sometimes presented on marital stability and children. On the one hand, children are said to provide a common interest and a focus for family life. On the other hand, children may serve to intensify an existing conflict. In any event, in recent years the proportion of divorcing couples with children has been rising. Whether the number of divorces would have been larger or smaller if there had been more or fewer couples with children is unknown.

6. The wealthy and the highly educated have a higher divorce rate than the poor and those of limited education.

Although comprehensive national statistics are not available on this point, a number of excellent research publications indicate that the higher professional and business groups have the lowest divorce rates, while the highest divorce rate is found among working-class families. The great publicity attending divorce actions of wealthy and prominent persons may account for the popular myth that these groups have the highest divorce rate.

7. Because of the high divorce rate, there are enormous numbers of divorced persons in the population.

Census figures do not support this view. A 1962 sample survey indicated about 3 million divorced persons—that is, about one divorced person in the population to every 29 married persons.

Remarriage, of course, is the main reason for the relatively small number of divorced persons. In the same survey, the Census Bureau reported more than 14 million persons who had been married more than once. Some had been widowed, but the majority had been divorced.

8. Divorced persons are less likely to remarry than are the widowed.

Just the opposite is true: About three out of four remarriages involve a divorced person. The reason is the early age of most couples at the time of divorce. Age at widowhood has been advancing in recent years and the likelihood of marriage declines with age. Most remarriages of persons past 55 years of age are of the widowed; however, the majority of remarriages occur at younger ages and involve divorced persons.

While it is easy to point out some of the obvious misinformation about divorce—the myths—it is not easy to obtain the comprehensive facts the importance of the subject warrants. An insurance actuary estimates the risk of death from a study of death statistics. Excellent divorce statistics would make it possible to calculate the risk of divorce from such facts as age at marriage, differences between ages of husband and wife, number of previous marriages and whether they were dissolved by divorce or death.

Unfortunately, persons interested in the stability of family life cannot get the needed facts from official sources. With considerable chagrin, after years of working to improve them, I must make it clear that the United States is far behind most countries of Western Europe in the accuracy of its divorce statistics.

Why is this true? For one thing, the vital statistics (including divorce statistics) of the United States are different from the national censuses of population. The latter are provided for in the Constitution as a responsibility of the Federal Government. Vital statistics are a responsibility of the states.

Early in this century births and deaths were not fully reported. That they are now is the result of a campaign led by public-health specialists and leading physicians. Similarly, the American Bar Association has urged its members to support the central registration of divorces. Leading social scientists in the 28 states not now participating in the Divorce Registration Area program are actively urging their states to join. It can be hoped that it will not be long until all 50 states are cooperating. Then there will be fewer myths and more solid facts about divorce.

Help Wanted: Divorce Counselor

by Morton M. Hunt

WHEN NEW YORK'S legislators drafted the new divorce law that becomes effective next September, they wrote into it a feature many people think of as modern and in tune with the times—a conciliation program designed to save as many disintegrating unions as possible through marriage counseling. This program is currently under fire, but only on the grounds of administrative complexity; what no one has admitted is that it is about as modern as the Welsbach mantle and about as attuned to the times as the matchlock harquebus. Not that conciliation is a bad thing in itself—but if the legislators had been genuinely responsive to the needs of modern citizens, they would have created not just a marriage counseling service, but its even more valuable obverse, a divorce counseling service.

If any legislator thought of it, however, he kept his peace. To espouse divorce counseling would be tantamount to saying that divorce is as valid and as moral an alternative to marital conflict as conciliation, and that people should be aided—at public expense—in choosing and carrying out that alternative; a legislator would as soon wear his hair shoulder-length or come out in

From the *New York Times Magazine,* January 1, 1956, copyright © 1956 by The New York Times Company favor of legalizing pot. Western Christian society has never admitted the possibility that marriage-until-death might be no better as a way of life—and might in many circumstances be worse—than marriage-divorce-remarriage. For roughly 1,000 years, divorce was totally impossible within Christendom, and after the Reformation it was permissible even in the Protestant nations only under very stringent circumstances, and always as the last and worst of possible choices.

In the United States divorce has become common and easy to obtain only in the last two generations, and our thoughts and feelings about it have not yet caught up to the realities of our behavior; on the surface, most of us are now tolerant and permissive toward divorcing people, but deep inside we still tend to be critical and disapproving of them. We have not yet opened our minds to the possibilities that divorce may be a creative rather than destructive act, that it may be a better choice for all concerned (including the children) than trying to repair a defunct marriage, and that divorcing people should be aided rather than impeded in their efforts to make the break and to live successfully in the post-marital world.

Such suggestions still cause in most Americans an immediate visceral "No"—the product not of reasoning, but of cultural conditioning; people "know" that such ideas are wrong and bad, even as certain primitive peoples "know" that it is evil and dangerous for a man to utter his mother-in-law's name or for a woman to step across her husband's pillow. One does not argue about such things; what is right is right, what is wrong is wrong, because it has always been so and because everyone knows it to be so.

No wonder, then, that the new divorce law of New York State empowers justices to force participants in a divorce action to submit to anywhere from one session to as much as a 60-day period of marital counseling—but offers the litigants no help, if they really want a divorce, in obtaining it with a minimum of emotional damage to themselves and their children. The new "liberal" law says, in effect, that all marriages should be saved, if possible, and that the effort to save them should be forced on people. This is, at the very least, unrealistic since it is a truism of psychotherapy that an unwilling patient is almost always impervious to therapy; if his goals are radically unlike those of the therapist, treatment is almost bound to fail.

In the case of people whose marriages have deteriorated enough for them to have begun legal action, the goal the great majority of them desire is escape, not reconciliation. Surveys made in two Midwestern states show that three out of four couples filing for divorce go through with it, while only one quarter withdraw their suits (many of the latter, it is likely, reinstituting them again later). Even more significant is the experience of the "Friend of the Court," an official agency in Detroit which offers marriage counseling on a voluntary basis to every couple filing for divorce in Wayne County; in 1965, although some 11,000 couples filed for divorce and were offered counseling designed to prevent it, only 401 couples accepted the offer—and only about a quarter of these were actually reconciled.

None of which is a criticism of marriage counseling per se, which has a pretty fair record with people who seek help earlier in the conflict process; it does, however, strongly suggest that our belief that all crumbling marriages should be saved is archaic, and that we are seriously at fault for not yet having provided any social mechanism to help people dissolve moribund marriages and adjust to post-marital life.

Professionals in the field, to be sure, have been aware of the need for divorce counseling for some time: sociologist William J. Goode first suggested it in an article in a professional journal 19 years ago, and quietly (and rather guiltily) a small but growing number of marriage counselors and psychotherapists have been adopting the view that where a bad marriage seems unlikely ever to become satisfying and reasonably free of conflicts, it is proper to help the client get out of it.

But most practitioners still speak of this as though it were making the best of failure, as if it were the counsel of despair, the inferior alternative. The moral distortion in this outlook is immediately apparent if we compare it to that of the physician whose patient has, say, a duodenal ulcer: the physician will try to cure it with drugs, diet control, and even psychotherapy—but if all these prove ineffective, and major surgery is necessary to save the patient's life or restore his health, neither the patient nor the doctor views the operation as an act of "failure" or as a somewhat disreputable alternative, but merely as a drastic one.

So it could be with divorce counselors: they would be the surgeons of marriage, wielding the knife when necessary, but managing the operation so as to minimize the damage, speed the convalescence, and maximize the chance of the patient's full health. Lacking such help at present, millions of people remain in unhappy and damaging marriages, unable to muster the courage to break away from them. Those who do break away usually manage to remake their lives afterward, but at immense cost in wasted time and needless pain. Although the great majority do eventually remarry, more than half of them require four or more years (from the time of separation) to regain enough hope and trust to commit themselves a second time.

Divorce counseling, as I envision it in practice in the future, would require thorough professional training in social casework technique or clinical psychology, plus special knowledge of divorce law, child psychology, and the sociology of the postmarital world—a segment of American life that I consider virtually a subculture, with its own attitudes, mores, institutions, and goals.

The divorce counselor (who might also be a marriage counselor) would first of all ascertain the real goals of his client and the degree of health or illness in the marital relationship: if the client's real desire (conscious or unconscious) were to repair the marriage, and if it seemed reparable, the divorce counselor would either undertake that task himself or refer the client to another specialist.

Very often, of course, he would find the client ambivalent, wanting both to escape and to remain married. But many a time the desire to remain married would be the product of guilt: a great many unhappily married Americans still believe that they should stay together, whatever their marital unhappiness, "for the sake of the children." Yet the evidence painstakingly gathered by social psychologists points to the precise opposite; almost every serious investigator of the subject has found that children, however distressed they are at first by the breakup of the home, are in the end less damaged by divorce than by the continuance of a bad parent relationship.

The sociologist F. Nye compared a large group of adolescents from broken homes with another large group from unhappy intact homes; it was the latter, not the former, who showed more delinquent behavior, poorer adjustment to the parents, and more psychosomatic ailments. Even more striking is a recent study by sociologist Lee Burchinal, comparing grade-school students whose parents had been divorced with students from the whole spectrum of intact homes (happy and unhappy). Dr. Burchinal could find no significant differences in the emotional health of the two groups. It is indisputable that children of divorce have emotional problems, but so do children of happy homes; the assumption that the physical and behavioral problems of children of divorce have been caused by the divorce is based not on real evidence but on the cultural premise that divorcing people are self-indulgent, sinful, and guilty of wrongdoing.

It would be the divorce counselor's task to educate his client to the facts, and so free him or her to make a truly rational choice to divorce or not to divorce. Especially, he would try to help the client see himself or herself more accurately, without the dreadful distortions of the marital conflict, and more nearly as he or she would seem in other, healthier circumstances. For some, simple reassurance would be enough; others might need many hours of psychotherapeutic repair. But the goal in either case would be enough strengthening of the ego to allow the client to let go of the wreckage and begin to swim. Without professional ego-support, many people are never able to do so, or tragically waste years in which they could have made and enjoyed a better marriage. John Cuber and Peggy Harroff, in their study of upper-middle-class marital patterns, "The Significant Americans," find that the actual decision to divorce often comes only after three, four, or even more years of knowing that the relationship is doomed.

In some cases, the fear of divorce might be based on practical problems—the question of money, the effects of divorce on one's career, or ostracism by the community. All these are down-to-earth matters about which the counselor could advise the client—yet quite often, even these seemingly practical and realistic problems are a facade for deeper fears. Consider the matter of money: people often say they have postponed divorce because they cannot afford to live in separate homes—yet in actual fact, and in spite of the cliché that "desertion is the poor man's divorce," low-income families are about twice as prone to legal divorce as those of average or above-average income. If lack of money does not hold the lower-class marriages together, it cannot be the real reason among the middle class; not basic financial problems, but the social meaning of reducing one's standard of living, is what inhibits them.

Some of the fears that bind people to unhappy marriage can be rather quickly dispelled by information when the informant has the special authoritative relationship of a counselor toward his client. One man, for instance, remained married to a frigid and extremely destructive woman for nearly 10 years because he considered himself too poor a lover ever to win another woman; his grounds for this belief were his wife's continual hints that he was sexually inadequate because he could delay himself no more than half an hour in the sexual act. Nothing he heard or read to the contrary reassured him. When his psychotherapist told him that his performance was not only adequate but remarkable, he was astonished, relieved, and then proud. He now felt free at last to believe in himself and to search for a better marriage.

Wherever the divorcing person is unsure of how to behave in his new situation, the educational aspects of divorce counseling can have profound effects with relatively little effort. One of the common difficulties in this respect is what to tell the children (in the Northeast, almost 70 per cent of divorcing couples have minor children). There is no "right" formula, of course, but there is a series of attitudes and caveats that minimize the emotional damage.

It is helpful, for instance, to be on the lookout for one's own guilt-produced tendency to offer longer and deeper explanations to children than they are equipped to accept, the net effect of which is only to bewilder and trouble them. What they need are answers matched to the level of their own questions—simple answers patiently and tirelessly repeated, reassurances patiently and tirelessly given that it is not the child who caused the break, not the child who is being avoided by the departing parent.

Even more important is a clear recognition of the child's need to love both parents, and of the intolerable hurt when either one says anything denigrating or harsh to him about the other. But it is not enough to get the client to see that he must not say bitter or destructive things about his ex-mate to the children; he must also be led to see that actions are as dangerous as words. A woman may require her ex-husband to wait outside when he comes to pick up the children for his weekly visit; the children understand her terrible unspoken comment, and it makes them almost ill. A man encourages his children to break all their usual rules about eating and sleeping when they visit him; they go home and fall into tantrums and fits of tears, because they feel within themselves his implied hostility to their mother.

As important as education in what to expect of the children is education in what to expect of oneself as a result of divorce. The divorce counselor would carefully prepare his client for the bewildering and even frightening feelings that so often accompany separation—the excruciating loneliness (even in those who longed to escape), the waves of indefinable anxiety, the recurrent sense of being lost, the upsurge of desire to rush back, at whatever cost, into the bad marriage.

All these symptoms are normal and, in healthy people, temporary, and it is immensely reassuring and relieving to be prepared for them in advance, and to be told again when they occur that they are quite usual under the circumstances. The same is true of physical symptoms; many newly separated people are alarmed by their own sleeplessness, lack of appetite, tremor of the hands, skin eruptions, inability to concentrate, and the like; it would be most helpful, at this time, to be told by a divorce counselor that these things are both common and transitory. Indeed, the counselor might even offer more positive encouragement: in the course of interviewing a large number of separated and divorced people for my recently published book, I found a majority of them reporting that after a few months of adjustment to separation, they were sleeping and eating better, feeling and looking younger, and having greater work capacity and sexual drive than they did in the latter stages of the failed marriages.

Both before and after the actual separation, the divorce counselor would help the Formerly Married—my own term for the population composed of the separated and the actually divorced— to see in over-all perspective the process they can expect to experience in postmarital life. Under normal circumstances, they will have to grieve for the dead love, even as one grieves for a dead lover, before they can feel new feelings for someone else; gradually they will test out their capacity for new feeling, entering into transient and very superficial relationships at first, and then into longer and deeper ones.

At first, the very thought of meeting people or going on dates may be frightening or disconcerting; for women in particular, the thought of having to handle sexual approaches may well be a source of anxiety. The woman who has led the somewhat sheltered life of marriage for years may be astonished, if not horrified, that suddenly she is considered fair game and quite boldly approached by married men—neighbors, husbands of friends, business acquaintances—who treat her as an easy mark and a desperate case; an advance briefing would help her prepare to deal deftly with this common experience and with her own feelings about it.

The divorce counselor, having alerted the novice to this sort of thing, may well try to make her or him see, however, that genuine interaction with appropriate partners is the road to recovery. Dating, infatuations, sexual experiences and genuine love relationships all play a central role in the adjustment to postmarital life; it is through rediscovering one's potential and exercising one's capacities that one is restored to complete health. Among the separated and divorced, a great many report that it was the trial-and-error experience of sex and love in postmarital life that taught them capacities in themselves they had not even known in marriage, brought them some measure of exhilaration and *joie de vivre,* and prepared them for a second and more meaningful marital relationship.

The divorce counselor will, to be sure, temper such advice according to his client's ethnic and religious background; in some areas of the country, and among some religious groups, any sanction given to sex outside of marriage—even among the divorced—would be immensely upsetting, and probably would be rejected out of hand, along with everything else the counselor had said.

Even in more permissive and sophisticated parts of the country, the Formerly Married need to be advised that their sexual and emotional experiences are not really acceptable to most married people; in effect, the Formerly Married need to be advised what social role they must play. As things now stand, it is chiefly by blundering and testing that they learn that their married friends will sympathize with their sorrows but resent and disapprove of their newfound joys. Relief, delight in one's freedom, the rediscovery of sensuality, the experience of infatuations and new loves —all these are hard for the married to tolerate in their formerly married friends; the result is that the married become critical and an unhappy estrangement results. A careful briefing of the newly separated person as to the role he or she must be prepared to play would avoid at least some of that alienation.

For many of the Formerly Married, all this will seem rather academic; they would gladly suffer the disapproval of their married friends if they could only find suitable unmarried people to do disapproved things with. The high divorce rate is so recent a phenomenon that our society has not yet developed any officially sanctioned marketplace in which separated and divorced people can meet and choose new partners.

But a number of makeshift mechanisms have recently come into existence, and the divorce counselor, though he cannot play the part of social director or matchmaker, could at least alert the client to their existence. He will tell them, for instance, that in addition to such standard methods as referral by friends, there now are numerous social organizations of the Formerly Married and the never-married; there are tennis clubs, ski clubs, cruises, resort hotels, dance studios, literary clubs, and public dances, all catering to just such people; many churches are beginning to organize special events for the unmarried; and even the computer-dating craze now sweeping the major cities may be useful to some venturesome ex-marrieds.

I envision the divorce counselor as, in part, a therapist and, in part, an advice-giver, to whom the formerly married man or woman may return from time to time for a consultation whenever some new crisis arises for which he or she is unprepared.

It may be, for instance, that divorce negotiations drag on interminably, with much bitterness developing; the counselor may then help by pointing out to the client that he, or his ex-mate, is making impossible demands, not to be vengeful, but in order to put off the dreadful finality of it all—to hold on, in other words, to the shreds of the relationship. If the client himself is doing this, he may then let go; if his ex-mate is doing it, he may be better able to cope with it.

Or it may be that from time to time the sexual experimentations and uncertainties of the special world of the Formerly Married will produce upsets that counseling can help with. All of these are matters which the skilled counselor could handle with special effectiveness because of his knowledge of the divorce process, in the context of which he regards such problems as normal, usually temporary, and not very serious, after all.

The need to love and be loved, and the pressure to fit into a society composed of married couples, eventually lead six out of seven of the divorced to remarry. But it takes years for most of them to come to this point—and even so, two-fifths of their second marriages again end in divorce.

Divorce counseling, I believe, could avoid much of the misery involved in the actual break, shorten the interregnum between the old love and the new, and maximize the chances of success in the second marriage. It will take a courageous—perhaps even foolhardy—legislator, philanthropist, or agency director to violate our national shibboleths and publicly sponsor a Division of Divorce Counseling, but such a man would deserve the gratitude of his society for an act genuinely contributing to the American ideal of happy marriage.

300,000,000 Americans Would Be Wrong

by David E. Lilienthal

BY THE YEAR 2000, just one generation away, the population of the United States will probably be about 300 million—100 million higher than it is now and 200 million higher than it was in 1920. Yet, in comparison with many underdeveloped nations, population growth would not seem to be a serious problem in America.

Certainly this vastly increased population will not lack for food. While population growth in Latin America, for example, has brought per capita food production below pre-World War II levels, we in the U.S. worry about overweight, spend huge sums to restrict farm production and give away enough food to prevent famine in poor nations throughout the world. In contrast to less developed nations, we have enough space, too. Just fly over this country and see the huge, sparsely populated areas that could easily accommodate additional tens of millions.

Great differences in resources, technology and education help explain why Americans regard overpopulation as a menace only to other peoples. It can't happen here, they think. I used to think so, too; I don't any more.

From the *New York Times Magazine*, January 9, 1966, copyright © 1966 by The New York Times Company

During the past 10 years, much of it spent overseas, I came to the easy conclusion that if we succeeded in tripling or quadrupling food production in hungry nations—and in some areas in which I worked we did just that—the problem of overpopulation could be solved. But gradually I learned I was mistaken to believe that increased food production was the complete answer to the crisis of population abroad. Gradually, I also learned that America's overflowing cornucopia has obscured a deeper crisis developing here: a population of at least 300 million by 2000 will, I now believe, threaten the very quality of life of individual Americans.

An additional 100 million people will undermine our most cherished traditions, erode our public services and impose a rate of taxation that will take current taxes seem tame. The new masses, concentrated (as they will be) in the already strangling urban centers, cannot avoid creating conditions that will make city life almost unbearable. San Francisco, to take a still tolerable example, once was one of my favorite cities—cosmopolitan, comfortable, lovely. Now the high-rise buildings have sprouted like weeds and suburban blight is advancing on the Golden Gate. The value of real estate has increased while people's enjoyment of life declines.

Historically the United States owes much of its vigor and power to population growth. (Only 50 million people rattled around in America in 1880.) Large markets, skilled manpower, huge factories, a country able to spend billions on war, space and social welfare—all this, plus 75 million passenger cars—is surely a consequence of rising population. But no economy and no physical environment can sustain infinite population growth. There comes a point at which a change in quantity becomes a change in quality—when we can no longer speak of "more of the same." And another 100 million people will, I fear, make just that change in the joy of life in America.

It is probably true that as the population will grow, so will the dollar value of our output. U.S. wealth, measured by Gross National Product, is now $670 billion; barring a major economic setback, total output will be doubled in about two decades. With G.N.P. climbing at the rate of $40 billion a year, the U.S. probably can afford to build the schools, housing projects, roads and other necessities of life for 300 million Americans.

But if our resources are mainly spent merely to survive, to cope with life in a congested America, then where is the enjoyment of living? Our teeming cities are not pleasant places today; imagine them by the middle of the next century when the areas of some might be 100 times larger than they are now. This is the real possibility envisioned by Roger Revelle, director of the newly established Center for Population Studies at the Harvard School of Public Health. And it will be to the cities that tomorrow's millions will flock. Or consider the picture, drawn with characteristic wit, by economist John Kenneth Galbraith: "It is hard to suppose that penultimate Western man, stalled in the ultimate traffic jam and slowly succumbing to carbon monoxide will be especially enchanted to hear from the last survivor that in the preceding year Gross National Product went up by a record amount."

Nor does the nightmare consist only of traffic jams and a bumper-to-bumper way of life. As we have seen in the history of the last 25 years, public services only the Federal Government can provide will continue to expand. Moreover, state governments, until now unable (or unwilling) to pay their share of the bills, show signs of awakening to their responsibilities. But bigger government efforts do not produce better results for human beings: they are simply a way of getting a job done when no more feasible methods exist.

Even today, most of the nation's most serious problems are caused largely by the pressures of a too rapidly rising population. In the next generation, the problems may become unmanageable. Take four basic needs: education, water, air and power.

The quality of education is closely related to the problem of numbers. Within the next five years, we are told, the number of high school students will rise to 15 million (a 50 per cent increase over 1960), forcing hundreds of communities to consider imposing stiff new taxes. Many taxpayers will refuse to accept the added burden and their children will attend even more crowded classes. Far-sighted citizens will approve new school bond issues, but the increased financial drain probably will not result in an improved education.

Our standard of democracy entitles everyone to free schooling through high school. But our educational standards are rising. Two-year junior colleges, many of them supported by cities and states, loom as the next step in our system of free, universal education. Along with the surge in enrollment at traditional four-year colleges and universities, higher education is expected to attract about 12 million students in 1980 (triple the 1960 figure).

Merely building the physical facilities for such huge increases is a formidable prospect. Creating a sympathetic atmosphere for education, and filling the need for qualified teachers is a much more staggering problem. Of course, we may argue for the radical reform of U.S. education. We may plead for overhauling the existing system of teacher training, as James B. Conant has eloquently done. But I see few signs we are about to undertake such vast changes in the machinery of U.S. education; nor does it seem possible, even if the mood for drastic reform was overwhelming, simply to order new procedures, new goals and new solutions and then put them into practice. Good teachers cannot be turned out by fiat. We do not live in a planner's paradise. Ask Robert Moses.

With increased urbanization and industrialization, demands on the water supply will be much greater than most Americans have remotely imagined. The drought in the northeast United States last summer was an indication of shortages even greater to come. And though engineers and scientists can, and will, tap new sources of water and devise ways to purify polluted rivers like the Hudson, the cost will be fantastic—hundreds of billions of dollars. Add to the current strain the pressure of a 50 per cent increase in population and the result may well be a chronic water shortage that can hardly be solved at any tolerable price.

Imaginative but impractical water schemes have been proposed, such as one to bring to the United States the almost limitless supply of far northern water, carrying it a thousand miles and more to our own boundaries. Assuming that Canada would agree to the politically prickly diversion of her waters, the cost is estimated in the neighborhood of $100-billion. But it has taken more than a generation of hot dispute and interminable litigation to decide priorities of water among our own sister states of the West. How much greater the difficulties of diverting Canada's water to care for U.S. needs?

As for nuclear-powered desalination plants, quite apart from the cost of constructing the huge installations we would need and the pipelines to carry the water inland, there is the additional problem of safety in disposing of radioactive waste. Technicians may solve the problem, but at what social cost? The conversion of precious open spaces into atomic garbage dumps?

Just as easily accessible water supplies dwindle, air pollution will increase. Air pollution is the result of congestion, industrialization and the multiplication of automobiles—factors in direct relation to population density in urban areas. Los Angeles is not an industrial city, yet at times its air is hardly fit to breathe. And with the spread of industry in the sprawling cities of the nation, more and more places will be Los Angelized.

We have long assumed that at least the air we breathe is free. It won't be for much longer as we expand our efforts to purify the atmosphere. In California, for example, an aroused public finally insisted that automobile manufacturers install exhaust filters to trap toxic chemicals. Keeping automobile fumes and industrial poisons out of the air we breathe is going to be an increasingly costly business. By the year 2000 the high cost of breathing will be a real issue, not just a phrase.

Packing too many people into an urban area increases the cost of providing still another essential of everyday living: electric power. Even more serious, such concentrations of people may make absolutely reliable electric service more and more difficult to maintain. I doubt if it was a mere coincidence, for example, that New York City needed 10 hours to restore electricity after the recent Northeast power failure while smaller communities were able to turn on their lights in a much shorter time. Growth is desirable up to a point; then the advantage of size diminishes and the multiplication of complexity multiplies the headaches. And by 1980 we can expect at least a 300 per cent increase in the nation's electrical energy needs. Most of this will flow into urban areas. The present difficulties of maintaining absolutely reliable service to such concentrations of people and industry, and holding down costs, will thus be magnified.

As chairman of T.V.A. and the Atomic Energy Commission, and in my present work in Asia and Latin America, I have become familiar with the problems of producing and distributing electricity on a large scale. Indeed, it was T.V.A. a generation ago that pioneered the concept that the greater the use of electricity the lower the cost per kilowatt hour. This is still generally true. But for great cities the exact contrary is coming to pass. To *distribute* electricity in a large, densely populated area such as New York is more costly than in smaller urban markets. Huge generating power plants produce ever lower generating costs; but to bring this power to the consumer in massive concentrations of population grows more and more expensive. Consequently, the price of this essential of modern life probably will go up in the great cities as population growth continues.

Without realizing it, we are fast approaching what may be called the population barrier beyond which lie unpredictability and, I fear, problems of unmanageable size. Consider, for example, the relationship between population growth and the poor.

The Federal Aid to Dependent Children program has doubled to more than four million cases during the last decade, while the costs have soared from about $600 million to more than $1.8 billion. Even more depressing than the numbers of families who cannot survive without welfare assistance is the phenomenon known as the "cycle of dependency."

More than 40 per cent of parents whose children receive A.D.C. funds themselves had parents who received relief checks. This cycle is sad but not surprising. Poor people tend to have more children than they want or can afford, and the children have less chance to receive the education and training they need to break the pattern. Thus, even the third generation appears on relief rolls in the U.S., the most socially mobile nation in the world. In America, reports the National Academy of Sciences in a recent study, "The Growth of U.S. Population," "the burden of unwanted children among impoverished and uneducated mothers . . . is much like that experienced by mothers in underdeveloped countries."

Since the poor cannot contribute their share of the mounting costs of education, medical care, public housing and similar necessary government enterprises, the money must be supplied by the rest of the population through taxation. But the most painful loss is not measured in dollars but in human resources. And one measure of the potential loss is the fact that one-fourth of America's children are the offspring of poor parents.

Belatedly, we are helping poor couples who need and want financial and medical help in family planning. The White House Conference on Health in November gave high priority to birth control as part of Federal efforts to halt the cycle of dependency and poverty. Tax-supported activities in 40 states, combined with such large-scale private efforts as Harvard's Center for Population Studies and the $14.5 million grant by the Ford Foundation for basic research by the Columbia-Presbyterian Medical Center and the Population Council, herald new progress in a long-neglected field.

We tend to patronize the poor by preaching to them about birth control; though poverty-stricken parents with four, five or six children are the most publicized aspect of population growth, they are by no means the most important numerical aspect of the problem. As a matter of simple arithmetic, the four-fifths of the nation's families who earn more than the poverty-line income of $3,000 a year—and who can afford two, three or four children—produce a greater total of children than the one poor couple out of five which may have six youngsters.

In fact, the latest census information reveals that though poor families may have more children than do better-off families, the difference is much smaller than many people believe. According to the National Academy of Sciences analysis, in 1960 married women 40 to 44 years old in families with incomes below $4,000 and above $4,000 differed in the average number of children by less than one. The postwar baby boom, for example, was more pronounced among middle- and upper-income families than among the poor.

Thus, these relatively well-off families are the ones mainly responsible for our rapidly rising population curve. They and their children are the ones who will account for most of the 100 million additional Americans by the end of the century.

How many children a couple should have is a decision only they should make; a government inducement or deterrent—a tax, for example—is morally repugnant and politically impossible. We cannot penalize the poor in order to limit the size of their families while we allow more prosperous parents to have as many children as they want. The large majority of middle- and upper-class parents need no birth-control help from government, nor will they welcome outside advice on so personal a matter. Yet it is this group of families who will want to have three, four or more children for the very natural reason that they like children and can afford to support them. The question is, can the *country* support them?

Any notion that The Pill or some other scientific device is the sole and complete answer is very dubious. At a symposium on birth control not long ago, Dr. Stephen J. Plank, a professor in the Harvard School of Public Health, cautioned against "the facile assumption . . . that we may be able to contracept our way to the Great Society." Birth control, he said, is a question of motivation rather than technology alone.

The neglected arithmetic of the population problem facing us is depressing. Look at this table showing the birth and death rates over the past quarter-century in the United States:

Year	Births	Rate (per 1,000 pop)	Deaths	Rate (per 1,000 pop)
1940	2,360,399	17.9	1,417,269	10.8
1945	2,735,456	19.5	1,401,719	10.6
1950	3,554,149	23.6	1,452,454	9.6
1955	4,047,295	24.6	1,528,717	9.3
1960	4,257,850	23.7	1,711,982	9.5
1964	4,027,490	21.0	1,798,051	9.4

Although the birth rate has been declining since the mid-50's, while the death rate has remained relatively stable, the drop in the birth rate is too little and too late to prevent an oversized population. The surge in the number of births over deaths continues (2.3 million were added to the population in 1964).

Or examine these low and high population projections prepared by the Census Bureau:

	Low	High
1970	206,000,000	211,000,000
1985	248,000,000	276,000,000
2010	322,000,000	438,000,000

The high figure would be reached if birth rates returned to the levels of the early 1950's. The low estimate—enormous as it is—is based on the possibility that the rates may decline by 1985 to the comparatively low levels of the early World War II years.

One theoretical way out of the dilemma would be to say that since America can no longer sustain complete "family freedom," some form of compulsory birth control is, regrettably, necessary. It would not be the first time in our history that government intervened to restrain individual impulse in the name of collective welfare. Yet, where children and parents are concerned, I do not believe we can yet advocate the sacrifice of one freedom for the sake of preserving another. Such a "solution" would make no sense at all, theoretically, practically or ethically.

Government policies and private programs must make plain the kind of life we all face if economically comfortable families reproduce at rates they personally can afford. With equal urgency we must make plain the dangers if poor families have children in numbers they cannot afford.

Obviously, a stationary population—one in which the birth rate matches the death rate—is out of the question for many years to come. It is probably not feasible, nor even desirable. All we can hope to achieve is a slower rise in the size of our population rather than the present steep increase. What is needed is a far more drastic cut in the birth rate—a voluntary curtailment of the right to breed. It is needed, but I have no great conviction that it will happen.

For though scientific ingenuity may be able to solve many of the technological problems, we are only beginning to understand people always change more slowly than technology. It is easier, after all, to design a new industrial process than redesign a cultural tradition. Yet that is the order of change we face if we are to preserve life's dignity and quality. Confronted by the crisis of population growth, we must, at present, appeal to private conscience for the sake of the general good.

Birth Rates Strain Developing Economies

by Juan de Onís

UNITED NATIONS, N. Y.

PRESIDENT ARTHUR da Costa e Silva of Brazil, where the economy is growing at a strong 6 per cent this year, lamented recently to a diplomatic visitor that the benefits of this growth are being diluted by a soaring population.

"If we didn't have so many more new people each year, we would rapidly be approaching decent living standards for everyone," he said.

Brazil, with a population of nearly 90 million, is growing at a rate of 3.5 per cent a year. This means a doubling of the population in 20 years.

Even with very strong economic growth performance, the increase in the size of the productive pie must be shared among so many new people that the benefits per capita are meager. Living standards remain low, and frustrations rise.

This is what Robert S. McNamara, President of the International Bank for Reconstruction and Development, called today

From the *New York Times,* October 1, 1968, copyright © 1968 by The New York Times Company

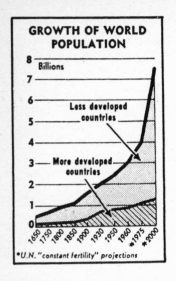

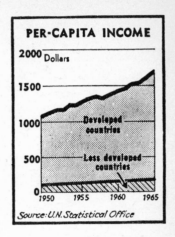

a "crippling effect" on the growth aspirations of developing countries where population is growing rapidly.

In announcing that the bank, for the first time, was prepared to finance national family-planning programs, Mr. McNamara opened an important new front in the international campaign to assist developing countries that want help in controlling their population growth.

There has been growing recognition in this decade that population growth represents a global problem of explosive potential. The present world population of 3.5 billion is expected to double by the end of this century.

Since the largest part of this increase by far will be in developing countries, which have per capita incomes of less than $300 a year, the population explosion threatens to aggravate the existing "poverty gap" between these countries and the wealthier, industrialized nations, where per capita income, as in the United States, exceeds $3,000 a year.

The massive distribution of modern drugs, particularly antibiotics, combined with higher levels of nutrition and sanitary medicine, such as malaria control, have brought a dramatic decline in death rates in developing countries.

This has not been accompanied, as yet, by any significant decline in birth rates. In developing nations, births annually run from 40 to 50 per 1,000 persons, compared with 17 to 20 per 1,000 in industrialized countries.

As a result, the poorest nations must spend the most proportionately on schools or medical facilities, instead of factories, roads or agriculture.

The only way to effectively cut the population growth rate, in the opinion of demographers and medical men, is to intensify greatly the national family-planning programs, usually with Government support.

Experts consider the use of modern contraceptives, such as the "pill," essential to achieve as strong an effect on birth control as the "wonder drugs" had in reducing mortality.

The International Planned Parenthood Federation, a private group that has pioneered in this field, maintains voluntary family-planning programs in some 60 countries, but the scope of the problem and the financial requirements are so large that public programs are considered vital.

Since 1968, the United Nations has officially recognized the problem, and has set up a population division, but it lacks resources. But the World Bank, which announced today it would enter the field, does have large resources and international experience in development financing.

The United States Government's assistance in international population programs has grown sharply—from $2-million in 1966 to $35-million this year for programs in 25 countries, the Pan-American Health Organization and the United Nations, as well as the Planned Parenthood Federation and other organizations.

Congress has approved a $50-million authorization for next year, and has authorized the distribution of contraceptive materials under United States-financed programs and the employment of funds generated by the sale of United States food in developing countries for local population programs.

The biggest United States-supported program is in India, where

$8-million in grants and $40-million from food sales are backing the national program.

The World Bank's program will supplement the United States international population efforts for countries that request family-planning assistance.

Family Planning
Is Called Futile

by Robert Reinhold

BERKELEY

"I CALL IT collective gold displacement," Kingsley Davis, the population expert, said with a sneer. "The Federal Government is spending millions of dollars under the illusion it is getting population control. All it is getting is bad advice."

Professor Davis, director of International Population and Urban Research at the University of California at Berkeley, reflects a growing conviction among demographers that "family planning" programs are a hopelessly futile means of controlling population explosion.

"The Government says all you need is 100 per cent effective birth control devices—this is nonsense," says the 61-year-old father of three. "You cannot just duck out and think by some technological gimmick you are going to solve the problem—the basic motivation to have children is very strong in society."

Unless this motivation is undermined by making large families undesirable or impossible, he believes, the availability of more and better contraceptives will do little to stem population growth.

To support this view, he cites evidence developed at Berkeley

From the *New York Times,* November 5, 1969, copyright © 1969 by The New York Times Company that fertility control has not been effective in lowering overall population growth in any country. Even in countries where stability has been achieved, such as Japan and Taiwan, the success is attributed not to distribution of contraceptive devices, but to motivations such as crowded living space that create demand for the devices.

Professor Davis does not suggest direct controls, such as compulsory sterilization or abortion. Rather, he poses two indirect approaches to population control policy through "selective restructuring of the family in relation to the rest of society."

First, he would have governments postpone the age of marriage, thus reducing the childbearing years, while maintaining current proscriptions against illegitimate birth. Second, he would impose conditions designed to motivate couples to keep their families small.

For example, he suggests, government could stop taxing single persons more heavily than married ones, end tax exemptions for children, pay the cost of abortions, levy a "child tax," and give women equality in educational and job opportunities so that they would develop interests competing with family interest.

Measures such as these, the population expert says, have stemmed population growth in the Communist countries of Eastern Europe, where married women generally must work and where housing and consumer goods are scarce and abortions are free.

"So, if you want to control population, there's your answer," he says. "How do you do it here? The social organization is the problem. That's why you are not going to get it."

In the meantime, he sees the world moving ostrich-like and inexorably toward disaster.

"We may have fewer people in the world all right," he says with more than a tinge of sarcasm. "Nigeria is trying to help out Africa's problem."

As for the argument that large populations are needed to maintain national strength, Professor Davis cited Israel.

"From the point of view of population control," he says, "we owe a great debt to Israel because she has shown that manpower is of very little importance militarily, that modern wars are pushing buttons and paper work—100 million people is perfectly adequate to defend any territory."

He is contemptuous of birth control projects that concentrate on poor minorities.

"The population problem does not lie in some group of blacks having more children than they want," the professor argues. "It lies in the great broad classes having more than they want. You cannot brush it off on some particular group. It lays itself open to the claim of genocide. How'd you feel if someone said you were having too many babies—it would get your back up."

What would he do if he were President Nixon?

"I would devote a lot more attention to goals," he explains. "What kind of population do we want in the United States? Until we get that straightened out, we cannot talk about means.

"I happen to think this country would be better off with half the population. With our present technology and the population of the 1930's the country would be a paradise. As it is, it's getting to be like hell—too many places getting like New York City."

Part 6

NEW FAMILY FORMS

IN THE final section, the possibility of new family forms is considered. One major set of forces comes from the women's liberation movement, which was analyzed in the Introduction, and another comes from the somewhat romantic search for microutopias, usually called communes. The latter is analyzed in the article by Robert Houriet.

Whenever a formerly subordinate group decides to revolt, the typical response on the part of those who were formerly dominant is surprise and hurt. Generally, they had not listened to earlier complaints, or had simply not taken them seriously, feeling that the system was itself just. Most men are therefore shocked to find that an increasing percentage of women are objecting to traditional social patterns of domination and discrimination. Susan Brownmiller describes this movement and expounds some of its philosophy. Perhaps, needless to say, most women would not accept this program as presented in her article, but an increasing percentage of American women do, and there is little likelihood that the women's liberation movement will diminish in power during this decade. How far it will go, and how much it will transform the American family, it is too soon to say. The reader may profitably reflect on just which changes in the American family would be introduced if women were given full equality and freedom and which of those changes he or she would personally now accept.

Most contemporary communes have a short life. Few groups have the necessary capital to set up an adequate physical organization, and often the romantic spirits who are attracted to such small-scale utopias are not willing to submit to the kind of discipline that seems to be necessary to carry on an effective division of labor, schedules of production, or modes of decision-making. If the group does become technically effective in these ways, the discipline may thereby destroy the very aims of its founders.

Communes vary considerably in their "family rules." Some attempt a rather complete community of sex, parenthood, child rearing, food preparation, and production. Others permit exclusive couples to exist. Some try to maintain themselves in city apartments, while others seek the greater beauty of rural areas. All, however, face the problem that they begin with adults who have been reared in a different family system, and thus must adjust to rules which are unfamiliar to them, not having been part of their own socialization process. Jealousies may emerge, in spite of their rules. Some may wish to command when others will not accept domination. Some will expect to be taken care of, instead of assuming adult responsibilities.

Descriptions of these difficulties do not argue against the exploration of such family forms. Although only a minority of the American population would denounce as a total failure the American family system, many do feel that it has failed in major areas, and that alternative family forms should be evolved, or at least explored. Perhaps most people could not adjust to those new family forms, either. Nevertheless, it is clear that over the next two generations many people will make the effort to develop, on a temporary or permanent basis, some new types of family arrangements in which they believe they could not only feel more comfortable but develop more fully as human beings.

"Sisterhood Is Powerful"

by Susan Brownmiller

"Women are an oppressed class. Our oppression is total, affecting every facet of our lives. We are exploited as sex objects, breeders, domestic servants and cheap labor. We are considered inferior beings whose only purpose is to enhance men's lives. . . ."
—REDSTOCKINGS MANIFESTO.

"While we realize that the liberation of women will ultimately mean the liberation of men from the destructive role as oppressor, we have no illusion that men will welcome this liberation without a struggle. . . ."
—MANIFESTO OF THE NEW YORK RADICAL FEMINISTS.

THERE IS a small group of women that gathers at my house or at the home of one or another of our 15 members each Sunday evening. Our ages range from the early twenties to the late forties. As it happens, all of us work for a living, some at jobs we truly like. Some of us are married, with families, and some are not. Some of us knew each other before we joined the group and some did not. Once we are settled on the sofa and the hard-

From the *New York Times Magazine,* March 15, 1970, copyright © 1970 by The New York Times Company

backed chairs brought in from the kitchen, and the late-comers have poured their own coffee and arranged themselves as best they can on the floor, we begin our meeting. Each week we explore another aspect of what we consider to be our fundamental oppression in a male-controlled society. Our conversation is always animated, often emotional. We rarely adjourn before midnight.

Although we are pleased with ourselves and our insights, we like to remind each other now and then that our small group is not unique. It is merely one of many such groups that have sprung up around the city in the last two years under the umbrella of that collective term, the women's liberation movement. In fact, we had been meeting as a group for exactly four Sundays when one of us got a call from a representative of C.B.S. asking if we would care to be filmed in our natural habitat for a segment on the evening news with Walter Cronkite. We discussed the invitation thoroughly, and then said no.

Women's liberation is hot stuff this season, in media terms, and no wonder. In the short space of two years, the new feminism has taken hold and rooted in territory that at first glance appears an unlikely breeding ground for revolutionary ideas: among urban, white, college-educated, middle-class women generally considered to be a rather "privileged" lot by those who thought they knew their politics, or knew their women. From the radical left to the Establishment middle, the women's movement has become a fact of life. The National Organization for Women (NOW), founded by Betty Friedan in 1966, has 35 chapters across the country. Radical feminist groups—creators of the concept of women's liberation, as opposed to women's *rights*—exist in all major cities side by side with their more conservative counterparts.

Without doubt, certain fringe aspects of the movement make "good copy," to use the kindest term available for how my brethren in the business approach the subject matter. ("Get the bra burning and the karate up front," an editor I know told a writer I know when preparing one news magazine's women's liberation story.)

But the irony of all this media attention is that while the minions of C.B.S. News can locate a genuine women's liberation group with relative ease (they ferreted out our little group before we had memorized each other's last names), hundreds of women in New York City have failed in their attempts to make contact with the movement. I have spoken to women who have spent as much as three months looking for a group that was open to new members. Unclaimed letters have piled up at certain post office box numbers hastily set up and thoughtlessly abandoned by here-today-and-gone-tomorrow "organizations" that disappeared as abruptly as they materialized. The elusive qualities of "women's lib" once prompted the writer Sally Kempton to remark, "It's not a movement, it's a state of mind." The surest way to affiliate with the movement these days is to form your own small group. That's the way it's happening.

Two years ago the 50 or so women in New York City who had taken to calling themselves the women's liberation movement met on Thursday evenings at a borrowed office on East 11th Street. The official title of the group was the New York Radical Women. There was some justification at the time for thinking grandly in national terms, for similar groups of women were beginning to form in Chicago, Boston, San Francisco and Washington. New York Radical Women came by its name quite simply: the women were young radicals, mostly under the age of 25, and they came out of the civil rights and/or peace movements, for which many of them had been full-time workers. A few years earlier, many of them might have been found on the campuses of Vassar, Radcliffe, Wellesley and the larger coed universities, a past they worked hard to deny. What brought them together to a women-only discussion and action group was a sense of abuse suffered at the hands of the very protest movements that had spawned them. As "movement women," they were tired of doing the typing and fixing the food while "movement men" did the writing and leading. Most were living with or married to movement men who, they believed, were treating them as convenient sex objects or as somewhat lesser beings.

Widely repeated quotations, such as Stokeley Carmichael's wisecrack dictum to SNCC, "The position of women in our movement should be prone," and, three years later, a similar observation by Black Panther Eldridge Cleaver had reinforced their uncomfortable suspicion that the social vision of radical men did not include equality for women. Black power, as practiced by black male leaders, appeared to mean that black women would step back while black men stepped forward. The white male radical's eager embrace of *machismo* appeared to include those backward aspects of male supremacy in the Latin culture from which the word *machismo* is derived. Within their one-to-one relationships with their men, the women felt, the highly touted "alternate life style" of the radical movement was working out no better than the "bourgeois" life style they had rejected. If man and wife in a suburban split-level was a symbol of all that was wrong with plastic, bourgeois America, "man and chick" in a Lower East Side tenement flat was hardly the new order they had dreamed of.

In short, "the movement" was reinforcing, not eliminating, their deepest insecurities and feelings of worthlessness as women —feelings which quite possibly had brought them into radical protest politics to begin with. So, in a small way, they had begun to rebel. They had decided to meet regularly—without their men —to talk about their common experience. "Our feminism was very underdeveloped in those days," says Anne Koedt, an early member of the group. "We didn't have any idea of what kind of action we could take. We couldn't stop talking about the blacks and Vietnam."

In Marxist canons, "the woman question" is one of many manifestations of a sick, capitalist society which "the revolution" is supposed to finish off smartly. Some of the women who devoted their Thursday evening meeting time to New York Radical Women believed they were merely dusting off and streamlining an orthodox, ideological issue. Feminism was bad politics and a dirty word since it excluded the larger picture.

But others in the group, like Anne Koedt and Shuli Firestone, an intense and talkative young activist, had begun to see things from a different, heretical perspective. Woman's oppressor was Man, they argued, and not a specific economic system. After all, they pointed out, male supremacy was still flourishing in the Soviet Union, Cuba and China, where power was still lodged in a male bureaucracy. Even the beloved Che wrote a guidebook for revolutionaries in which he waxed ecstatic over the advantages to a guerrilla movement of having women along in the mountains—to prepare and cook the food. The heretics tentatively put forward the idea that feminism must be a separate movement of its own.

New York Radical Women's split in perspective—was the ultimate oppressor Man or Capitalism?—occupied endless hours of debate at the Thursday evening meetings. Two warring factions emerged, dubbing each other "the feminists" and "the politicos." But other things were happening as well. For one thing, new women were coming in droves to the Thursday evening talk fest, and a growing feeling of sisterhood was permeating the room. Meetings began awkwardly and shyly, with no recognized chairman and no discernible agenda. Often the suggestion, "Let's sit closer together, sisters," helped break the ice. But once the evening's initial awkwardness had passed, volubility was never a problem. "We had so much to say," an early member relates, "and most of us had never said it to another woman before."

Soon *how* to say it became an important question. Young women like Carol Hanisch, a titian-haired recruit to the civil rights movement from a farm in Iowa, and her friend Kathie Amatniek, a Radcliffe graduate and a working film editor, had spent over a year in Mississippi working with SNCC. There they had been impressed with the Southern-revival-style mass meeting at which blacks got up and "testified" about their own experience with "the Man." Might the technique also work for women? And wasn't it the same sort of thing that Mao Tse-tung had advocated to raise political consciousness in Chinese villages? As Carol Hanisch reminded the group, Mao's slogan had been "Speak pain to recall pain"—precisely what New York Radical Women was doing!

The personal-testimony method encouraged *all* women who came to the meeting to speak their thoughts. The technique of "going around the room" in turn brought responses from many who had never opened their mouths at male-dominated meetings and were experiencing the same difficulty in a room full of articulate members of their own sex. Specific questions such as, "If you've thought of having a baby, do you want a girl or a boy?"

touched off accounts of what it meant to be a girl-child—the second choice in a society that prizes boys. An examination of "What happens to your relationship when your man earns more money than you, and what happens when *you* earn more money than him?" brought a flood of anecdotes about the male ego and money. "We all told similar stories," relates a member of the group. "We discovered that, to a man, they all felt challenged if we were the breadwinners. It meant that we were no longer dependent. We had somehow robbed them of their 'rightful' role."

"We began to see our 'feminization' as a two-level process," says Anne Koedt. "On one level, a woman is brought up to believe that she is a girl and that is her biological destiny. She isn't supposed to want to achieve anything. If, by some chance, she manages to escape the psychological damage, she finds that the structure is prohibitive. Even though she wants to achieve, she finds she is discouraged at every turn and she still can't become President."

Few topics, the women found, were unfruitful. Humiliations that each of them had suffered privately—from being turned down for a job with the comment, "We were looking for a man," to catcalls and wolf whistles on the street—turned out to be universal agonies. "I had always felt degraded, actually turned into an object," said one woman. "I was no longer a human being when a guy on the street would start to make those incredible animal noises at me. I never was flattered by it, I always understood that behind that whistle was a masked hostility. When we started to talk about it in the group, I discovered that every woman in the room had similar feelings. None of us knew how to cope with this street hostility. We had always had to grin and bear it. We had always been told to dress as women, to be very sexy and alluring to men, and what did it get us? Comments like 'Look at the legs on that babe' and 'would I like to—her.' " *

"Consciousness-raising," in which a woman's personal experi-

---

* My small group has discussed holding a street action of our own on the first warm day of spring. We intend to take up stations on the corner of Broadway and 45th Street and whistle at the male passersby. The confrontation, we feel, will be educational for all concerned.

ence at the hands of men was analyzed as a *political* phenomenon, soon became a keystone of the women's liberation movement.

In 1963, *before* there was a women's movement, Betty Friedan published what eventually became an American classic, "The Feminine Mystique." The book was a brilliant, factual examination of the post-World War II "back to the home" movement that tore apart the myth of the fulfilled and happy American housewife. Though "The Feminine Mystique" held an unquestioned place as *the* intellectual mind-opener for most of the young feminists—de Beauvoir's "The Second Sex," a broad, philosophical analysis of the cultural restraints on women, was runner-up in popularity—few members of New York Radical Women had ever felt motivated to attend a meeting of Friedan's National Organization for Women, the parliamentary-style organization of professional women and housewives that she founded in 1966. Friedan, the mother of the movement, and the organization that recruited in her image were considered hopelessly bourgeois. NOW's emphasis on legislative change left the radicals cold. The generation gap created real barriers to communication.

"Actually, we had a lot in common with the NOW women," reflects Anne Koedt. "The women who started NOW were achievement-oriented in their professions. They began with the employment issue because that's what they were up against. The ones who started New York Radical Women were achievement-oriented in the radical movement. From both ends we were fighting a male structure that prevented us from achieving."

Friedan's book had not envisioned a movement of young feminists emerging from the college campus and radical politics. "If I had it to do all over again," she says, "I would rewrite my last chapter." She came to an early meeting of New York Radical Women to listen, ask questions and take notes, and went away convinced that her approach—and NOW's—was more valid. "As far as I'm concerned, we're *still* the radicals," she says emphatically. "We raised our consciousness a long time ago. I get along with the women's lib people because they're the way the troops we need come up. But the name of the game is confrontation and action, and equal employment *is* the gut issue. The legal fight is enormously important. Desegregating The New York Times help-wanted ads was an important step, don't you think? And NOW did it. The women's movement *needs* its Browns versus Boards of Education."

Other older women, writers and lifetime feminists, also came around to observe, and stayed to develop a kinship with girls young enough to be their daughters. "I almost wept after my first meeting. I went home and filled my diary," says Ruth Herschberger, poet and author of "Adam's Rib," a witty and unheeded expostulation of women's rights published in 1948. "When I wrote 'Adam's Rib,' I was writing for readers who wouldn't accept the first premise. Now there was a whole roomful of people and a whole new vocabulary. I could go a whole month on the ammunition I'd get at one meeting."

In June of 1968, New York Radical Women produced a mimeographed booklet of some 20 pages entitled "Notes from the First Year." It sold for 50 cents to women and $1.00 to men. "Notes" was a compendium of speeches, essays and transcriptions of tape-recorded "rap sessions" of the Thursday evening group on such subjects as sex, abortion and orgasm. Several mimeographed editions later, it remains the most widely circulated source material on the New York women's liberation movement.

The contribution to "Notes" that attracted the most attention from both male and female readers was a one-page essay by Anne Koedt entitled, "The Myth of Vaginal Orgasm." In it she wrote:

"Frigidity has generally been defined by men as the failure of women to have vaginal orgasms. Actually, the vagina is not a highly sensitive area and is not physiologically constructed to achieve orgasm. The clitoris is the sensitive area and is the female equivalent of the penis. All orgasms [in women] are extensions of sensations from this area. This leads to some interesting questions about conventional sex and our role in it. Men have orgasms essentially by friction with the vagina, not with the clitoris. Women have thus been defined sexually in terms of what pleases men; our own biology has not been properly analyzed. Instead we have been fed a myth of the liberated woman and her vaginal orgasm, an orgasm which in fact does not exist. What we must do is redefine our sexuality. We must discard the 'normal' concepts of sex and create new guidelines which take into account mutual sexual enjoyment. We must begin to demand that if a certain sexual position or technique now defined as 'standard' is not mutually conducive to orgasm, then it should no longer be defined as standard."

Anne Koedt's essay went further than many other women in the movement would have preferred to go, but she was dealing with a subject that every woman understood. "For years I suffered under a male-imposed definition of my sexual responses," one woman says. "From Freud on down, it was *men* who set the standard of my sexual enjoyment. *Their* way was the way I should achieve nirvana, because their way was the way it worked for them. Me? Oh, I was simply an 'inadequate woman.' "

By September, 1968, New York Radical Women felt strong enough to attempt a major action. Sixty women went to Atlantic City in chartered buses to picket the Miss America pageant. The beauty contest was chosen as a target because of the ideal of American womanhood it extolled—vacuous, coiffed, cosmeticized and with a smidgin of talent.

But New York Radical Women did not survive its second year. For one thing, the number of new women who flocked to the Thursday evening meetings made consciousness-raising and "going around the room" an impossibility. The politico-feminist split and other internal conflicts—charges of "domination" by one or another of the stronger women were thrown back and forth—put a damper on the sisterly euphoria. An attempt to break up the one large group into three smaller ones—by lot—proved disastrous.

Several women felt the need for a new group. They had become intrigued with the role of the witch in world history as representing society's persecution of women who dared to be different. From Joan of Arc, who dared to wear men's clothes and lead a men's army, to the women of Salem who dared to defy accepted political, religious mores, the "witch" was punished for deviations. Out of this thinking grew WITCH, a handy acronym that the organizers announced, half tongue-in-cheek, stood for Women's International Terrorist Conspiracy from Hell.

Much of WITCH was always tongue-in-cheek, and from its inception its members were at great pains to deny that they were feminists. The Yippie movement had made outrageous disruption a respectable political tactic of the left, and the women of WITCH decided it was more compatible with their thinking to be labeled "kooks" by outsiders than to be labeled man-haters by movement men.

In the WITCH philosophy, the patriarchy of the nuclear family was synonymous with the patriarchy of the American business corporation. Thus, four women took jobs at a branch of the Travelers Insurance Company, where a fifth member was working, and attempted to establish a secret coven of clerical workers on the premises. (For the Travelers' project, WITCH became "Women Incensed at Travelers' Corporate Hell.") In short order, the infiltrators were fired for such infractions of office rules as wearing slacks to work. Undaunted, a new quintet of operatives gained employment in the vast typing pools at A.T. & T. "Women Into Telephone Company Harassment" gained three sympathizers to the cause before Ma Bell got wise and exorcised the coven from her midst. Two WITCHes were fired for insubordination; the rest were smoked out and dismissed for being "overqualified" for the typing pool.

WITCH's spell over the women's movement did not hold. "At this point," says Judith Duffet, an original member, "you could say that WITCH is just another small group in women's liberation. We're concerned with consciousness-raising and developing an ideology through collective thinking. We don't do the freaky, hippie stuff any more."

While WITCH was brewing its unusual recipe for liberation, another offshoot of New York Radical Women emerged. The new group was called Redstockings, a play on *bluestockings,* with the blue replaced by the color of revolution. Organized by Shuli Firestone and Ellen Willis, an articulate rock-music columnist for the New Yorker and a serious student of Engels's "Origins of the Family," Redstockings made no bones about where it stood. It was firmly committed to feminism and action.

Redstockings made its first public appearance at a New York legislative hearing on abortion law reform in February, 1969, when several women sought to gain the microphone to testify about their own abortions. The hearing, set up to take testimony from 15 medical and psychiatric "experts"—14 were men—was hastily adjourned. The following month, Redstockings held its *own* abortion hearing at the Washington Square Methodist Church. Using the consciousness-raising technique, 12 women "testified" about abortion, from their own personal experience, before an audience of 300 men and women. The political message of the emotion-charged evening was that *women* were the only true experts on unwanted pregnancy and abortion, and that every woman has an inalienable right to decide whether or not she wishes to bear a child.

Redstockings' membership counts are a closely held secret, but I would estimate that the number does not exceed 100. Within the movement, Redstockings push what they call "the pro-woman line." "What it means," says a member, "is that we take the woman's side in *everything*. A woman is never to blame for her own submission. None of us need to change ourselves, we need to change men." Redstockings are also devout about consciousness-raising. "Whatever else we may do, consciousness-raising is the ongoing political work," says Kathie Amatniek. For the last few months, the various Redstocking groups have been raising their consciousness on what they call "the divisions between women that keep us apart"—married women *vs.* single, black women *vs.* white, middle class *vs.* working class, etc.

While Redstockings organized its abortion speak-out, the New York chapter of NOW formed a committee to lobby for repeal of restrictive abortion legislation. These dissimilar approaches to the same problem illustrate the difference in style between the two wings of the women's movement.

But within New York NOW itself, a newer, wilder brand of feminism made an appearance. Ti-Grace Atkinson, a Friedan protégée and the president of New York NOW, found herself in increasing conflict with her own local chapter and Friedan over NOW's hierarchical structure, a typical organization plan with an executive board on top. Ti-Grace, a tall blonde who has been described in print as "aristocratic looking," had come to view the power relationship between NOW's executive board and the general membership as a copycat extension of the standard forms of male domination over women in the society at large. She proposed to NOW that all executive offices be abolished in favor of rotating chairmen chosen by lot from the general membership. When Atkinson's proposal came up for a vote by the general membership of the New York chapter in October, 1968, and was defeated, Ti-Grace resigned her presidency on the spot and went out and formed her own organization. Named the October 17th Movement—the date of Ti-Grace's walkout from NOW —it made a second debut this summer as The Feminists, and took its place as the most radical of the women's liberation groups. (New York NOW suffered no apparent effects from its first organizational split. Over the last year it has *gained* in membership as feminism has gained acceptability among wider circles of women.)

The Feminists made anti-élitism and rigorous discipline cardinal principles of their organization. As the only radical feminist group to take a stand against the institution of marriage they held a sit-in at the city marriage license bureau last year, raising the slogan that "Marriage Is Slavery." Married women or women living with men may not exceed one-third of the total membership.

Differences over such matters as internal democracy, and the usual personality conflicts that plague all political movements, caused yet another feminist group and another manifesto to make their appearance this fall. In November, Shuli Firestone and Anne Koedt set up a plan for organizing small groups—or "brigades," as they prefer to call them—on a neighborhood basis, and named their over-all structure the New York Radical Feminists. Eleven decentralized neighborhood units (three are in the West Village) meet jointly once a month.

The Radical Feminists coexist with the Feminists and the Redstockings without much rivalry, although when pressed, partisans of the various groups will tell you, for instance, that Redstockings do too much consciousness-raising and not enough action, or that the Feminists are "fascistic," or that the Radical Feminists are publicity hungry. But in general, since interest in the women's liberation movement has always exceeded organizational capacity, the various groups take the attitude of "the more the merrier."

Despite the existence of three formal "pure radical feminist" organizations, hundreds of women who consider themselves women's liberationists have not yet felt the need to affiliate with any body larger than their own small group. The small group, averaging 8 to 15 members and organized spontaneously by friends calling friends has become *the* organizational form of the amorphous movement. Its intimacy seems to suit women. Fear of expressing new or half-formed thoughts vanishes in a friendly living-room atmosphere. "After years of psychoanalysis in which my doctor kept telling me my problem was that I wouldn't accept —quote—*my female role,"* says a married woman with two children who holds a master's degree in philosophy, "the small group was a revelation to me. Suddenly, for the first time in my life, it was *O.K.* to express feelings of hostility to men." Says another woman: "In the small group I have the courage to think things and feel feelings, that I would never have dared to think and feel as an individual."

The meetings have often been compared to group therapy, a description that most of the women find irritating. "Group therapy isn't political and what we're doing is highly political," is the general response. In an early paper on the nature and function of the small group, Carol Hanisch once wrote, "Group therapy implies that we are sick and messed up, but the first function of the small group is to get rid of self-blame. We start with the assumption that women are really 'neat' people. Therapy means adjusting. We desire to change the objective conditions."

The groups are usually leaderless and structureless, and the subjects discussed at the weekly meetings run the gamut of female experience. The Radical Feminists offer to new groups they organize a list of consciousness-raising topics that includes:

Discuss your relationships with men. Have you noticed any recurring patterns?

Have you ever felt that men have pressured you into sexual relationships? Have you ever lied about orgasm?

Discuss your relationships with other women. Do you compete with women for men?

Growing up as a girl, were you treated differently from your brother?

What would you most like to do in life? What has stopped you?

"Three months of this sort of thing," says Shuli Firestone, "is enough to make a feminist out of any woman."

The kind of collective thinking that has come out of the women's liberation movement is qualitatively different from the kinds of theorems and analyses that other political movements have generated. "Women are different from all other oppressed classes," says Anne Koedt. "We live in isolation, not in ghettos, and we are in the totally unique position of having a master in our own houses." It is not surprising, therefore, that marriage and child care are two subjects that receive intensive scrutiny in the small group.

If few in the women's movement are willing to go as far as the Feminists and say that marriage is slavery, it is hard to find a women's liberationist who is not in some way disaffected by the sound of wedding bells. Loss of personal identity and the division of labor within the standard marriage (the husband's role as provider, the wife's role as home maintenance and child care) are the basic points at issue. "I have come to view marriage as a built-in self-destruct for women," says one divorcée after 12 years of marriage. "I married early, right after college, because it was expected of me. I never had a chance to discover who I was. I was programmed into the housewife pattern." Many married women's liberationists will no longer use their husbands' last names; some have gone back to their maiden names, and some even to their mothers' maiden names.

One paper that has been widely circulated within the movement is entitled "The Politics of Housework," by Pat Mainardi, a Redstocking who is a teacher and painter. "Men recognize the essential fact of housework right from the beginning," she wrote. "Which is that it stinks. You both work, you both have careers, but *you* are expected to do the housework. Your husband tells you, 'Don't talk to me about housework. It's too trivial to discuss.' MEANING: *His* purpose is to deal with matters of significance. *Your* purpose is to deal with matters of insignificance. So *you* do the housework. Housework trivial? Just try getting him to share the burden. The measure of his resistance is the measure of your oppression."

Not only the oppression of housework, but the oppression of child care has become a focus of the women's movement. Much of the energy of young mothers in the movement has gone into setting up day-care collectives that are staffed on an equal basis by mothers and fathers. (Thus far they have proved difficult to sustain.) "Some of the men have actually come to understand that sharing equally in child care is a political responsibility," says Rosalyn Baxandall, a social worker and an early women's liberationist. Rosalyn and her husband, Lee, a playwright, put in a morning a week at an informal cooperative day nursery on the Lower East Side where their 2-year-old, Finn, is a charter member.

In November, at the Congress to Unite Women, a conference that drew over 500 women's liberationists of various persuasions from the New York area, a resolution demanding 24-hour-a-day child care centers was overwhelmingly endorsed. Women in the movement have also suggested plans for a new kind of life style in which a husband and wife would each work half-day and devote the other half of the day to caring for their children. Another possibility would be for the man to work for six months of the year while the woman takes care of the child-rearing responsibilities—with the roles reversed for the next six months.

The "movement women" who did not endorse the separatism of an independent radical feminist movement last year and chose to remain in what the feminists now call "the male left" have this year made women's liberation a major issue in their own political groups. Even the weatherwomen of Weatherman meet separately to discuss how to combat male chauvinism among their fellow revolutionaries. The women of Rat, the farthest out of the underground radical newspapers, formed a collective and took over editorial management of their paper last month, charging that their men had put out a product filled with sexist, women-as-degraded-object pornography. Twenty-two-year-old Jane Alpert, free on bail and facing conspiracy charges for a series of terrorist bombings, was spokesman for the Rat women's *putsch.* A black women's liberation committee functions within SNCC, and its leader, Frances M. Beal, has said publicly, "To be black and female is double jeopardy, the slave of a slave."

The new feminism has moved into some surprisingly Establishment quarters. A spirited women's caucus at New York University Law School forced the university to open its select national scholarship program to women students. Women's caucuses exist among the editorial employes at McGraw Hill and Newsweek. Last month, 59 women in city government sent a petition to Mayor Lindsay demanding that he actively seek qualified women for policy-making posts.

The movement is a story without an end, because it has just begun. The goals of liberation go beyond a simple concept of equality. Looking through my notebook, I see them expressed simply and directly. *Betty Friedan: "We're going to redefine the sex roles." Anne Koedt: "We're going to be redefining politics."* Brave words for a new movement, and braver still for a movement that has been met with laughter and hostility. Each time a man sloughs off the women's movement with the comment, "They're nothing but a bunch of lesbians and frustrated bitches," we quiver with collective rage. How can such a charge be answered in rational terms? It cannot be. (The supersensitivity of the movement to the lesbian issue, and the existence of a few militant lesbians within the movement once prompted Friedan herself to grouse about "the lavender menace" that was threatening to warp the image of women's rights. A lavender *herring,* perhaps, but surely no clear and present danger.)

The small skirmishes and tugs of war that used to be called "the battle of the sexes" have now assumed ideological proportions. It is the aim of the movement to *turn men around,* and the implications in that aim are staggering. "Men have used us all their lives as ego fodder," says Anne Koedt. "They not only control economics and the government, they control us. There are the women's pages and the rest of the world." It is that rest of the world, of course, that we are concerned with. There is a women's rights button that I sometimes wear and the slogan on it reads, "Sisterhood is Powerful." If sisterhood were powerful, what a different world it would be.

Women as a class have never subjugated another group; we have never marched off to wars of conquest in the name of the fatherland. We have never been involved in a decision to annex the territory of a neighboring country, or to fight for foreign markets on distant shores. Those are the games men play, not us. *We* see it differently. We want to be neither oppressor nor oppressed. The women's revolution is the final revolution of them all.

How does a sympathetic man relate to a feminist woman? Thus far, it has not been easy for those who are trying. The existence of a couple of *men's* consciousness-raising groups—the participants are mostly husbands of activist women—is too new to be labeled a trend. "When our movement gets strong, when men are forced to see us as a conscious issue, *what are they going to do?*" asks Anne Koedt. And then she answers: "I don't know, but I think there's a part of men that really wants a human relationship, and that's going to be the saving grace for all of us."

The Family,
to Lorenz, Is All

by Walter Sullivan

DR. KONRAD LORENZ, author of the widely read book "On Aggression" and a founder of the young science of ethology (the study of animal behavior in the wild) argued yesterday that large and stable family groupings were essential to the survival of human society.

"The father-mother family with two children isolated in a city flat," he said with a chuckle, "is already insufficient."

The need to surround the child with enough people to make it feel secure, he said, even makes grandmothers desirable.

Dr. Lorenz, who heads the Max Planck Institute for the Physiology of Behavior at Seewiesen in Bavaria, was not arguing for many-child families. Rather, he said, an individual child should have intimate association with several adults in an extended family group.

Thus he advocated "artificial" families in which several young couples associate closely, baby-sitting for one another and providing their children with a feeling of community.

From the *New York Times,* January 22, 1970, copyright © 1970 by The New York Times Company

Violence in Fairy Tales

Dr. Lorenz, here to receive a medal for his work with birds, spoke on a wide range of subjects in an interview, his thoughts pouring forth in a stream of ideas and anecdotes, broken occasionally by gentle interventions of his diminutive wife.

Asked about various aspects of contemporary violence, he and his wife, a physician, both spoke in favor of violence in fairy tales. The children love it, they said, and are well aware that it is not real.

Concerning Vietnam, Dr. Lorenz commented that television was at last bringing warring peoples face to face with their victims, making war less palatable.

He discussed various aspects of fear, citing evidence within his own family that fear of lightning was largely acquired from the parents. Experiments with institutionalized children in Vienna, he said, have shown that, without conditioning about snakes, the children, though disgusted, were not fearful of them.

"Strange to say," he added, the fear of snakes in some species of monkey "is entirely traditional," that is, learned.

The aggressive instincts common to all higher animals, he said, normally lead to violence only when fear is aroused. Thus, aggressiveness in human beings generates ambition, but current fear of the blacks and an impatient younger generation has led to violence and may result in a dangerous swing to the right in this country.

Dr. Lorenz, now a vigorous 66, wears a robust beard and speaks excellent English, part of his fluency dating back to a year of study at Columbia University in 1922. He was born in Vienna, but in recent years he has been most active in Germany.

Asked about survival of the family in a modern, technological society, Dr. Lorenz said:

"The survival of society at all—of human society—is in doubt, particularly if the family structure is not kept up.

"I believe that the innate program of the human individual is such that he cannot deploy all his possibilities and evolve all his inherent faculties unless it's done within the frame of the normal family. And the normal family even implies the grand-mother."

Of the family limited to two children, mother and a father, he said:

"The young child must know more than two people that are friendly. Because if you have just two people who are your friends—that 'we' are only four and the rest are 'they,' then 'we' are in a frightening minority."

This is particularly true, Dr. Lorenz said, if the parents fear frustrating their children. "Then visualize the situation of the child," he said, "defended by two despicable cowards in a world of hostile people."

Neurosis is almost sure to follow when such a child goes to school or college "and is suddenly subjected to the full impact of very cold public opinion, which rejects him," he said.

Effect of Love or Mercy

Like other members of his school, Dr. Lorenz argued that men are willing to kill one another in war because modern weapons keep them from seeing their victims at close hand.

Aggressive behavior in animals, he said, normally stops short of violence because of an instinct manifest in man as love or mercy.

Love of humanity (as opposed to sexual love), he said, "is a response which definitely is there only in aggressive animals. And it has evolved as a means of mitigating and inhibiting aggression. That is quite indubitable."

Thus, he argued, animals fighting for a female, to guard their territory or to establish their dominance in a group, normally stop short of killing.

In fact, the "fighting" tends to be ritualistic unless fear enters in. Fear may come from being cornered or from being so closely matched with a rival that a panic reaction sets in.

He told of a tropical fish known as the Dempsey child be-cause, like the boxer Jack Dempsey, it is a gentlemanly fighter.

But Dr. Lorenz has found that, when two evenly matched fish of this species confront each other and their ritual combat fails to settle the rivalry, they begin biting off one another's fins in all-out combat.

"The prerequisite for loving," Dr. Lorenz continued, "is certainly personal acquaintanceship—that you know the chap." The world situation demands that we all love one another, "but we can't do it," he went on. "And the less you know a chap, the more easy you find it to kill him."

Despite the drawbacks of television, he said, "there are great blessings coming from the mass media—for instance, that the whole antagonism against the war in Vietnam which you find in America—the very just antagonism—is largely based on the fact that people actually see the atrocities."

On Tuesday evening Dr. Lorenz was presented with the newly established Delacour Medal at the American Museum of Natural History. The medal was awarded by the United States section of the International Council for Bird Preservation and is named for Jean Delacour, a noted French ornithologist.

Life and Death of
a Commune Called Oz

by Robert Houriet

AROUND 9 O'CLOCK of a sun-filled morning last summer, in a ramshackle farmhouse near Meadville, Pa., 23-year-old Kathy crawled out of a sleeping bag to make breakfast for her 35-member communal family.

She slipped into her well-worn Mother-Hubbard-like dress, quietly. Ten men and women of the family were still asleep on mattresses strewn about the floor of the large room.

After a visit to the bathroom—a tin pail set inside a closet—she went downstairs and out the back door. Her kitchen was around an open fire in the field behind the farmhouse.

David had started the fire and now sat Buddha-like, strumming his guitar and looking out over the rolling hills of Western Pennsylvania. Kathy leaned down and kissed him companionably, then turned to preparing breakfast: a pot of oatmeal from grain provided by neighboring farmers, apples picked from their own trees and milk from their own goat, Carol.

One by one, members of the family appeared. They sniffed the air, saluted the day, greeted each other with embraces and caresses.

Patty-Pooh returned nude and glistening from a bath in the

From the *New York Times Magazine,* February 16, 1969, copyright ©️ 1969 by The New York Times Company nearby creek and knelt to warm herself by the fire. Dan held 3-year-old Amy on his knee and talked with her mother Rebecca, a divorcee, of how children can teach adults to perceive clearly and fully without interference from their egos.

It was a typical morning at Oz, as the family called its 130-acre homestead. For four months they stayed there—from June until late September—sharing food, clothing, shelter and life experiences. When they left, it was against their will—the result of a campaign of harassment by some irate citizens of Meadville.

Today, the members of the family are scattered across the country. Some of the younger ones are back with their parents, but many have joined other communes. For in the last five years, since the first hippie settlements sprang up in California, the commune movement has spread—first to the Southwest and, within the past year, to the colder and more puritanical climates of the Northeast. Wandering flower children are welcomed now in communes in New York State, Massachusetts and Vermont.

"In a few years," says an Oz family member, "there'll be a whole network of communes from coast to coast—like Howard Johnsons." Maybe. But the movement must first find a formula for dealing with the "straight" society. For Oz and Meadville, coexistence proved impossible.

The nucleus of the commune came together in Southern California, united by a common aversion to the urban scene with its air pollution, and commercialization. "About the only way to make it in a city is to hold some kind of job," Kathy, the breakfast-maker, added disapprovingly. She is a University of Iowa dropout who was majoring in creative writing before she joined the commune.

For about 18 months, the family lived in a lodge and several small cabins near Santa Cruz. The high rent ($500 a month) sent them searching for another site. Then a friend and sometime merchant seaman, William Close, offered them free use of his newly-inherited farm, and they headed east for the promised land.

Their new home was a rundown, three-story farmhouse of Charles Addams design, set on a dirt road a mile uphill from State Highway 102. It was in Summit Township, a few miles from the village of Harmonsburg and some eight miles from

Meadville (population: 20,000). It lacked windows, a working stove, indoor plumbing, electricity.

There were 20 men and 14 women in the family—plus little Amy. Seven of the women were married or had an "old man" with whom they regularly shared a mattress. The oldest of the family was Cora, a woman in her 40's who, before her divorce, had followed a standard suburban way of life in Mill Valley, Calif. During her stay at Oz, she held a part-time job as a domestic to earn money to support her macrobiotic diet. Aside from Amy, the youngest was Vesta, a 16-year-old, sylph-like blonde recruit from Meadville. Most family members were in their early 20's.

Though the family had no leader as such, it had a kind of guru —a heavily bearded, 30-year-old student of philosophy named George Hurd. He described Oz as a "working anarchy," without officers or work schedules and with few "tribal councils." When the tribe did meet, matters were decided by consensus rather than majority vote. All of which helps explain why some of the work of repairing the house was never accomplished, to the annoyance of those farmers who had lent the family tools which were never put to use.

The family did, however, organize enough to maintain themselves. They cooked out with scrap wood gathered from a nearby sawmill. They molded scented paraffin candles into fantastic, freeform shapes to provide light. They built an outdoor privy and repaired the broken-down well. The neighboring creek served them as bathtub and washtub, though clothing wasn't much of a problem. The men wore little but jeans, the women wore the long, loose dresses and there was a considerable amount of group nudity. Dirty clothes were tossed into a corner of the downstairs room called the "free store," available to all for the washing.

The family's financial resources were limited. The only regular income came from allowances. Marko, for example, received a $30-a-month allowance from his father, a West Coast Litton Industries executive. Said Marko, as he sat beside the fire one night, munching an apple: "My father spends a quarter of his life in a car on the freeway breathing sulphur dioxide and cursing the pollution. I'm living the way he secretly wishes he was."

Patty-Pooh, the daughter of a New York advertising executive, left the farm to work in New York, modeling for a pornography photographer, then dutifully returned home to Oz. She used the money she'd earned to buy Carol, the goat.

The family also depended on handouts from tourists, birthday gifts and the sale of beads and other handicrafts to visitors. A favorite product was the God's eye—a woven, diamond-shaped mobile.

But work in the usual sense—eight hours a day, 40 hours a week, for money—was shunned. "When people work for profit," said Deja, a slender girl with pigtails who acquired her name from a Ouija board, "they deny their very brotherhood. The capitalist system forces people into boring activity and cuts them off from nature by forcing them to live in cities. It goes against the order of God."

Most of the men did work for neighboring farmers, but they labored intermittently, and then only five hours a day. They were paid not in dollars but in kind—a share of the farmer's crops. They harvested corn and beans, milked cows, picked blueberries, hayed, painted and repaired barns.

A garden was planted at Oz, though not in time to harvest such crops as corn. But home-grown squash, turnips and tomatoes added some variety to the usual family diet—brown rice, bread made in a pressure cooker from flour they ground themselves, fried soybeans, a perpetual pot of vegetable soup (unfinished portions were poured back into the common pot), goat's milk and ice cream brought by newspaper reporters. The family in general sought to avoid chemically treated foods.

So there was a substantial amount of purposeful activity at Oz, but it was a sometime thing. At any given moment, a visitor to the farm was likely to confront this kind of scene:

Adolph, the son of a wealthy family near Carmel, Calif., is sitting on the porch, composing separate songs for each card of the tarot pack. Nearby, Ruthie is charting a horoscope. Michael, son of a humanities professor, is engrossed in a comic book beside his wife Kathy, who's crocheting. Another Michael is reading aloud from a Doctor Seuss book, and Parmel is napping, his head cushioned on the goat Carol.

From out of the woods comes Morgan, back from one of his long, solitary walks. He stops to watch naked little Amy frolicking in the front yard with some of the family's 11 dogs. In the backyard Danny, Bodyless George, Ludwig and Dancing Bear are playing at being a rampaging motorcycle gang, revving around on imaginary bikes, grunting biker phrases.

Such activities satisfied the purpose of the commune—the furthering of its members' psychological and spiritual growth. Unlike many European communes, the family of Oz ignored politics altogether. At the time of the Democratic convention in Chicago, few knew or cared who the candidates were. As one member of the family put it: "It's where your head is that counts."

Said Deja: "You can say this is one 24-hour group therapy session." When she met a newcomer, Deja would take his hand and say, "I'm Deja. I'm a girl."

David felt that life in the family was "like having to look yourself in the mirror all the time." Kathy observed: "We all came into the family with ego hangups of one sort. Our life together wears down these hangups until a sort of group spirit takes over."

Ross was a case in point. He joined the family with a set of "tough guy" defenses picked up during his adolescence in the Bronx. He was in a biker phase when he arrived in black leather jacket and boots; then he dropped that pose for Indian dress, complete with head band. But he took to carrying a sawed-off shotgun and shooting up trees, signs and cats. Finally the family, which was nonviolent on principle, expelled him. They told him he was on an "ego trip" and that his gun was simply a substitute for his inability to love and be loved. By the end of the summer, Ross had reformed; he sold his gun, was readmitted to the family and performed communal tasks he had shirked before.

Twenty-year-old Ken had dropped out of high school in East Palestine, Ohio, about 50 miles south of Meadville, and lived in a drug pad in Youngstown before joining the Oz family. He assumed the name of Dancing Bear, which came to him, he says, during an acid trip while romping through the woods: "It sorta fits my vibrations." Looking back on the summer, he said, "We all went through changes. I had always wanted to be famous, to be recognized by Time magazine as a leading hip figure. At the farm I grew out of that, learning to live in the now, not worrying about being anybody. I'm much happier."

Along with defenses and egos, the family of Oz often discarded individual surnames and family-given first names as if to symbolize the transfer of identity from their former families of blood relation to their new-found family of communal experience. Guru Hurd recalled, "We toyed with the idea of taking the same last name—Om, after the Hindu concept—but we rejected the idea. Names, after all, just divide people."

Group "happenings" enhanced the family's almost mystical feeling of oneness. One moonlit night they stood outdoors, hand in hand, and chanted, "Hare Krishna. . . ." Then they were silent for long minutes, just listening to the sound of their own breathing. Once, in the midst of a thunderstorm, they did a rain dance to the accompaniment of recorders, a clarinet and a saxophone. There were also a few nude love-ins in the creek. "It was beautiful," recalled Josh, 36, a bearded refugee of the beat generation who looks like an Old Testament prophet. "The minnows nibbled at your feet, and you could reach out and touch another body so you felt there was no difference anymore between what you thought and what you did, as there was no difference between what the minnow felt of himself and the water."

Such happenings were part of the family's search for inner peace and exaltation by natural means, including yoga, rather than relying on drugs to achieve an artificial "high." L.S.D. and marijuana were sometimes used, but it was usually a family affair. One morning while the rest of the family still slept, Patty-Pooh returned from New York with some L.S.D. She and Debbie, a local girl, dispensed it gaily, running from one person to another, awakening them and popping pills in their mouths. "We attained a group high that wouldn't have been possible if we had taken separate trips," Michael said. There were two or three such occasions during the summer.

A few of the family members used strong drugs—one was on morphine, another on methadrine—but no one was hooked. In the isolation of Oz, it was difficult to get drugs. Some marijuana was brought in by visiting Allegheny College students, though the family limited its use to once or twice a weekend. And when one visitor arrived with a huge jar filled with pills, he was bodily thrown off the property.

In some hippie communes, group sex is standard procedure. At a few in the Southwest, newcomers are given to understand from the outset that property and bodies are to be shared freely, on demand. But at Oz, orgies were few and far between.

Not that the Oz family was straitlaced. In addition to the few "stable" relationships among unmarried men and women, there were perhaps four girls who shared their beds occasionally with two or three other men. And there were two girls who, by summer's end, had slept with all but the two men who lived as celibates (there was also a woman who lived alone in her own tent). Such girls lived dangerously, for there was a fairly widespread feeling in the family, among both men and women, that birth-control devices were unnatural. Marko, for one, refused to have intercourse with a girl who he knew was taking the pill or using a diaphragm. Over the past few years there have been several pregnancies in the family.

Among the married couples, there was one who had agreed to allow each other sexual freedom. Once, when an orgy did take place, the wife walked out while the husband participated. They both insisted later that the experience had not weakened their strong bond. Said the wife:

"We've known each other since high school and have learned to accept everything that happens. Group living creates new relationships—not just sexual. I've become close to other men besides my husband. When you can get past the cat-and-mouse stage—the seductive way women treat men—then you can learn to be friends as human beings. There's not much difference between men and women after all. Like Bob Dylan says, 'Baby, I just wanta be friends with you.' "

In general, the family's relationships with neighboring farmers were good. "They were great workers and good people," says Elmer Taylor of Springboro. "I had them over to my house many times, and they have a standing invitation to come back." The feeling was mutual. Said Marko: "The farmers have the same respect for nature we do. Some of them were the most spiritually high people I ever met."

Some farmers dumped bags of surplus commodities on their porch—soy beans, potatoes, wheat—and gave the family instructions on how to plant and raise their own crops. A particular farmer friend was Theodore Everett, a man in his 60's with silver hair and the weathered face of a Robert Frost. Everett advised the family on matters both agricultural and spiritual. One day he waded out into the creek with some of the family and applied his faith-healing techniques to their burns and skin diseases. "I'd like to come here more often," he told a reporter, "but I'm afraid of what my friends might say."

The attitudes of the townspeople of Meadville were not always so friendly. Tucked away in the northwest corner of Pennsylvania, Meadville is the seat of Crawford County, an area of scraggly woods, dwindling dairy farms and close-knit towns. Meadville has few bars and many green-and-white litter cans. At noon on Sunday, the air is filled with hymns from the First Baptist Church.

A Republican citadel for years, the brick and pillared courthouse of Meadville looks out on a pleasant mall of criss-crossing walkways, ancient trees and a bubbling fountain. Gov. Raymond P. Shafer began his political climb here, and another Shafer has followed him—his nephew, Paul D. Shafer Jr., serves as district attorney.

Meadville's first view of the family of Oz came shortly after their arrival when a school bus owned by one of the commune's couples drove into town. The hippies disembarked and set forth on a barefoot stroll, beards flapping.

Traffic halted. Women stopped pushing their baby carriages. Store clerks ignored their customers. Townsfolk lined the hippies' route—and stared.

Just what the commune's relationship with the outside world should be had been a matter of great discussion among the family—and it would continue to be a bone of contention throughout their stay. The only fist fight of the summer occurred after one of the men had accepted a visitor's gift of beer and another had objected.

A minority wanted the farm to keep to itself. It should become as self-sufficient as possible; hand-outs should not be accepted; "no trespassing" signs should be erected. Visitors, specifically including teen-age runaways and reporters, should be discouraged.

But the majority maintained that it was Oz's destiny to be

a pilot project for the communal society. "From the first," said George Hurd, "we decided not to keep our community a secret. We had nothing to hide, and we didn't want any false rumors started about what we were up to."

So the hippies visited Meadville, and the townspeople returned the favor. At first, they journeyed to the farm simply out of curiosity. Sunday afternoons, they packed their kids into the family auto and went to gape. The slow procession of cars, with children's faces pasted to the windows, crept past the farm, churning up a continual dust cloud. Some days more than a thousand cars filed past, so many that state police had to be assigned there to direct traffic and post "no parking" signs along a strip of road.

Stories in The Meadville Tribune described the way of life at Oz and spelled out the family's plans. They were there to develop "true brotherhood" by throwing off ties to the "capitalist system" and thereby attain "cosmic consciousness." These were disquieting images and ideas for the residents of Crawford County, for the women in their spic-and-span one-family houses, for the men who worked eight hours a day at Viscose and Tallon and American Brake Shoe. But the visitors kept coming to Oz, where they were greeted by the family with kisses, Zen sayings and put-ons ("I'd like you to meet Susan, one of my six wives").

Though some of his critics in the commune sneered that he was trying to "turn on the world, beginning with Meadville," George Hurd persisted in his efforts to win over the townspeople. He served as spokesman for the family, leading visitors to a large clearing where he would "rap" on the meaning of communal life.

Hurd grew up in a middle-class family on the outskirts of Suffield, Conn., a staid town of expensively restored colonial homes. He was an ardent member of the local N.A.A.C.P. chapter in high school and went off to college fully intending to fulfill his mother's dream of his becoming a physician. But it was not to be. After attending several colleges and studying mathematics and psychology, at San Francisco State and the University of California at Berkeley, he worked briefly as a computer programer and then dropped out to live the communal life on the West Coast.

It was in the role of a philosopher that Hurd spoke to visitors to Oz. The commune, he said, was an extension of a new religion. The disaffection of the younger generation grew from religious discontent, which eventually took the form of protest against the lack of genuine spirituality and brotherhood in the adult world. A new religious synthesis would emerge, ideally blending the best of Christian ethics—nonviolence and love—with the mind-expanding disciplines of Eastern faiths.

Hurd often referred to Oz as a new denomination, which he called the "Anthropodeic" church—a term with its roots in Greek ("man") and Latin ("God"). But most of the family later admitted that the "church" reference was little more than a ruse to obtain tax exemption and greater understanding from the state and its citizenry.

Hurd's efforts at first seemed to bear fruit. He won some support for his idea to build a coffeehouse discussion center where members of the "straight" and communal cultures might meet. The center was to be in the form of a geodesic dome, and the foundation for the building was actually dug. Moreover, Hurd's talks, and the example of Oz, won disciples for the communal life.

Most of his converts were teen-agers. One was Ellen, 16, the daughter of an art professor at Allegheny College in Meadville. "We were all going through the rebellion stage," she said. "Our parents were down on us for the way we dressed. We knew what we didn't want—living like our parents who were brought up to hate. The hating begins with cliques in high school and carries over to the Apple Valley Country Club. George gave us a positive alternative. He talked on the similarities of Zen and Christianity which both try to throw off self-consciousness and replace it with cosmic consciousness."

Another Meadville girl, Debbie, first came to the farm with a casserole of spaghetti. She stayed most of the summer. Debbie explained, "It wasn't what George said so much as his quiet conviction. He wasn't pushing anything, no product, no drugs, just spiritual awareness. And when you have this awareness, you don't need things or governments or marriage certificates. All you need is a group of people who feel the same way."

Hurd estimated that there were 30 teen-agers who regularly

visited the farm; four—three girls and a boy—left home to live there. As the summer wore on, the farm attracted more and more runaways who, in the opinion of the family, were "nowhere, just mixed-up kids." Hurd found himself in the awkward role of a guidance counselor ministering to confused youths and placating indignant parents who came out to the farm in search of their missing offspring.

Ellen's father had at first defended the family of Oz against the small-town intolerance they met. When several of the family were overnight guests in his house, his neighbors drew up a petition threatening legal action against him. He was indignant. But he modified his support of the family as his daughter spent more time at the farm.

Today, afraid that he has lost touch with Ellen and fearful she might drop out of high school, he speaks of George Hurd as a "Pied Piper" who divided his daughter's loyalties between her primary family and the family of Oz. This exchange occurred between them:

Father: "I just don't want you to spend the rest of your life contemplating your navel. We're living in an exciting time, a new Renaissance, when technology is pushing out frontiers for man. Look at the space shot."

Ellen: "It doesn't impress me that we sent men around the moon. It's internal discovery that's important."

Father: "I don't care what experiences you have. As long as they don't destroy you and you do something productive."

Ellen: "What's productive? As long as I'm perceiving the world in all its beauty and dimension, I don't have to paint pictures."

The farm also made some adult converts. A biochemistry professor from Edinboro State College, just divorced and on the verge of committing suicide, spent many weekends at the farm. "We replaced the family he had just lost and gave him a new grasp on life," said Dancing Bear. The professor returned to teaching in the fall.

Debbie met a family who drove up to talk about their son who had just received orders to go to Vietnam: "They were very religious people and believed that killing, even in a uniform, violated Christ's teachings. We talked for a long time. Six days later, the son returned alone. He had gone AWOL." She didn't know the end of his story. Other overnight guests at the farm included ministers, college teachers, doctors, realtors and car dealers. Many of them came away with new perspectives.

"Although most people wouldn't admit it, the farm changed a lot of preconceptions in this town," said Ken P. Williams, managing editor of The Meadville Tribune. "For the most, it was good for this town."

Toward August, the weekend crowds at the farm began to get out of hand. Members of the family threatened to leave, to "split." But Hurd's philosophy of an open community prevailed —there were to be no "no trespassing" signs. Hippies came from as far away as Cleveland and Pittsburgh, and much occurred without the family's knowledge that they were nonetheless held responsible for. One night, for example, two teeny-boppers set up what amounted to a tent of ill repute on the grounds. Naturally, many of their clients spread the word throughout the county that the hippies supported themselves by selling their own women.

Hamlets in a 50-mile radius of Harmonsburg buzzed with other rumors as well: "All drug addicts." "There've been a lot of thefts around here since that group moved in." "I saw a pack of them drag a 16-year-old into the weeds."

The stories multiplied, fed by fears that the farm was converting (or, as the residents put, "corrupting") numbers of local youth to a radical life style. For most of Meadville, the "live-and-let-live" days were over. There was talk of organizing a vigilante gang to run the hippies off the farm. Ugly incidents occurred there.

A drunken trio of motorcyclists shot off a rifle near the farmhouse and grappled with Theodore Everett, the elderly faith healer, who had stopped by to check on the progress of the family's garden. The bikers took off when the state police arrived; Everett was treated for a badly scratched hand.

Early one morning, as the family slept, someone stole into the farmhouse and set a mattress on fire. A family member awakened in time to keep the fire from spreading.

One of the family's dogs was shot. A gang of youths tried to haul one of the commune girls into their car; her face was scratched with a razor when she struggled, but she finally escaped.

When one of the family was admitted to the hospital with a case of infectious hepatitis, the regional health officer went on the radio to urge all residents to keep away from Oz. The broadcast precipitated a hepatitis scare of bubonic plague proportions though, as it turned out, there were only nine cases of hepatitis in Crawford County in 1968 as compared to 15 the previous year.

A protest meeting was conducted at the Summit Township Fire Hall. A sign posted outside read, "All Citizens Welcome," but when 20 hippies appeared, entrance was denied. Only Hurd and a girl who acted as the family's secretary were allowed inside; they were given only a brief time to ask and answer questions.

During the meeting, a woman resident bluntly expressed her view on the free inoculations of gamma globulin given the family against hepatitis: "I would let them live there and die." Later, State Senator James E. Willard pledged he would do all in his power to move the hippies out of the county, hinting that he might even introduce a special law into the State Legislature if he had to.

On Aug. 12, four members of the family were arrested as vagrants in Cambridge Springs, a small town north of Meadville. They were accused of dangling their feet in a public fountain and of having a total bankroll of two cents.

Four days later, around 9:30 A.M., Oz was raided by the state police. The sleepy family, plus some visitors (including a divorcee and her 3-year-old girl), were packed into a school bus and driven off to Meadville. There, a jeering crowd of 200 surrounded the bus as the police led the family into the office of an alderman to be arraigned. They were charged with "maintaining a disorderly house" in violation of an 1860 statute: "Whoever keeps and maintains a common, ill-governed and disorderly house or place to the encouragement of idleness, gaming, drinking or misbehavior and to the common nuisance and disturbance of the neighborhood and orderly citizens is guilty of a misbehavior. . . ." A second charge was that the family was corrupting the morals of a 16-year-old girl who had been living at the farm with her parents' knowledge and tacit consent.

Amy was taken away from Rebecca's custody and placed in a foster home. The other 3-year-old was placed in the custody of her grandmother. The Juvenile Court charged that the girls had been exposed to male nudity and foul language, left to wander about without supervision and allowed to live amid filthy housing conditions (the house was a haven for flies). Evidence for this neglect and for the charges against the family was based on information gained by a police undercover agent who first showed up with a goat (Ed) which he offered to the family and which was gladly accepted. He posed as a retarded, guileless animal keeper and returned for several short visits at the farm but did not stay overnight. Other evidence was furnished by two itinerants in hippie attire who said they were freelance writers. They took many photographs, one of them a portrait showing the family posing nude in the woods in a feigned Victorian attitude. They sold the photographs to the district attorney and vanished from Meadville.

An injunction was nailed to the front of the farmhouse, forbidding the use of the premises for "fornication, assignation and lewdness." But with the aid of a court-appointed attorney, the family returned and continued to live there—for a time.

Storekeepers began refusing to serve the family. When some of the hippies decided they would sign a complaint against the small grocery store in Harmonsburg, they walked to the home of the justice of the peace, only to be confronted by his wife. The judge was not home, she said, and she blocked the doorway. "They were filthy," she later explained. "I wouldn't let them in the house."

By September, there was not a store in the Harmonsburg vicinity that would sell them food. The community was so hostile toward the family that professors at Allegheny College hesitated to shop in Meadville in sandals and sunglasses for fear of being publicly berated.

Nevertheless, there were some citizens who continued to preach toleration for the hippies. Letters to the editor of The Meadville Tribune ran three to two in favor of the family. Some observers spoke critically of the police raid; and Allan Crane, an associate professor of sociology at Allegheny, compared the public in its attitude toward Oz with the viewers of TV's "Peyton Place," who watch the program because of their "suppressed desires which they're afraid to satisfy."

Yet communalism in Crawford County was dead, and the family knew it. "The harassment was making it impossible," Hurd said later. "We could be dragged in and out of courts indefinitely." At a hearing in Meadville on Sept. 6, the Commonwealth and the family reached an agreement: the district attorney would drop charges against them and the family would leave the farm within two weeks and not return for a year.

So the family scattered. Michael and Susie set out to track down rumors that Timothy Leary's Millbrook colony had relocated in Arizona. Adolph and Deja set out on a tour of the country in a new Cadillac, purchased with part of the $10,000 he inherited. Parmel is living in a community in New York State, owned by a couple who accept people willing to engage in an unknown kind of eugenics experiment; the community is known to hippies as the "animal farm." David, Muffin and their newborn child live in a walk-up apartment on Manhattan's West Side; their lone piece of furniture is a mattress. After visiting at communes in Woodstock, N. Y., Patty-Pooh is back in New York, living off and on in her parents' plush East Side duplex. Eric, a teen-ager who ran away from home to stay briefly at the farm, is said to have been committed by his parents to a mental hospital in Ohio. Rebecca when last heard of was in Florida, working as a waitress; Amy is in the custody of her grandmother, and Rebecca sees her daughter on weekends.

George Hurd stayed around Meadville for a time, but in January he, Josh, Kathy and Michael headed for California in search of a new homestead. They had kept in touch with various other members of the family by mail and telephone—the phone calls paid for by using a credit card said to belong to an executive in a large defense industry. Hippies are known to possess a large number of credit cards, which they pass around among their friends as needed.

Only Marko is still on the farm in Harmonsburg. He lives alone in a shack he built himself, for the main house of Oz is no more. It was set afire by persons unknown, after the family left, and all that remains of the homestead today is a pile of charred timbers.

Suggested Reading

E. Digby Baltzell, *Philadelphia Gentlemen,* New York, Free Press, 1958.

Norman W. Bell and Ezra F. Vogel, eds., *The Family,* rev. ed., New York, Free Press, 1968.

Jessie Bernard, *Remarriage,* New York, Dryden Press, 1956.

Robert O. Blood and Donald M. Wolfe, *Husbands and Wives,* New York, Free Press, 1960 (paperback).

Elizabeth Bott, *Family and Social Networks,* London, Tavistock, 1957 (paperback).

John N. Edwards, ed., *The Family and Change,* New York, Knopf, 1969 (paperback).

Cynthia Fuchs Epstein, *Woman's Place,* Berkeley, University of California Press, 1970.

Betty Friedan, *The Feminine Mystique,* New York, Norton, 1963 (Dell paperback).

William J. Goode, *World Revolution and Family Patterns,* New York, Free Press, 1963.

William J. Goode, *The Family,* New York, Prentice-Hall, 1964 (paperback).

Andrew M. Greeley, *Why Can't They Be Like Us?,* New York, Institute of Human Relations Press, 1969.

Mirra Komarovsky, *Blue-Collar Marriage,* New York, Random House, 1962 (paperback).

Louis Kriesberg, *Mothers in Poverty,* Chicago, Aldine, 1970.

E. E. Le Masters, *Parents in Modern America,* Homewood, Ill., Dorsey Press, 1970.

Oscar Lewis, *La Vida,* New York, Random House, 1965 (paperback).

Elliot Liebow, *Tally's Corner,* Boston, Little, Brown, 1963 (paperback).

Charles Nordhoff, *The Communistic Societies of the United States,* New York, Schocken, 1965 (paperback).

Herbert A. Otto, *Family in Search of a Future: Alternate Models for Moderns,* New York, Appleton-Century-Crofts, 1970 (paperback).

Ira L. Reiss, *Premarital Sexual Standards in America,* New York, Free Press, 1960 (paperback).

Index

A Note on the Editor

William J. Goode is Professor of Sociology at Columbia University and president of the American Sociological Association. Born in Houston, Texas, he studied at the University of Texas and at Pennsylvania State University, and was a Guggenheim Fellow. Mr. Goode's books include *World Revolution and Family Patterns, The Family, Women in Divorce, Family and Society,* and *Dynamics of Modern Society.*

NEW YORK TIMES BOOKS published by QUADRANGLE BOOKS